Allegorical Architecture

Xing Ruan

Allegorical Architecture

LIVING MYTH AND ARCHITECTONICS
IN SOUTHERN CHINA

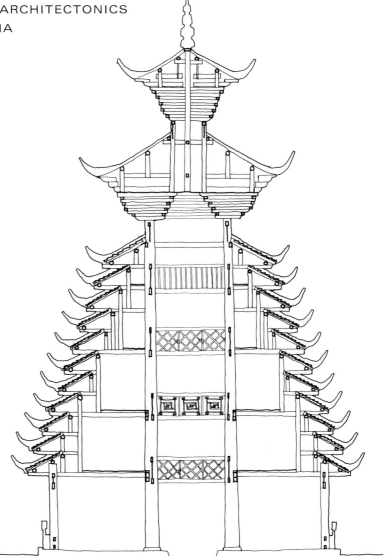

spatial habitus

University of Hawai'i Press
Honolulu

© 2006 University of Hawai'i Press
All rights reserved
Printed in the United States of America

11   10   09   08   07   06   6   5   4   3   2   1

LIBRARY OF CONGRESS CATALOGING-IN-PUBLICATION DATA

Ruan, Xing.
Allegorical architecture : living myth and architectonics
in southern China / Xing Ruan.
    p. cm.—(Spatial habitus—making and meaning in Asia's architecture)
Includes bibliographical references and index.

ISBN-13: 978-0-8248-2151-7 (hardcover : alk. paper)
ISBN-10: 0-8248-2151-3 (hardcover : alk. paper)

    1. Architecture, Dong. 2. Ethnic architecture—China, Southwest.
3. Vernacular architecture—China, Southwest. 4. Symbolism in architecture—
China, Southwest. I. Title. II. Title: Living myth and architectonics in southern
China. III. Series: Spatial habitus (Series)

    NA1546.S66R83 2006
    728.0951'3—dc22

                                    2006015042

University of Hawai'i Press books are printed on acid-free paper and meet the
guidelines for permanence and durability of the Council on Library Resources.

Book design and composition by Diane Gleba Hall

Printed by Thomson-Shore, Inc.

TO THE MEMORY OF MY MOTHER,
WHO HAD FAITH IN THE GOOD

Contents

Preface

This book has had a long gestation period: the primary research and field-work were conducted between 1989 and 1993; my PhD dissertation of 1997 grew out of the fieldwork; and a great deal of the fieldwork has been used in the current book, which was written between 2003 and 2004. Although I did not have the opportunity to write this book immediately after the dis-sertation—that would have been a quite different book—in retrospect I am grateful for this delay. When the project was first conceived in the late 1980s, the so-called postmodernism in architecture was largely about a free use of historic motifs in architectural facades. I thought there was a need to discuss the meaning of the built form beyond its look.

Now almost two decades have gone past, during which time we have seen several phases of architectural vogue. While the revival of the austere in modern architecture is still with us, the current digital frenzy seems to predict that buildings and even large city fabrics will have to turn and twist. Whatever the looks of the built forms, however, the fundamental concern of my early research—the legibility of our built world—has, to my surprise, remained unchanged. But it was not until I had the time to sort and order the materials into various themes for the book that I realized that the conceptual frame is more important than the materials: I wanted to combine the study of the physical laws of the built forms, or the artifice so to speak, with their "circulation" in social life. It was a realization that architects, planners, and environmental designers are not solely responsible for a meaningful built world—and the inhabitants are not completely free from the "control" of a formal configuration either. The book, therefore, is written for the form givers as much as for the inhabitants. For the processes of making and inhabiting, as I have attempted to demonstrate in the built world of the minority groups in southern China, cannot be separated. This is a reminder that meaningful engagement of the inhabitants with their built world requires conscious efforts from the designers as well as from the inhabitants themselves. And indeed there is artifice on both sides that needs to be learned.

■

During the long period of this book's making, I inevitably owe thanks and debts to many individuals and institutions. First and foremost, I am grateful to my teacher Professor Clarence Aasen: when I was a graduate student in Nanjing in the late 1980s, Clarence and Gail took me on a wondrous journey into the minority regions of southern China, which was the starting point for the current book. I would like to thank him for bearing with me during my days in Wellington when I could hardly express myself in English. The early fieldwork was assisted by an Internal Grant Committee Grand-in-Aid from the Victoria University of Wellington. The New Zealand Vice-Chancellor Scholarship enabled me to pursue my early research based in New Zealand. I also appreciate the encouragement from Dr. Paul Walker during my stay in Wellington. Many scholars and friends assisted me during my fieldwork in southern China; I wish to acknowledge Long Yuxiao in Guiyang, Wu Quanxin and Shi Tingzhang in Congjiang, Wang Shengxian and Yang Guoren in Kaili, and Yang Tongshan in Sanjiang. Above all, I would like to thank all these wonderful people in the field who welcomed me and opened the doors of their world to this curious outsider. My parents provided all the support I needed during my early research of the book. My late mother, on her holiday in Australia, sorted out in longhand the Chinese bibliography for the early version. This book is dedicated to the memory of her love.

Professor Roxana Waterson and Professor Kim Dovey offered perceptive and thorough readings of my early work. I hope the book is a worthy response to their comments. It was Roxana who first told me that there was a book here, and for this I must thank her. Over the last six years, Professor Ronald Knapp has become a mentor. At a time when I thought I would never finish this book, Ron urged me to get it done. More than once, May and Ron graciously welcomed me to their home in New Paltz to discuss this book and the Spatial Habitus series. The scholarship of Professor Joseph Rykwert has been an inspiration, not only for this book, but also for my academic career. Five years ago Joseph took the trouble to English my book proposal and write recommendation letters to grants committees so that I might get some teaching relief in order to write the book. Joseph and Anne over the years have shown me that a scholarly career is actually a way of life. Professor Yi-Fu Tuan may not know that my rereading of his works, and our recent conversations, have provided some reassurance for my tangential thoughts in the book. Misunderstandings and errors of course remain my own.

My students Rachel Trigg and Min-chia Young provided invaluable assistance. Rachel was an enthusiastic reader of the late drafts and offered professional editorial advice; Min's computer skills made the preparation of the manuscript a joy. Here I would like to thank Patricia Crosby, executive editor at the University of Hawai'i Press, for her vision for the Spatial Habitus series and for her patience. One anonymous reader offered not only great encouragement but also, I must say, penetrating readings; the other reader scrutinized some of my loose ends with care. The presentation of the book has benefited from the meticulous copyediting of Don Yoder. I also would like to acknowledge three institutions—Curtin University, University of Technology Sydney, and the University of New South Wales (UNSW)—as well as two deans, Professor Laurie Hegvold and Professor Peter Murphy, for providing me with academic homes. I wish to thank Professor Martin Loosemore, and his Research Committee in Faculty of the Built Environment, UNSW, for granting me a book subsidy.

Finally, I owe the greatest debts to Dongmin, who was my collaborator for the fieldwork, literature research, and some of the fieldwork drawings. Dongmin, along with Shumi and Shuyi, has put up with my frequent weekend and holiday absences with love and humor.

A Note on Names and Terms

Most personal and place names in China, including those of the minority groups in southern China, as well as architectural terms are romanized in pinyin except where a different romanization was used in the original source. This also applies to the bibliography. Dong names and terms are romanized in the standard romanization that was introduced to the Dong in 1958. It is similar to pinyin, but the last letter indicates the tone only. Since there are nine tones in the Dong language (there are four tones in the Chinese-language *putong hua*), they are indicated, namely, by *l, p, c, s, t, x, v, k,* and *h.* The goddess Sax, for example, pronounces as *sa,* similar to that of pinyin, and the end letter *x* is silent. Chinese characters, both in simplified and full form, occasionally appear in the text when the visual aspects of the words are necessary to illustrate a point. In the bibliography, Chinese-language materials appear both in pinyin and simplified Chinese characters.

PROLOGUE

The American architect Louis Kahn contemplated a romantic picture when he designed the Salk Institute (1959–1965), a science laboratory for biological studies in La Jolla, California. In the central plaza, which is bound by two rows of concrete buildings and is open to the infinite Pacific Ocean on the cliff edge, scientists would walk up and down between the laboratory building and the plaza; they would engage in heated debates about the problems of the world; they would pause to "chalk an equation or draw a diagram" on the slabs of slate that Kahn had placed there for their convenience. But as Arthur Danto has observed: "[No]body was ever there . . . nobody but architectural tourists. . . . Kahn was almost hopeless in his romanticism, hoped people would rise to the architecture, but they rarely did or do" (Danto 1999, 202).

Kahn, like any great architect, envisaged life in a building that would unfold according to design. A history of architecture—that of the twentieth century in particular—has proved that this indeed is heroic romanticism, for there is often a poor chance that the intention of the architect, as materialized into a spatial disposition in a building, would be taken in the same way by the inhabitants. The disengagement between architect and inhabitants in the twentieth century has made this "mutual understanding" even more difficult. Despite this near impossibility, and the original intent of the architect, buildings in one way or another still *work!* Kahn's Salk Institute will continue to attract architectural tourists and, perhaps, increasingly general tourists. It will eventually become a ruin, like the mysterious Stonehenge (as Danto predicted), where the original intent has long become undecipherable. Although the Salk Institute never works, like a text, in a didactic manner to illustrate the intention of the architect, Danto obviously hopes that its potency, like an allegory, will increase as it ages, though its meaning remains tacit.

This book is concerned with the *workings* of architecture. It views the built world, from an individual building to a settlement, as not merely passive templates on which life is staged by itself but meaningful instruments within which the life of the inhabitants may be activated. The instrumental capacity (Evans 1997, 35–91) of a building is often neglected when a history of architecture is only concerned with grandeur and splendor and architecture is only studied and measured by its formal and physical laws. If architecture works, questions then arise: How does life unfold in the man-made habitat? How does a building animate individual as well as social life? The interactive and yet legible relationship between the built world and its inhabitants is the major theme of this book.

The workings of architecture, I should think, depend on an understanding of the meaning of the built world that the inhabitants are able to gain. Before I move into the subject matter of this book—the vernacular architecture of minority groups in southern China—let me first look into the history of how architects and social anthropologists, roughly grouped for the convenience of discussion, have wrestled with this problem from the vantage point of their disciplines.

Form and Meaning

Substantiated by more than a century of anthropological and ethnographic findings, vernacular architecture has commonly been considered among the richest and the most meaningful of architectural forms. Ironically, however, vernacular architecture is not made or designed by individuals or groups intentionally to produce meaning. On the contrary, it is an "architecture without architects" (Rudofsky 1964). While it may be culturally meaningful, it is not seen to be meaningful as a result of conscious design. The architect-designed habitat, by contrast, often takes full credit for abundant meaning.

Architect Bernard Tschumi's 1987 follies in Parc de la Villette in Paris are an outcome of such conscious design: they were a winning entry of a major international architectural competition that was judged by a panel of renowned architects, architectural historians, and theorists, as well as painters, musicians, and representatives from ministries and the city.[1] Tschumi's design, among other competition entries, stood out as the most convincing and meaning-laden artifact, for a piece of great architecture must be a great concept that is materialized as spaces and forms. But Michael Benedikt observes after the successful completion of the project: "If you don't know the critical/theoretical narrative background, [the follies] are simply nice little red Neo-constructivist buildings upon which to climb—which is how the people of Paris see them" (1991, 1). This statement implies that "sophisticated architecture" is understandable only if people, through text and narrative, know how it was meaningfully conceived. It also suggests that this is a level of understanding, and kind of meaning, that is beyond the abilities of ordinary people, who are, incidentally, the inhabitants of the built world.

This statement also represents a common theoretical position—that the basis for understanding architecture is through a preexisting and superimposed text; that text is regarded as the analogy of architecture and a precursor to a meaningful architecture. Hence the understanding of architecture is seen as explaining, reading, interpreting, and decoding the *hidden* meanings behind the built form. In other words, architecture is seen to carry, transmit, and communicate meanings in a linguistic sense. The linguistic pairs of "words/ signifier" and "referents/signified" are thus arbitrarily associated with "form/ meaning" in architecture.

Arguably the separation of form from meaning only occurred in the late eighteenth century, and architecture ever since has become a formal problem for architects (Vesely 1985). It is all too easy to be impressed by the architecture of antiquity, and the classical periods in Europe, simply because of their grandeur and splendor. Monumentality, to use architectural jargon, is usually how our contemporary eyes perceive the history of architecture. To take a cynical view, monumentality heightens not only our awareness of the built world but also our vanity. But the architecture of the ancient world could have served other purposes. Some argue that the emergence of modern science—an instrumental, or mathematical, representation of the universe—in the seventeenth century replaced the role of architecture in Europe, which used to play a role in reconciling the transcendent and the world, or the cosmos and man (Pérez-Gómez 1983). Science, however, is only a partial representation of reality; the transcendental and symbolic aspects of science often are not fully acknowledged. If architecture no longer plays a critical role in this "reconciliation," one must admit that it has retreated into the realm of technology and aesthetics. (Nietzsche sees their affinities for the will and the pleasure to power.) The formal problem in eighteenth-century Europe, to take the extreme case of Jacques-Nicolas-Louis Durand's teaching as an example, is that of economy and efficiency. A round plan, for Durand, is the ideal prototype, for it is the most economical and efficient plan type in terms of its floor area and hence should be aesthetically most pleasing. Technology and aesthetics thus fit each other. Meaning and form remain a pair.

The good intention of structuralism in the 1960s (Lévi-Strauss 1963) in its faith in a culturally independent human common ground, a deep structure so to speak, has had a crude reception in architecture, for it coincided with the modern belief in architecture as a formal problem. Architecture, following the easy analogy of a language (which itself comes from linguistic structuralism), becomes a spatial "syntax." When reaching this point, the formal problem of architecture is already devoid of any worldly meaning, for in a syntactic structure, like the grammar of a language, any meanings that remain are abstract. What then can be said about the "formal language" of a building? Can one only decipher void, solid, recession, oblique, or frontality, as suggested by Peter Eisenman (1971)? What then can be pursued in the realm of a formal language? Newness! Artistic endeavor, in the twentieth century in particular, has been a business of denying the past and inventing the new.

Newness or novelty thus becomes the only measure of art—rather than a pursuit of instrumental virtuosity, or morality, which any artwork inevitably carries (Gell 1998; 1999, 159–186). Architecture has been no exception in this regard since it is clear that the invention of new form has almost exclusively occupied architects over the past century. When artists and architects were busy in their revolutionary invention of new forms, genres, styles, or whatever they might be termed, social anthropologists quietly went into the "field" to examine preindustrial and nonliterate societies ("primitive societies" as they once were called). One of their discoveries was that, in addition to imitating the universe, buildings actually imitated their inhabitants. A house, for example, could be seen as society at the macro level, and it embodies its occupier at the micro level.

Towards the end of the nineteenth century and the beginning of the twentieth, social anthropologists saw the built fabric of "primitive societies" as a *reflection* of their social structures. This view was largely due to the continuing legacy of European modern science since the seventeenth century. The "scientific absolute" in social theories had been replaced by social organization, social structure, and cosmology (Durkheim and Mauss 1963). The concept of "primitive communism," for example, was deduced from aboriginal housing forms, simply because those dwellings made it possible for a large number of household members to produce and consume food jointly (Morgan 1965). For social scientists, society—in terms of kinship structures and social organization—was actually represented by architecture, the built form. Thus a conclusion could be reached that the larger winter houses of Eskimos were caused by the need to accommodate a collective intensification of ritual during the winter months, rather than by explanations such as the conservation of heat, diffusion of technology, or requirements of collective hunting (Mauss and Beuchat 1979). No matter what the cause was, the ritual practice became the cultural meaning of the larger winter houses, and this was inferred from the house form itself. Even for social anthropologists, it seemed that the appeal of an austerity of the scientific truth, and its consequential splendor, were just too irresistible.

Beginning after World War II and continuing to the present, architects have evinced an increasing interest in the vernacular built world. In part, this interest is due to a widespread disappointment with modernist architectural solutions, which are largely based on faith in efficiency and efficacy. It is also due to an increasing fascination with the powerful, often "organic," formal qualities of vernacular architecture in premodern societies. But this interest has been predominantly visual, which is evident in the effective use of photographic and architectural drawing techniques. They capture, rather subconsciously, only the picturesque and idyllic images of romanticism and nostalgia. Cultural, climatic, economic, and social facets are mentioned, but often without sufficient elaboration. The most representative example of such visual admiration of the vernacular built world is Bernard Rudofsky's *Architecture Without Architects* (1964), a collection of striking black and white photographs, selected by the cultivated eye of a modernist architectural taste, of vernacular built environments around the world. First published as a catalogue of a photographic exhibition at the Museum of Modern Art in New York from 1964 to 1965, it has since seen five printings. In a similar vein, Le Corbusier's travelogue, *Journey to the East* (1987), which recorded his tour of the exotic "oriental world" in 1911, would be incomplete if it were not accompanied with his masterful sketches of architecture.

This visual appreciation of vernacular architecture continued with much popularity in the second half of the twentieth century. African villages and their huts, for example, were depicted with meticulous architectural drawings (Prussin 1969). More works were produced, and attempts were also made to include vernacular architecture in the writing of orthodox architectural history (Oliver 1969, 1971, 1975). The scope of the survey, assisted by color and more sophisticated photographic techniques, expanded to every corner of the world (Oliver 1987, 1997; Guidoni 1978). Chinese architects, too, showed great admiration for their vernacular forms, as well as their housing types (Liu 1957), while the study of imperial and religious architecture was in vogue in the first half of the twentieth century. The trend was resumed in the 1980s after the Cultural Revolution and reached a level of prosperity in the late 1980s when the China Architecture and Building Press published a book series of regional surveys of vernacular architecture in China (Knapp 2000, 7–18). The value of the survey material notwithstanding, these books, filled with ample illustrations of architectural drawings and sketches, to my mind, became a "beauty contest" among the pictorial vernacular buildings (as well as the drawing skills of the architects who recorded them).

Surely not all architects in the modern period are merely "visual animals." Social and anthropological angles have, to a certain degree, infiltrated their minds. English architect William Lethaby's nineteenth-century book *Architecture, Mysticism, and Myth* (1974) showed a great "anthropological" fascination with symbolic expressions in architectural forms. Unlike anthropologists and ethnographers, Lethaby used only secondhand material rather than fieldwork observations. Although this book has remained relatively obscure among architects, Lethaby nonetheless has a kindred spirit in our time. Joseph Rykwert's *The Idea of a Town: The Anthropology of Urban Form in Rome, Italy, and the Ancient World* (1988) reminded architects and planners that there was a mutual and yet symbolic understanding between citizens and town patterns in the ancient world. The book in fact was conceived and first published in the late 1950s as a special issue of the Dutch magazine *Forum,* which was edited by architect Aldo van Eyck. Incidentally, it was a time when city planning and building design were considered rational outcomes of production, marketing, traffic circulation, and hygiene; the idea of an interactive and symbolic relationship between the inhabitants and their built world was, not surprisingly, seen as "ridiculously passé" (Rykwert 1988). Since the publication of that book, Rykwert has continued to remind architects of the humane aspects of the ancient built world, where the fabrication of buildings and societies were engaged with each other, and in particular the salutary power of myth in a meaningful negotiation between people and their built world (Rykwert 1996).

Although architects have been preoccupied by formal problems for more than two centuries, they have also attempted to deal with a variety of vernacular built forms from sociocultural perspectives. Questions are asked: Why are forms different? What meanings might be responsible for the variation? In his *House Form and Culture* Amos Rapoport (1969b) makes an explicit statement that the integration of all cultural, material, spiritual, and social aspects shapes built form and, moreover, that such factors best explain variations in such forms. For Rapoport, the deterministic "cause" of built form should be seen as arising not from a single factor but from multidimensional aspects. While believing that built form responds both to climatic conditions and to limitations in construction materials and methods, for him the sociocultural causes are paramount.

Rapoport, however, warns scholars to be careful "not to speak of forces determining form." He suggests that, instead of causal relations, "coincidences" be used because "the complexity of forces precludes our being able to attribute form to given forces or variables" (1969b, 17). Nevertheless, he proposes a comprehensive conceptual framework to explain the variety of house types and forms and the forces that affect them. He also attempts to reach a better understanding of formal determinants of dwellings. As he proceeds to point out:

> The specific task, then, becomes to select those features of the house
> which seem most universal, and to examine them in different contexts

so that we can best understand what it is that affects the forms taken by dwellings and groups of dwellings, and also what it is that so easily enables us to tell, often at a glance, the area, culture, or even subculture to which a dwelling or settlement belongs. Instead of trying to describe or classify differences in house forms, their materials, and parts, I will ask to what these differences can be attributed, and will try to relate them to the way of life, the image of the good life, social organization, concepts of territoriality, way of handling "basic needs," the link between the dwelling and the settlement pattern, and so forth. [1969b, 17]

Despite being an architect, Rapoport, like Rykwert, begins to ponder the impact of built form on the invisible, such as way of life and social organization. Social anthropologists, naturally, are more concerned with the conceptual attributes of built form than with the physical laws of the man-made habitat. The symbolic approaches, interpreting built form as a representation or expression of a cultural code system, are perhaps the most developed ones. For most symbolic theorists, meanings encompass cultural aspects such as cosmology, myth, or social structure, intangible cultural abstractions that are often hard to grasp. For such theorists, the role of architecture is to communicate or transmit these intangible meanings by giving them tangible and concrete form.

Most symbolic approaches are deeply rooted in structuralist thinking that is concerned with finding out the facts that are true of the human mind, rather than facts about the organization of any particular society or class of societies. The structured collective unconsciousness is in fact a hypothetical mental structure. This mental structure is seen to be capable of generating patterned cultural behavior, including built forms (Lévi-Strauss 1963). At the same time, this mental structure can be understood and realized through a myriad of sociocultural manifestations such as architecture. Drawing on this approach, built form and architecture most commonly are considered as a reflection of conceptual ideas.

To interpret and decode implicit meanings, architectural semiotics is probably the most extreme strategy. As a method, it reduces architectural characteristics to systems of signs or codes. Despite the acknowledgment that architectural elements have no linguistic functions, may not be analogous to linguistic signs, and are more complex to interpret (Eco 1972), built form in this approach often is assumed to have a cultural function similar to that of a language, with symbols becoming signs. As the next step, it is not difficult to propose that space be seen as a text that can be read (Moore 1986).

Taking the position of culture as abstraction and architecture as representation, James Fernandez sees metaphor as a medium to move culture from the abstract and inchoate to the concrete, tangible, and reachable. These metaphors are what Fernandez calls "cultural architectonics." In *Fang Architectonics,* he writes:

> How have they built themselves into the spaces available to them and what is represented in the "buildings"? We shall concentrate on the buildings in the literal sense of the term but we shall argue that these buildings cannot be completely understood without a large sense of the architectonics of Fang culture and Fang culture history. Cosmology and legend are, thus, essential parts of Fang architectonics. [1977, 1]

In conclusion, the symbolic and metaphoric analysis of built environment "merges the strength of cultural meanings and interpretation with concrete architecture. The built form thus becomes a vehicle for expressing and communicating cultural meaning—that is, a meaning system itself that is interpreted within the context of isomorphic meanings of body, personhood, and social structure" (Lawrence and Low 1990, 473–474).

For architects, the role of built form as a *reflection* of cultural meanings remains nonetheless dubious. Kahn obviously could not stand in front of his Salk Institute to tell people how the building was meant to be inhabited. A building, after all, is mute. Its social life, after it leaves the hands of the architect, is unpredictable. Pierre Bourdieu (1977) sees this problem, but he tackles it from his field of ethnography and sociology. He asks: how does one act in social as well as physical space? Bourdieu realizes that human beings act neither like mechanical puppets nor like calculating game players in space. The clever Frenchman then reinvented the practice-based notion of "habitus" to replace a linguistic conceptualization. His ethnographic findings prove that "natives" (in his own words) use habitus to reproduce existing structures without being fully aware of how these structures are in turn affected. In generating practices—say building a building—habitus reproduces the conditions that gave rise to it initially; habitus, therefore, is both the product and the producer of history. Instead of a linguistic reading, the process in practice is emphasized to remind people that *inhabitation* combines mind and body. Bourdieu may not solve the problems of the modern architect, but he offers hope that a meaningful relationship between the built world and its inhabitants does exist.

This relationship indeed exists in the vernacular built world, where inhabitants still build for themselves and the processes of making and inhabiting the habitat are still engaged with each other. Drawing on firsthand fieldwork experience, social anthropologists and cultural geographers increasingly shift their focus from mere objects to more fluid but lively social relations. In the case of the human habitat, it is a conceptual interest in the symbolic and ritualistic engagement between the inhabitants and the built world. In her book *The Living House: An Anthropology of Architecture in South-East Asia*, Roxana Waterson (1990) believes that inhabited spaces are not neutral but rather are cultural constructions of one kind or another. In her own words: "Any building, in any culture, must inevitably carry some symbolic load" (p. xvi). As an approach, she chooses the house as a fully saturated cultural embodiment and goes on to examine and reveal the ideas and beliefs enacted in building and living in such a house. These social and symbolic aspects of architecture include kinship systems, gender symbolism, and cosmological ideas. For Waterson, it is the meaningful relationship between the creators and their creations that matters.

In a similar vein, and for a period of over thirty years, Ronald Knapp has written extensively on China's vernacular architecture in terms of its living state (1986, 1989, 1999, 2000). In *China's Living Houses: Folk Beliefs, Symbols, and Household Ornamentation* (1999), Knapp demonstrates that, much more than merely a shelter against the elements, a house plays a vital role in enshrining the hopes and fears of its inhabitants when they are able to symbolically engage with it. Although he does not use them in any simplistic sense, for Knapp the workings of a house in its living state can even be didactic in guiding the proper behavior of its occupiers.

Legibility and Instrumental Form

The architect studies the physical laws of built fabric without being fully aware that his behavior may have been affected by a spatial disposition; the social anthropologist speculates with anxiety about how the human figure acts in space without much knowledge of the artifice of built form and its contribution to social space. My approach in this book, rather, is to contest formal analysis in a social milieu. In order to make the book "manageable," in the sense that the material receives due loving care (through both literature and fieldwork research), this book focuses on a range of architecture of the minority groups in southern China—that of the Dong nationality in particular. But the main reason for focusing primarily on Dong architectonics is that, despite its striking visual radiance, Dong architecture is tremendously instrumental, beyond its picturesqueness, in animating their social life. Architectonics in this book is used in a literal sense to refer to a wide range of elements that construct the built world of minority groups in southern China. These elements include village patterns (blocks, streets, compounds, and plazas), landscape ensembles, houses, public building structures (opera stages, bridges, and towers), graves, shrines, gates, thresholds, doors, windows, and floor plans and sections. My purpose is to expand the conventional confinement of architecture that may refer only to individual buildings.

Chinese terminology defines the world in terms of Han—the majority population—and non-Han relations. There are fifty-five officially acknowledged "minority nationalities" *(shaoshu minzu)* and thus fifty-six "nationalities" *(minzu)* including the Han. The Dong, one of these minority nationalities, belong to one of the six Tai linguistic groups in southern China that are related to the Austronesian cultures found elsewhere in Southeast Asia and the South Pacific region.[2] Although the focus of the book is the architectonics of the Dong and other related minorities in southern China—which, geographically, includes Guangxi, Guizhou, Hunan, and Yunnan provinces—the context throughout the book covers Han architecture and indigenous architecture in Southeast Asia, as well as Western architectural modernity in the twentieth century.

Having coexisted with the Han for many thousands of years, the minorities in southern China remain largely nonliterate; but they make and inhabit, to a "cultivated" eye, a strikingly picturesque built world. The public structures of the Dong, for example, include splendid drum towers and roofed wind-and-rain bridges. Despite their relatively poor economic and, arguably, inferior political status in the context of the majority Han in China, the minority groups in southern China still invest enormously in their built world. They do so, clearly, to make tangible their ethnic identity. But going beyond the picturesque splendor of Dong architecture, this book focuses on the instrumental role their architecture plays in making lively their own social life.

In fact, in addition to representing, or expressing, its inhabitants to the Han and others, minority architecture in southern China also symbolically resembles its inhabitants in many ways. It is an architecture that "speaks" to them, and it is an architecture that is primarily *for* its inhabitants. The built world indeed is the extension of their body and mind; their experience with architecture is figurative, and their understanding of the built world is allegorical. Allegorical architecture does not merely represent, or symbolize, something else; rather, it is a story about its makers and inhabitants. Unlike the symbolism of historical architecture, which needs to be decoded through a speculative reconstruction of the past, among the minority groups in southern China stories about inhabitants are made legible in a *living* state—that is, the recurrent process of the ritualistic making and inhabiting of their built world. This book thus offers architectural analysis of both spatial dispositions (building types) and social life (the workings of the buildings). It is, in other words, a figurative experience that reconciles the inhabitants with their built world and, as well, the objectification of this experience as myth and architectonics.

My basic approach to the study of the built world is to offer "thick description" (Geertz 1973) of Dong architectonics in an effort to understand the workings of architecture in the social world. The focus on Dong architectonics within its regional as well as the global context makes it possible to combine detailed formal analysis of building types and their spatial dispositions with their effects in a social context. Architecture is assumed to be an art form in which the feelings and lives of its makers and inhabitants are embodied. The artifice of architecture—its physical laws—is thus analyzed and contested in terms of its instrumental capacity. The "biographical" undertone of Dong architectonics by no means results in a monograph. On the contrary, it uses the Dong as a case study in order to play out the paradox of universal human conditions and ethnic specificity. My aim, therefore, is to provide an "intermediate writing" that "incorporates ethnography but is not subordinated to it" (Thomas 1991, 316). It is this human common ground that transcends culture and ethnicity; it ensures that no society at any point in history is immune to the desire for progress—and now the overarching Western modernity. Progress and modernity surely have not bypassed rural societies of the minority groups in southern China. The writing of the book thus carries this ambivalence: romanticism and cultural renewal. For minority groups in southern China, romanticism, materialized via architectonics, is a necessity for making a home and identity in the Han and global cosmos; it is in the meantime desired by the Han and others as an exotic cultural counterpart. Progress and cultural renewal inevitably infiltrate into the rural areas but are usually disguised by the mask of ethnicity.

Analogous to this approach is a nondiscriminative and yet strategic juxtaposition of "secondhand" literature and "firsthand" fieldwork observations throughout the book in order to offer not only a personal but hopefully also a discerning view on the workings of architecture. Since the book is neither a monograph on one type of vernacular architecture, nor a comprehensive survey of several of them, the selective use of material serves, in my own conceptual frame, to address the workings of architecture and our built world in general. I begin by outlining a historical and political context of the minority groups in southern China against the background of the majority population Han. The history and ethnicity of the Dong, for example, have been for thousands of years under recurrent fabrications by the Han majority and other groups. These fabrications, however, are only objectified meaningfully through Dong architectonics and their built world—ranging from small shrines to housing, from public structures to settlement patterns.

A settlement pattern in southern China often assumes a posture of human or animal bodies. For the Dong and other minority groups in southern China, an intimate sense of home, and belonging to such a place amid the preeminent Han world, is achieved through ritualistic engagement with their settlements. The myths of migration, ancestors, and their worldviews are in this way allegorically materialized. A settlement pattern enacts figurative imagining in which the extraordinary Dong wind-and-rain bridge is symbolically reified.

The artifice and the symbolic honor of the highly elaborate Dong drum tower, as well as other public structures, are examined in detail from three sources: historical literature, archaeological evidence, and their living state in the process of making and inhabiting. The paradoxical role of the drum tower as both the hearth and the mask of the Dong is made knowable as "choral symbolic power," and in this sense it is empowering in the structuring of Dong society.

As a building type, the pile-built dwellings—houses that are elevated above the ground on timber posts—are widely found throughout southern China, Southeast Asia, and the Pacific region. The universal meaning and its ethnic specificity are placed in such a context to examine the relationship between a building type and its heterogeneity. The way a type is inhabited makes slight differences significant among the similarities within one particular building type and indeed gives life to such a type.

Through a series of self-initiated events in promoting Dong culture, the role of architecture in driving an ethnicity is, rather accidentally, realized by the minority groups in southern China. "Ancient" allegories are seen as symbolic justifications for cultural renewal and progress. "Origin" is reinvented out of time, since many of the old building types continue to be made by the Dong and others in southern China. Political fabrications and textualizations from the Han, the presence of anthropologists and architects in the region, and the transformation from honor to capital in tourism are discussed in relation to the making of architecture in southern China.

If social scientists and anthropologists are led by habitus to examine the interactive relationship between human beings and their built world, a larger purpose of this book is to ask whether the constitution of a human person, in an anthropological sense, is also an essential task of architects, planners, and environmental designers.

1

ARCHITECTONIC FABRICATIONS OF MINORITIES   The Dong and Others

Lu You from the Southern Song dynasty (1127–1279), well known for his poems and extensive travelling experiences, had the following observations on the southern minority groups in his *Laoxue an biji,* or "Notes from an Old Study Shed":

> Unmarried young men are decked with golden chicken feathers in their hair, and unmarried young women wear necklaces made of spiral shells. . . . Men and women sing and dance together when drunk. In the slack season, a parade of about 100 to 200 people is often staged. They sing together, hand in hand, with some people playing *lusheng* at the head of the parade.[1] [Dongzu Jianshi Bianxie Zu 1985, 145]

A taste for exoticism notwithstanding, a certain sense of admiration for the free spirit is also evident between these lines. Lu You may only represent the more liberal views of the Han literati; the minority groups in southern China, however, have also been widely regarded by the Han as *nanman* (literally "southern barbarians"). Historically, there has always been this paradoxical consciousness among the Han about non-Han peoples on their frontiers. The Han, by contrast, being the majority, are known to have a self-assured ethnocentrism, not only against the background of minority groups within China, but also the rest of the world: the meaning of "China," literally the "Middle Kingdom," says it all to some.

Through a long history of contact with the Han, and effectively having been ruled by Han state power for more than two millennia, the minority groups in southern China are very aware of the fact that they cannot afford to indulge themselves with any degree of ethnocentrism. One of the main reasons for the Han to see the southern minority groups as *nanman* is that they historically were, and many of them still are, nonliterate cultures. Though ancient with a history that can be readily traced back many thousands of years, very few of the minority groups have developed a written language of their own, although some of them are now literate in Chinese. The sunny effect of this paradox between the majority Han and the minority groups is this: the Han expect an exoticism from the minorities, which indeed is a necessary counterpart to the mainstream culture that seems to need to draw inspiration from them to renew its own culture; the minority groups, in the meantime, also need a distinctive ethnicity in order to create a legitimate home amid the Han. Without a written language, the development of material culture has as a result flourished largely to reflect this paradox.

Among the most striking aspects of the Dong, for instance, is the richness and intricacy of their material culture. Since their culture has never been made into a "text," it has developed into oral literature, music, dance, and a variety of artifacts, the most dominant, and indeed the most instrumental, of which are rituals and architecture. The Dong possess a meaningful and understandable relationship with their built world, a relationship rarely found between modern citizens and their urban habitat. To provide a context for an architecture-based culture, I shall first explore the historical and political fabrications, mainly from the Han, of the Dong before I give an overall picture of their architecturally disposed culture in this chapter.

Historical and Political Fabrications

A RECORDED HISTORY

The Dong are an ancient but little-known ethnic group who today number more than 2.9 million, a little less than the population of, say, Jamaica. All existing historical records on the Dong are in Chinese, which, as mentioned earlier, was based on various "travel notes" from adventurous Han literati like Lu You.[2] The polarization of the self-centric Han and the *man* or "barbarians" was a widely adopted intellectual framework for Han historical writings on minorities. Although there are few historical references to the Dong, the earliest found in historical Chinese sources dates from the Qin dynasty (221–206 BC). At that time, the ancient inhabitants in today's Dong area were referred to as Qianzhong *man*. During the Han dynasty (206 BC–AD 220) they were known as Wuxi *man*, or Wuling *man*. *Man*, as stated earlier, refers to barbarians in the Chinese language. In the Northern and Southern dynasties (420–589), the minority groups in this region were called Liao. These people were considered to be the descendants of the ancient Baiyue. The Dong were thus thought to be part of that group, for they share similar customs.

In the Song dynasty (960–1279), a number of minorities were recorded living in the cross-border area of today's Hunan and Guizhou provinces. In the middle of the Southern Song dynasty (1127–1279), a Chinese official recorded Wuxi *man* (five-water barbarians) in a book called *Ximan Congxiao*. The five groups were designated variously as Miao, Yao, Liao, Ge-ling, and Ge-lao. According to this book, these five minority groups shared the same customs and language. The name Ge-lao pronounces reasonably similarly to the Dong self-identification of Gaeml, or Geml. The Dong might have been one of those language groups. They, however, have customs and language that are distinctively different from those of the Miao and the Yao. The minority people described by Lu You were referred to as the Geling, the Gelao, the Gelan, the Gelou, and the Shanyao (mountain Yao) in *Laoxue an biji*. Lu You believed that the customs of these *man* were similar to those of the aborigines. Although it is unclear who were the aborigines in that region, Lu You suspected that the *man* were migrants. Since these customs are identical with the contemporary Dong, it is likely that he was in fact referring to the Dong.

No specific records concerning the Dong were found from the Yuan dynasty (1271–1368), and the picture of the Dong was somewhat confusing in that period. Yet during that period, for unknown reasons, an interesting twist occurred: when some Yuan scholars cited the previous historical sources, the name Gelin was changed into Dong (峒), a different character from "侗" but with the same pronunciation. In the Ming dynasty (1368–1644), the name Lin appeared as an abbreviation of Gelin. Also a variety of "Dongs" were indicated in the use of different radicals. It was at this time that the Dong began to be regarded as a branch of the Liao. In the Qing dynasty (1644–1911), these same people were variously termed the Dongmiao, the Dongmin, the Dongjia, or simply the Miao.

Although no monographs were produced, a number of arguments had been advanced about the Dong through ethnographic research in the Republican period (1912–1949). One of the most intriguing propositions was that the Dong were the living remnants of the ancient Han (Zhang Min 1989). This argument was initiated by observation of the Dong language, folk songs, mourning apparel, and even physique and facial features. Extended further, the following historical interpretation was advanced: the earliest Han invasions of the southern regions were carried out by small tribes who fought against heavy odds and were no match for the Miao already living in that region. Hence these tribes were ruled and slowly assimilated by the

Miao, a larger group, which is today found in greater numbers in Thailand, Laos, Vietnam, and Burma where they are known as Hmong. When the large-scale Han invasions occurred between 1376 and 1397 in the Ming dynasty, the Miao, with the assimilated Han tribes, migrated farther south to mountainous jungle areas (Zhang Min 1989, 24). Another Republican-period argument contended that the Dong had always lived together with the Miao and never mixed with two other groups, the Yao and the Zhuang. As in the Ming dynasty, the Dong were still regarded as a branch of the Liao. Some speculations proposed that the Dong came from the Dongting Lake plain and were of the Chu culture (475–221 BC); others simply treated them as part of the Miao (Zhang Min 1989).

DEFINITIONS OF ETHNICITY

The Dong are today one of the fifty-five "minority nationalities" *(shaoshu minzu)* officially acknowledged by the Chinese central government. "Nationality" *(minzu)* and "minority nationality" *(shaoshu minzu)* are the two prevalently used terms to define the relationship between the majority Han and non-Han nationalities. Within this categorization, fifty-six *minzu* have been recorded in the official census of today's China: the Han nationality plus fifty-five *shaoshu minzu*.

The definition of a minority group in the Han context depends on the "nationality policy" of the dynastic power at different periods and has a history that reaches back to before the Qin dynasty, beginning in 221 BC, when China was united by Emperor Qinshihuangdi. To achieve unification, various definitions and categories for the "non-Han nationalities" were invented by the Han state. The present policy defines a minority nationality, such as the Dong, in terms of five criteria: common language *(gongtong yuyan)*; residing both historically and at present in a defined, common territory *(gongtong diyu)*; with a common economic base *(gongtong jingji)*; sharing blood and tradition and possessing a common psychological sentiment *(gongtong xinli suzhi)*—all expressed in a common culture *(gongtong wenhua tedian)* (Liscák 1993, 12–16). In addition, "respecting the minority nationalities' desire" was a vital strategy in implementing the policy. Yet even with these criteria, a community speaking the Dong language and with Dong architecture, particularly a drum tower, could have been officially defined as Miao and vice versa.[3] Such political fabrications of minority groups by the ruling power affect the way they define themselves. Architecture, nonetheless, serves as one of the most potent means of both self and other identification, a point I shall return to later.

The names Dong and Dongjia are Chinese terms. In older literature, the reader might find that these terms were spelled as Tung, Tung-chia, or Tung-jie before pinyin became prevalent. The Chinese character for the Dong previously had *shan* (山 mountain) or *shui* (氵 water) as radicals and was written as "峒" or "洞," characters that literally mean cave. Occasionally the radical *quan* 犭, meaning dog, was attached. In the Sui and Tang dynasties (581–907), the word Dong meant the administrative zone belonging to the local government Jimi Zhou. Since Chinese script is pictographic, however, the implication of such meanings is usually supported by the meaning of their radicals. After 1949, when the new Communist government produced its official definition of minority nationalities, a new character, "侗," was created. It was combined with *ren* 亻, meaning people or person, as the radical to replace those used earlier, which were thought to denigrate the Dong people.[4]

The Dong call themselves Gaeml. Within the variety of local dialects they are also called Jaeml and Jeml. Early English literature sometimes referred to them as Nin Kam (Beauclair 1960, 172) and Kam (Li Fangkuei 1943). With the exception of the Han, other neighboring ethnic groups refer to the Dong in a manner similar to what they call themselves: the Sui call them Kam; the Zhuang, Pu Kjam; the Gelao, Kjam; and the Miao, Ta Ku.

The remote mountain valley region in southwestern China where Guizhou, Guangxi, and Hunan provinces meet constitutes the habitat of the Dong (Figure 1.1). This rugged topography is higher in the northwest and lower to the southeast with elevations ranging from 300 to 2,000 meters. Mountains, basins, plains, and rivers constitute the complicated configuration of this area, with about 1,200 millimeters annual rainfall and 16°C average air temperature. The current Dong population, according to the 2000 census, is 2.96 million.[5] The total population of the Dong in early 1991, for example, already exceeded 2.5 million: some 1.4 million live in Guizhou province as compact communities in Liping, Rongjiang, Congjiang, Tianzhu, Jinping, Jianhe, and Cengong (within the Miao and Dong Autonomous Prefecture of Southeast Guizhou) and also in Yuping, Tongren, and Jiangkou (in the Tongren Area and Wanshan Special Zone); 0.7 million scatter in Tongdao, Xinhuang, Zangjiang, Jingzhou, Chenbu, Huitong, Hongjiang, Qianyang, and Suining in Hunan province; Guangxi province has a population of 0.4 million Dong living in Sanjiang, Longsheng, Rongsui, and Luochen; and about 40,000 Dong live in Enshi, Xuanen, and Xianfeng in Hubei province (Yang Quan 1992, 2). Historical Dong population estimates range from 200,000 (Beauclair 1960, 137) to 700,000 (Bruk 1960, 25) in the 1960s and perhaps 1.4 million in 1982.[6] The birth control policy of one child per family was readjusted to a limit of two children per family for minorities. This supposedly is the policy for the Dong regions, although figures indicating the rapidly increasing Dong population suggest a greater birthrate than that.

The Dong speak their own language, which in some areas is thought to be a musical language with about fifteen tones. Their language is classified by Li Fangkuei (1943) as belonging to the Dong-Shui (Kam-Sui) dialect group

Figure 1.1 *Above:* The Dong are scattered in the southern provinces of Guizhou, Guangxi, and Hunan. This map shows their distribution in the main regions and counties of this cross-border area. The Dong are intermingled with the Han and other minority groups, mainly the Miao and the Zhuang. The shaded areas show the concentrations of Dong populations in this region. The main areas of my fieldwork include Kaili, Rongjiang, Congjiang, and Sanjiang. Source: Drawn by Xing Ruan. *Opposite:* The topography in the Sanjiang area showing mountain river valleys as a distinctive feature of the Dong habitat. Source: *Sanjing Dongzu Zizhixian Zhi* Guangxi Sanjiang Dongzu Zizhixian Zhi Bianzuan Weiyuanhui (1992, 80).

in the Zhuang-Dong branch of the Sino-Tibetan language family. Their language is affiliated with the language of the Zhuang, Buyi, and Dai, but particularly with the Maonan, Gelao, and Shui. Although related to modern Tai dialects such as Dioi (Chung-chia, Zhuang-jia), Tho, and Thai, the Dong-Shui (Kam-Sui) dialects represent an early separation from the mainstream of Tai linguistic development (Li Fangkuei 1943). With the exception of groups such as the Dai in Yunnan, the Li in Hainan Island, and the Thai

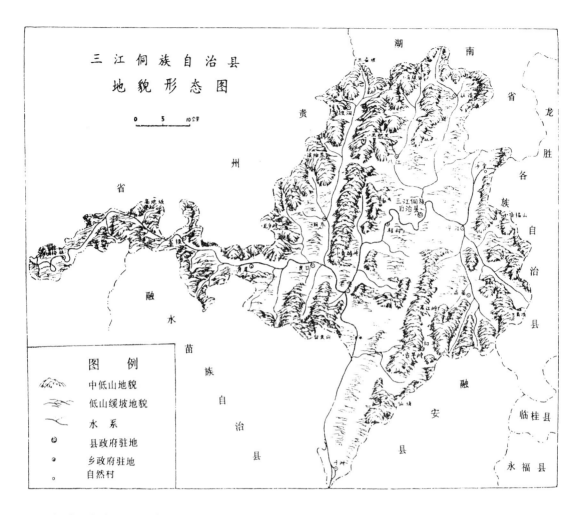

in Thailand, the Dong live in contiguous areas with these related linguistic communities.

There are basically two Dong dialects, northern and southern, each containing three subdialects. The northern dialect includes Dong living in Tianzhu, Xinhuang, Jinxian, Jianhe, Sansui, and northern Jinping, while the southern dialect is found in Liping, Rongjiang, Congjiang, Tongdao, Long-sheng, Sanjiang, Rongshui, Zhenyuan, and southern Jinping. The northern dialect is more influenced by the Chinese language, and most people in this area in fact speak Chinese. In some areas, the Dong language has even been replaced by Chinese. Because of the relatively less frequent contact with the Han, the southern dialect is considered closer to the original.

Using Chinese characters to phonetically record the Dong language was once the only way of writing for a small number of literate Dong. The Han influence started in the Tang dynasty (618–907) when Chinese culture reached a splendid prosperity that radiated widely beyond the Han domain. In the Song dynasty (960–1279), the central government began to establish schools in Chenzhou and Huizhou (today's Liping, Jingzhou, Tongdao, and Suining). This tradition has been maintained. In the Qing dynasty (1636–1911), the creation of a Dong oral literature reached a historical peak. A few Han-educated Dong literati attempted to use Chinese characters to record oral folk traditions in the Dong language, treating Chinese characters simply as phonetic letters. Books written in this way were called "*leec* Gaeml" (Dong books). Following the invention of this method, numerous Dong books such as *Folk Songs, Calendar, Agriculture Book, Medicine, The Book of Family Genealogy,* and *The Book of the Clan Tree* were produced (Yang Quan 1992, 6–11).

In 1952, incited by the new Communist central government, a group of linguists began to research the Dong language and educate the so-called Dong language cadres. A working team investigated twenty-two Dong dialects in fourteen counties and in 1955 decided to use the Zhanglu dialect of Rongjiang as the standard pronunciation. A Latin alphabetic system, designed on the basis of the Zhanglu dialect as a romanization of the Dong language, was made public in 1958. But the implementation of this written language has not been successful. Both strategies—using Chinese characters to phonetically record the Dong language and applying an arbitrary, new Latin alphabetic romanization—remain luxuries for an elitist Chinese-educated Dong group. Overall *the Dong* remain a minority people without a "text."

In 1958, the Minority Nationality Research Institute of the China Science Academy organized field investigations and literature research on the Dong. As a result, *The Brief History of the Dong*, with a Chinese Marxist theoretical framework, was produced in the autumn of 1959. Twenty years later, this version was revised and published in 1985 as the first history book in Chinese on the Dong. The revision and publishing of this book evoked new debates on such issues as the ethnographic names and origins of the Dong, particularly among Dong scholars and local officials educated by and in the manner of Han Chinese.

ORIGIN AND MIGRATION

There are two totally different hypothetical constructions of Dong origins and history, as well as a number of variations (Zhang Min 1989, 35–53). One propounds that while they had different names in different periods, the Dong are an indigenous people and migration never happened. There are several supportive arguments:

- The Dong are believed to have originated from Luoyue of Xiou, a branch of ancient Yue. They were called Liao after the Wei Jin dynasty (220–420).
- The language and customs of the ancient Yue and Liao in historical literature have close connections with the Dong, particularly

the pile-built houses, bronze drums, chicken divination, and young married women not living at their husbands' homes.

■ In the local dialect the Dong name is pronounced "Qian," Guizhou's ancient name; they even have the same meaning (a place enclosed by tree branches).

■ The Dong have been living in the cross-border area of Hunan, Guizhou, and Guangxi for thousands of years. Their language, social structure, and customs are very stable, and there are no historical records of migrations caused by wars or natural disasters.

■ Although some folk songs describe the Dong migration from Wuzhou (a place in today's Guangxi), these refer to the internal migrations of the ancient Yue and the Liao. One folk song also proves that there were Dong ancestors already living in this region before the migrations from Wuzhou (Yang and Wu 1981).

But there is another migration interpretation based on the following arguments:

■ Some folk songs, such as "The Grandfather Going to the Upper Reaches," "The Origin of Ancestors," and "The Ancestor Founding the Village," popular in the Liping, Rongjiang, and Congjiang areas, are very important oral histories of the Dong. These folk songs describe the places where their ancestors used to live. The transliteration of these place-names is very similar to the Tang-dynasty (618–907) place-names of today's Wuzhou and Liuzhou area. Due to population pressures, some ancient Dong migrated via the rivers to the upper reaches to look for new lands.

■ A Qing-dynasty (1636–1911) publication, "The Book of Wu Family Genealogy," unearthed in Enshi, Hubei province, was written in the Dong language with Chinese characters. The book mentions the migration and indicates the Dong homeland as Liuzhou in Guangxi province. It also describes the landscape at the time when their ancestors first arrived.

■ Sax is the Dong goddess enshrined in the southern area. Both "The Song of Sax" and the chants to found a Sax altar tell the story of Sax migrating with Dong ancestors from the Wuzhou area to a place called Daeml Heic Maix Mags, near Longer and Liping. In the past, when setting up a new Sax altar or refurbishing an old one, the villagers had to go to the Daeml Heic Maix Mags to fetch a pinch of soil and put it on the altar.

■ Social customs in southern Guangxi (the Wuzhou and Liuzhou area recorded in Han literature) can be found in the present

Dong area: festivals, food, architecture, dress, social activities, weddings, funerals, music, divination, and so on.

- The Dong migration stories can be found in many local annals and county annals. This is particularly important in relation to the Wuzhou and Liuzhou annals, where the Dong were recorded as local inhabitants.
- In the Rongjiang, Congjiang, Liping, and Sanjiang areas, some names of mountains, places, rivers, graveyards, and villages are still Miao names. Legends of Miao moving away from this area are widespread.

In summary, then, the Dong are largely believed to be migrants.

Another proposition of migration contends that the Dong are from Jianfu in Jiangxi province. This migration story is quite popular in the Dong area, particularly in Liping, Congjiang, and Sanjiang. The Dong with family names of Yang, Wu, Shi, Lu, Li, and Ou usually believe that their ancestors came from Jianfu and that they were Han. This surely is not coincidental with the interpretation in the Republican period (1912–1949) that treated the Dong as living but ancient Han. Historical records are dug out to support this argument. As early as the Song and Yuan dynasties (960–1368), some Han Chinese migrated to the Dong area from the lower reaches of the Yangzi River. In the Ming dynasty (1368–1644), Emperor Zhu Yuanzhang, wanting to strengthen the rule of the central government, executed military control in the Dong area. For this reason, many Han soldiers and officials were sent to the Dong region. According to the "Lipingfu Annals," most of them were from Jianfu in Jiangxi province.

In addition to the question of migration, other debates center on the issue of the ethnic origins of the Dong. Generally speaking, the Dong are believed to have originated from a branch of the ancient Luoyue, who are known to have lived in Guizhou at the end of the Eastern Han dynasty (25–220). The Luoyue were native people of the area now inhabited by the Dong. The historically recorded Luoyue customs—tattoos, bronze drums, men and women bathing together in rivers, and the like—are still alive in today's Dong social life. In some places, even mountains and clans are named Luo. Through time, the ancient Baiyue migrated into this region, mingling with the native population. Other propositions regarding the origins of the Dong associate them with the ancient Yue, the Ouyue, the Ganyue, the Jinyue, and others. In all of these cases, the Dong are thought to have derived from these people.

All these propositions are historical as well as political, and they remain speculative. It is impossible and, at least for the Dong, unnecessary to trace the origins of these hypotheses. In any case, the written constructions of the Dong and the associated debates remain the concerns of the literate Dong, an elitist group within a minority group. But the historical and political fabrications of the Dong have been materialized, indirectly and yet intricately, through architecture, which is instrumentally empowering in the life of the Dong. Since architecture is not a text, meanings are transmitted through a nonlinguistic but allegorical manner. The distinctive workings of architecture are most evident in the case of the Dong among other nonliterate minority groups in southern China, which indeed is an architecture-based culture.

An Architecture-Based Culture

Although the Dong continue to display richness in their material culture, they do share many cultural affinities with other minority groups and with the Han. As examples, both the Dong and the Miao have traditions of water buffalo fighting and playing the *lusheng,* a mouth organ; the way the Dong hold ceremonies to their goddess Sax can also be found among the Miao; the Dong share language similarities with other Tai linguistic groups; the Daoist *fengshui*—a form of geomancy mainly used by the Han to decide the siting of buildings, graves, and settlements, as well as their spatial disposition—is also practiced by the Dong; they celebrate Han Chinese New Year; they transplant Han historical stories into their Dong opera; they borrow Han gods for practical needs; even their architecture is more or less built in a Han manner—elaborate roofed bridges, for example, can be widely found among the Han in Zhejiang, Anhui, and Jiangxi provinces. From these perspectives, it might appear that nothing is quintessentially Dong.

But all these material cultural fragments are staged into a composite disposition through their architecture: the Dong and their culture are architecturally objectified in the process of inhabiting and making their built world. Framed in their architecture, the eclectic cultural artifacts and associated activities are given a grounding confinement, and the overall cultural experience thus becomes tangible and real.

SOCIAL ORGANIZATION AND SETTLEMENT

Regardless of their origins, the Dong and their cultural features are closely tied to water. They have traditionally dwelt in mountain river valleys where, with the help of water buffaloes, they practice rice cultivation in irrigated fields and along steep mountain terraces. They raise fish in flooded rice paddies, go fishing in rivers, and wash long lengths of indigo-dyed cloth in mountain streams. Dong architecture and settlements are usually built on mountainous terrain to leave more flat land for cultivation (Figure 1.2). A Dong village is typically composed of some public structures, housing, rice storage, and a graveyard. Public structures include Sax altars, or shrines, the drum tower, the opera stage, and the wind-and-rain bridges. These structures

Figure 1.2 Zuolong village of the Sanjiang region in Guangxi province showing flat rice paddies along the river as well as housing and drum towers on one side of the river valley, all built on mountainous terrain. Source: Photograph by Xing Ruan, 1992.

are all delegated with their own role and place in the Dong's daily routines and seasonal festive activities, and they work together to make legible a Dong architectural narrative.

The basic unit of Dong settlements is the *zhai*, which might once have been a stockade village but is today a hamlet or small settlement. In the past, one *zhai* commonly contained only one clan's surname. This surname was thought of as a "big surname" for all the families of that clan with a drum tower built to signify the single surname. With a growing population and increasing migration over time, different surnames began to mix with each other, even within one *zhai*. It was necessary for a rite to be performed in order for outsiders to be adopted under the *zhai*'s original big surname in such a way that they could still keep their original family surnames. The *zhai*'s collective activities, however, continued to be conducted under the *zhai*'s big surname, which was the original clan's surname. Often several *zhai* were interconnected, usually inhabiting a mountain river valley, to make a village. Each *zhai* in the village thus had its own drum tower to signify the clan. Roads, brooks, or some other identification device served as the boundary markers, but in an indicative rather than an absolute demarcation.

The *zhai* is also the basic unit of Dong social organization in that living together under the clan's surname probably indicates the historical remains of a Dong patriarchal system. In a village, every *zhai* was supposed to have its own clan name, customary law and regulations, and a chief. The chief is called *nyens laox* or *yangp laox*, which means a venerated old man. This chief was the head of the clan and the head of the *zhai* and naturally was the leader. The chief was in charge of daily disputes and outside contacts, and he also coordinated the collective decision making. In cases of collective decision making, the drum tower was used as the tribunal and public meetinghouse, which still is the case. If a *zhai* does not have a drum tower, a public house, called *dangc kah* or *dangc wagx*, is used for these purposes. Once a resolution is passed through the public meeting in the drum tower, it is meant to be enacted without reservation.

Dong customary law usually has both tangible and invisible forms. The physical embodiment is a stone tablet engraved with the content (in Chinese) of this law, which is erected at the edge of the *zhai* or in some public area (Figure 1.3). The nonphysical form is the so-called oral tablet—a customary law made up as chants for the public to recite. Even so, a large piece of stone, called *jinl bial*, has to be set up as a physical empowerment of this law. The content of Dong customary law includes issues relating to the family, marriage, land,

Figure 1.3 Stone tablet of customary law at the gate of Xindi village in the Congjiang region, Guizhou province. In Chinese it reads: "Xindi New Regulations." The use of simplified Chinese characters and poor calligraphy indicate that this stone tablet was erected not long before my fieldwork in 1993. Source: Photograph by Xing Ruan, 1993.

house, property, forest, safety, and protocols of social conduct between young men and women.[7] For the Dong, the significance of such meanings does not take the form of a text; rather, it is always materialized as architectonic elements. Drum towers and stone tablets are examples of this point. In Dong society, a punishment for someone who breaks customary law is to exclude this person from access to the drum tower.

A different social organization, called the *kuanx,* tied the *zhai* to a village and linked villages to a larger Dong region. The *kuanx* was in fact a military alliance. Ten to twenty *zhai* and villages made up a small *kuanx,* and several small *kuanx* formed a big *kuanx.* A Dong folk song states that a big *kuanx* "starts from Guzhou (Rongjiang) and ends at Liuzhou (in Guangxi)" (Yang Quan 1992, 129). Both small *kuanx* and big *kuanx* had their own *kuanx* ground as a place of congregation. The head of a small *kuanx* was chosen from *zhai* chiefs; the head of a big *kuanx* was elected from the heads of small *kuanx.* These heads of *kuanx* also took care of the daily routines of the *zhai;* their main task, however, was to direct villagers to resist foreign aggression in the event of war. *Kuanx* heads did not receive any remuneration for their work, but a man called the *kuanx leg* was hired to do the routine work. This man was fed by all the villagers and did not need to do farming. In peacetime, the *kuanx leg* looked after the drum tower and supplied firewood for the fire pit in the tower. In an emergency, he climbed the tower to beat the drum, solicited villagers' attention, fired iron cannons as a signal, and called people together; the *kuanx leg* also served as a messenger between the *kuanx.*

Whether in peacetime or during war, the *kuanx* activities were staged through the drum tower and the *kuanx* ground. In the *kuanx* alliance, once a *zhai* or a village in the same *kuanx* received a piece of plank on which was tied a chicken feather, a piece of charcoal, and a chili, it was obliged to dispatch troops to join the battle and fire iron cannons to inform neighboring *zhai.* According to *kuanx* regulations, a *zhai* ought to be punished if it failed to respond. Every three to five years, the Dong would have a *kuanx* assembly. All adult men were required to attend the meeting, where the *kuanx* regulations were revised, explained, and publicized, particularly for young members. A water buffalo was slaughtered and shared by all the participants. The *kuanx* continued to work until the early Republican period. But now the system of village chief *(nyens laox)* still operates, coexisting with the Communist administrative system.

CULTURAL LIFE AND ARCHITECTURE

Dong architecture is built with China fir, a tree that they call *shan,* or *sha.* The Dong are believed to have had a long history of planting and cultivating China fir. The Dong region is also one of the best-known forest zones in China. China fir has many species. Favored by the Dong is one called "eighteen-year

China fir," a species that matures in about eighteen years. The Dong usually plant a number of these trees when they have a newborn child. Over eighteen years as the child matures and reaches the age of marriage, the trees should have grown to a size where they can be harvested to build the new home for the newly wed couple.

The trunk of the China fir is the basic element of Dong architecture. Closely tied to their built world, the China fir is also thought to be a holy tree that protects the Dong settlement. Dong daily life dwells on a variety of animistic religious beliefs and practices. Benevolent and malevolent spirits are seen to exist everywhere in nature. Valleys, rivers, mountains, rocks, and, most important, fir trees, all have spiritual significance. It is necessary to acknowledge and attend to these spirits in a proper way so as not to destroy an existing balance. For this reason, some fir trees hundreds of years old have survived and not been cut. It is believed that disaster is sure to follow if people trespass against these beliefs.

An architectonic analogy—that of an umbrella—has been derived from the fir tree. A village needs an "umbrella" to cast shade for the comfort of its people. The drum tower, a dominant multistoried structure, certainly has the capacity to protect villagers and cast shade for them. The form of the drum tower appears to serve as the analogy of the fir tree, giving it architectonic significance (Figure 1.4). When a drum tower is burnt down or destroyed by accident, the Dong erect the trunk of a fir tree on the site of the drum tower as a temporary replacement before the new one is built. In some Dong areas, real umbrellas are commonly used to crown their goddess Sax altar (Figure 1.5). The Sax altar is supposed to be protected in the shade of the umbrella. The Dong believe that the umbrella used to be the weapon of their Sax when she was alive. Quite literally, the power of the architectonics of this fir tree has been transformed into the weapon of the Sax.

Sax's name varies from place to place: Sax Sis, Sax Mags, Sax Pingl, Sax Daengc. In the Dong language they all mean grandmother. She is thought to be a historical heroine known as Xinni who died for the freedom of the Dong over a thousand years ago. In the southern Dong area, almost every *zhai* or village has a Sax altar, or a shrine, and a temple (Figure 1.6). Nobody is allowed to enter the Sax altar except on a ceremony day. An annual ritual of Sax worship is practiced early in the first month of the Chinese lunar year. It seems the whole ritual is a performance of war combat (Figure 1.7). A procession of young men and women carrying hunting rifles mimics going off to battle. The ritual starts from and ends at the drum tower. Tea, meat, incense paper, and candles are offered to Sax. Before the procession begins, the elder members of the *zhai* gather together at the altar to share food and sing praises to Sax. *Lusheng* are played and brass gongs are beaten. The procession usually follows the track of the *zhai*'s boundary. During the procession, the young

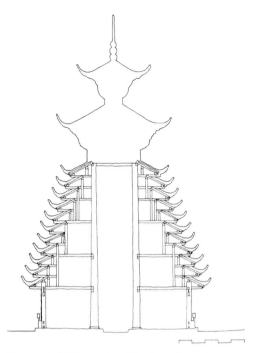

Figure 1.4 This section of the Zengchong drum tower does look like an architectonic tree. Zengchong village is in the Congjiang region, Guizhou province. Source: Drawn by Xing Ruan.

people stop along the way to fire off shots and let off firecrackers. Small iron cannons placed in the fields are likewise set off, creating a cacophony of noise. Men carry flags and guns decorated with leaves and paper streamers. Each *zhai* has its own unique form of decoration. A straw head is brought back to hang up at Sax's altar after the procession. Young women dance hand in hand in a circle in front of the drum tower to celebrate the victory of the battle. The architectonic elements, such as the drum tower, the Sax altar, and the boundary of the *zhai,* play critical roles in structuring the ritual. A special tea ceremony is sometimes held at the time when one *zhai* is to fight against other *zhai* or to repel a foreign invasion. If the annual Sax ceremony is an imagined war combat, it is more than an occasional compensation for the quiet sedentary life. It claims the meaning and pattern of the settlement, which will be elaborated on in the next chapter.

Sax is thought to be the most powerful goddess: she controls everything, including maintaining the peace of the village and making Dong life prosperous. Most of the other Dong gods are also female. For example, the mountain goddess is Sax Tiuk, the bridge and bed goddesses are called Saxgaos Jiuc, or Saxgaos Xangc, the soul goddess is Sax Liagx, the smallpox goddess is Sax Doh, and the goddess of the distiller's yeast is Sax Bins. A number of male gods are borrowed from the Han. These Dong gods include Leizhu, Wuchang, Nangyeu, Feishan, Tudi, Wenchang, and Guansheng. Each god is supposed to be worshipped on a specific date; generally, however, the Dong worship them whenever they have a practical problem to solve. The gods all take architectonic forms. For example, Tudi, the earth god, is represented in various small shrines scattered

Figure 1.5 A sheltered Sax altar in Chejiang village of the Rongjiang region in Guizhou province showing the altar protected and indeed "shaded" by an umbrella. Source: Photograph by Xing Ruan, 1992.

Figure 1.6 This Sax altar is a round hillock constructed of stones; the boxwood tree provides "shade" for the Sax. Zengchong village, Congjiang region, Guizhou province. Source: Photograph by Xing Ruan, 1993.

Figure 1.7 The Sax ritual performed on 23 January 1993 in Longtu village of the Congjiang region showing young men firing off shots in front of the Sax temple after the procession. Source: Photograph by Xing Ruan, 1993.

Figure 1.8 This Tudi (earth god) shrine in Mapang village of the Sanjiang region in Guangxi province is a miniature of a Han temple. Source: Photograph by Xing Ruan, 1992.

throughout the village (Figure 1.8). Guansheng, or Guandi,[8] is another popular Han god in the Dong area. For the Han, he was venerated as a god of war and also as a god of justice and righteousness: parties to a dispute take their case to his temple to be settled. For the Dong, Guandi is interpreted as an omnipotent god who can solve all practical problems. Unlike the Han, the Dong do not have temples dedicated to Guandi; he does, however, have a special place since he is usually housed in wind-and-rain bridges.

Dong bridges are significant public structures in the settlements: they are usually large-scale, roofed wooden structures known as wind-and-rain bridges (Figure 1.9). Seemingly, wind-and-rain bridges offer sheltered rest for weary travelers and protection from the elements. Since Guandi (and sometimes other gods; but they are, surprisingly, mainly Han gods) is housed in these bridges, they become temples on necessary occasions (Figure 1.10). Small bridges are known as flower bridges in the southern Dong region. They are usually built to span tiny, meandering streams (Figure 1.11) or simply built on the ground without spanning a river. Although Dong bridges sometimes serve as temples, generally they house worldly activities. These bridges are frequently the scenes of social gatherings on hot or rainy days as well as locations for chance, romantic meetings under the moonlight. Dong bridges are found both outside and inside the villages. A *zhai,* or a village, may have several bridges. Some bridges form an integral part of a composite structure with the drum tower and the opera stage as the center of a village (Figure 1.12). The position of bridges within the overall settlement pattern has to be carefully chosen, however, for the bridges are believed to have *fengshui* powers that can protect the village's wealth from being dissipated through rivers.

Dong daily activities, such as family life, marriage, textile making, and antiphonal singing, are largely framed and displayed within their houses. In most Dong areas, the houses are on piles called *ganlan* in Chinese. The upper floors are raised above the ground and serve as living quarters, while the ground floor is kept for domestic animals and storage. Dong homes are usually built as three bays. On the second level of what is considered to be the front of the house is a roofed but open and well-lit porch; at the back are rooms (Figure 1.13). Normally the Dong have relatively small, two-generation families; occasionally three or even four generations live together. Brothers and their families take turns to host and feed their elderly parents. The center

Figure 1.9 The Pingyan wind-and-rain bridge near Ma'an village of the Sanjiang region, Guangxi province. Source: Photograph by Xing Ruan, 1992.

Figure 1.10
One of the Han god shrines housed in the Badou wind-and-rain bridge, Sanjiang region in Guangxi province. Wind-and-rain bridges become temples on necessary occasions. Source: Photograph by Xing Ruan, 1992.

Figure 1.11 The Ouyang bridge in Heli village, Sanjiang region of Guangxi province, is a large-scale elaborate structure but spans only a small stream. Source: Photograph by Xing Ruan, 1992.

Figure 1.12 One of the centers in Zhaoxin village is formed by a combination of a drum tower, a wind-and-rain bridge, and an open square. Liping region of Guizhou province. Source: Photograph by Xing Ruan, 1993.

of each room on the second level contains an open fire pit on the floor. Except for some very special occasions, such as the moment the Sax ritual is being practiced, the fire has to be carefully protected at all times in order to keep the family's genesis alive. In this sense, the fire pit signifies the continuity of a family.

In addition to the balcony and fire pit room, the remainder of the house consists of bedrooms off the main room. These rooms occur mainly on the second and third levels; occasionally there is also a fourth level. Ten to twelve rooms are about the average for one house. The elderly are provided with heated bedrooms in the back part of the house. In Dong areas such as Tianzhu and Rongjiang, because of the greater Han influence, the houses are built on the ground: the family live downstairs, and the second floor is used for storage; animals then live in rooms to the side of the downstairs room (Figure 1.14).

Textile making plays an important role in a Dong woman's life. Not only the house but porches, bridges, and roadside pavilions frequently serve as textile workshops. On sweltering summer days, Dong girls sit on low stools set in mountain brooks under the shade of roofed wind-and-rain bridges, embroidering intricate designs on strips of white cloth, handwoven from threads finely spun from cotton grown in nearby fields.[9]

Although the drum is rarely beaten to solicit attention from villagers, the Dong drum tower is typically the highest, and symbolically the most revered, structure in the village. The plan shapes vary from that of a nine-square grid to a hexagon or octagon. The multistoried, pagoda-like roofs are always odd numbers, however, ranging from three to fifteen levels. In most cases, the ground level of the lower pavilion is where the drum tower is inhabited and there are no upper floors. A fire pit is directly at the center. Long benches are

Figure 1.14 A
"grounded" Dong
house in Chejiang
village of the Rong-
jiang region. Source:
Photograph by Xing
Ruan, 1992.

Figure 1.15 The interior of the lower pavilion in the Gaozeng drum tower, Congjiang region in Guizhou province, showing the central fire pit and long benches around it. Source: Photograph by Xing Ruan, 1993.

placed around the fire (Figure 1.15). A shrine is sometimes constructed on the wall opposite the front gate of the tower. In addition to serving as a public meetinghouse, dispute tribunal, and symbol of a clan's surname, almost all aspects of Dong social life and cultural practice are centered in and around the drum tower. It is not only a place where villagers congregate for festivals and rituals and special meetings but also where Dong people often gather in the evenings to listen to the elders' stories of their past and to practice their folk songs.

The Dong have a rich oral tradition in poems and legendary stories. Poems sung as folk songs, as well as stories handed down to the younger generations, all occur in the drum tower. The drum tower is also one of the stages to display the musical talents of the Dong. During festivals, the unique Dong polyphonic chorus called *al laox* (literally, the big songs) is often performed in the drum tower (Figure 1.16). Dong festivals are frequent and occur throughout the whole year, providing opportunities for singing contests, dances, music, opera plays, water buffalo and bird fights, and a variety of rituals and ceremonies.

Festive activities are traditional steps for young people towards courtship and marriage. The drum tower is almost always the center in these festivals. In an old custom, several weeks before an important festival village elders send their young men to nearby villages to invite the unmarried girls to attend. On the eve of the festival, the young men come to the village of the invited women with flutes and drums, bringing them back to meet in their village's drum tower. After a rich feast, the young men and women sit in parallel rows in the drum tower, facing one another under the eyes of their elders and becoming acquainted by spontaneously singing to each other. Until dawn, traditional songs mingle with the playing of the flute and *pipa*. The next morning, dressed in their finest woven and embroidered clothing and adorned with handmade silver bangles, the women assemble in their own village drum tower to wait. From the other village, the young men deliberately walk back and forth three times, playing flutes and drums, before the women are coaxed into accompanying them to their village for more festivities.

Another popular musical form of the Dong is the folk opera. A man named Wu Wencai wrote and performed the first Dong operatic play about 150 years ago (Li Ruiqi 1989). Accompanied by lyric *pipa* songs, this play marked the formation of a Dong tradition that is still being carried out today. Stories of Dong operas come from both Han and Dong narrative poems. Some are historical plays, such as that of Wu Mian, a hero from the Ming dynasty (1368–1644) who led the Dong and the Miao in a series of uprisings covering a period of eight years. In this play, Wu Mian takes on mythical properties. The form, content, and style of Dong folk operas are similar to a variety of Han rural operas.

Figure 1.16 A Dong *al laox* performed on 21 January 1993 during the Chinese New Year in the drum tower of Xiao-huang village, Congjiang region, Guizhou province. Source: Photograph by Xing Ruan, 1993.

Figure 1.17 The Dong opera stage in Baxie village, Sanjiang region of Guangxi province. It is often like a pile-built house that opens at the front. Source: Photograph by Xing Ruan, 1992.

The basic Dong opera stage is a pile-built house that is open at the front with some additional rooms wrapping around the open stage. The roof is often designed as a variation of a drum tower roof (Figure 1.17). Usually located near the drum tower, the opera stage commonly shares the square to form the center of a village. The opera stage occasionally has its own square that becomes another open space in the settlement. Village amateur opera troupes, which are often invited to perform in neighboring villages and towns, are warmly received by young and old. An opera performance attracts a mass gathering, which keeps Dong oral tradition alive.

In the chapters that follow, the workings of architecture among the minority groups in southern China—in the case of the Dong the settlement pattern, public structures, and housing, as well as the transformation of their roles due to modernization—are framed in detail in a succession of movements between the analysis of the built habitat as spatial dispositions and that of their "social life" in the process of making and inhabiting. The built world, as we tend to believe, shapes us as human persons. But to what extent is a community afforded a character through its buildings and streets? How does the making and inhabiting of a habitat interact with the cultivation of a human person and his or her habitus—be it a minority in southern China or an ethnic ghetto in a contemporary Western city? And how in general should the workings of our built world be discerned? These questions will be examined by situating the living myth and architectonics in southern China within a broad historical as well as contemporary context.

2

MYTH AND RITUALISTIC POSTURES
The Workings of the Settlement

The Italian architect Giuseppe Terragni, in 1936, depicted his newly completed Casa del Fascio (Fascist Party local headquarters) in Como with a famous photomontage: the building, with a coffer-grid open frontage, is presented as the central stage of a mass rally in an open square (Figure 2.1). The scene is so singularly compelling, it is as if Casa del Fascio, the building itself, were addressing this massive congregation. A rally of this scale perhaps never happened in reality, but the architect was hopelessly romantic, for this is the kind of instrumental capacity of the building that Terragni had hoped for.

The instrumental role that the built world plays in animating social life is most evident at the scale of a settlement pattern, that is, the scale of a village or a town. Settlement is used here to emphasize the process of making the built fabric, or formal structure, of a village, which I call pattern. This level of social animation is especially true for the village and town patterns of the minorities in southern China, which serve as templates for meaningful and legible social interactions, predominantly at a collective level. These patterns in which architectural elements are articulated together are indeed a materialization of allegories related to origins and migrations, which are reasserted through recurrent rituals. Architectural elements and the settlement pattern itself sometimes assume anthropomorphic and zoomorphic connotations that assist villagers in gaining a figurative understanding of, and hence an intimate relationship with, their settlements. A striking aspect of such a settlement is that it also allows Han settlement features, such as *fengshui* patterns, to be absorbed as an integral part of its own structures.

This chapter focuses on the relationships between architectural elements and their disposition within Dong settlements. It is divided into four main sections: the first describes myths of origin and migration and relates them to Dong settlement; the second describes the main architectural elements and their disposition in Dong settlements; the third examines some of the main rituals that enact these elements as integral aspects of Dong culture; finally, the settlement of Ma'an is used as a case study to summarize the key points.

The "regional" character of a Dong settlement is not merely geographic. Carol Burns (1991, 159) points out that a region is not a broadly homogeneous or indefinite geographical area: "The derivation of region stems from the Latin 'regere,' meaning 'to rule,' recalling the precise relationship between the land and the power of the ruler or king. Today, we must choose to be ruled by the region. The architectural implications of this term underline the

Figure 2.1 Photomontage by Giuseppe Terragni depicting a mass rally in front of the newly completed Casa del Fascio. Source: This image first appeared in the Italian journal *Quadrante,* October 1936.

power of political and ideological control in shaping physical areas." Having been ruled by the majority Han for many thousands of years, the Dong are an ethnic group that has never established a state power. Even now, the Dong exist under Han Chinese state power. The Dong region is an area historically considered remote from the center of China. This "remoteness" is more a political and cultural designation than a geographic one. The southern minorities, as a result of this perceived remoteness, were seen as and called *nanman* by the Han, and the region is described in Chinese idiom as "Heaven is high, and the Emperor is far away" *(Tian gao Huangdi yuan).*[1] Although politically ruled by Han state power, the Dong are some of those "southern barbarians" existing far from the civilized world. This regional and historical remoteness allowed, and still allows, the Dong to culturally identify themselves in a number of respects. Dwellings, and settlements in particular, are among the most decisive means of creating a cultural ethnicity. Dwelling, therefore, forms a critical part of Dong habitus, allowing them to strategically react to the political and historical fabrications imposed by the Han.

Despite the diverse and rugged topography of the region, the Dong only locate themselves in the mountain river valleys. These valleys are not neutral but preoccupied by the allegories of Dong myths of origin and migration and by "water-based" boatman's dreams. According to Sumet (1988), these "water-based" people lived on the Asian coast. They created pile-built structures and other water-related artifacts. The pile-built structure is one of the most important cultural artifacts they have retained since migrating to the interior of the mainland by boat via rivers. Based on some common features in architecture (pile-built structures in particular) and other artifacts, and perhaps even linguistic affiliations, the Dong and other Tai linguistic groups are believed to be culturally tied to Austronesian cultures.[2] The terraced rice paddies and settlements of pile-built structures are two major human creations that the Dong bring to the natural site of this region. These distinctively occupied and claimed mountain river valleys stand in sharp contrast to the highland Miao settlements in the same region.

The location, position, and general morphology of Dong settlements result from a combination of Dong myths of origin and migration plus an economy based on rice paddy farming—in other words, a combination of cultural production and local circumstances. Settlement is not, however, only an outcome. It is also an ongoing action, a constant mapping and remapping of the site through the processes of making and inhabiting. As noted in Chapter 1, the architectural elements of a Dong settlement usually include a drum tower and square, housing, wind-and-rain bridges, Sax altars or shrines, an opera stage, a graveyard, earth god shrines, village gates, well shelters, roadside pavilions, and barns. The location and general morphology of a Dong settlement—and, more important, the disposition and composite order of these architectural elements—construct a legacy of the past for the Dong. This legacy is made tangible in the sense that it is experienced directly and given concrete meaning when the Dong make and inhabit their settlements. For the Dong, making and inhabiting their settlements are symbolic journeys that connect them experientially to their migration myth, to the goddess Sax, to *kuanx* defense, to their ancestor's clan, to *fengshui,* to anthropomorphic and zoomorphic legends.

Myth and Settlement

Historical facts and issues—such as the ethnic origin of the Dong, whether they are an indigenous or migratory people, and from where they migrated (Wuzhou in Guangxi province, or Jianfu in Jiangxi province, as covered in Chapter 1)—are not the concern here. The origins and migrations of the Dong in this chapter are viewed as allegorical myths. They either take form as oral literature or they are made "real" in the sense that they are empowered through settlement and architecture.[3]

Settlement and architecture are not illustrations of myths. Myths become knowable in the processes of making and inhabiting. At the scale of a settlement, it is the mapping and settling on a large site. A site is culturally preoccupied; the actions of mapping a site are also enacted as historically and culturally preoccupied rituals. But there are no precise correspondences between rituals and what the settlement and architecture accommodate. As well, myth and architecture generate each other. Before proceeding to a discussion of the mapping of a site, a brief consideration of Dong myths of origin and migration in relation to the site is in order. In a quite universal sense shared by many premodern cultures, the Dong believe that the experience of human beings is ordered in relation to a sequence of origination, extermination, rebirth, and settlement. The Dong view themselves as only one of many reborn groups; other such groups include the Han, the Miao, the Shui, and the Yao. Rebirth is relevant to each group's distinctive character and to their final settlement.[4]

According to Dong myth, a devastating natural disaster caused a human extermination; human beings were reborn from the first baby of the only surviving couple, a brother and sister. The blood of the baby turned into the Han, who chose to live on vast river plains because blood flowed in big rivers. The Miao were made from bones; since bones are like hard trees that should grow on mountains, the Miao chose to live on high land. Flesh became the Dong, who were to be nourished by both water and land; that is why the Dong chose to live in mountain river valleys.[5] The Dong myth of origin gives anthropomorphic and zoomorphic features to those mountain-river-valley sites and establishes an intimate relationship between water and land. For the Dong, different sites and settlements are arbitrarily associated with the characters of their inhabitants. Sites are thus preoccupied by thoughts.

The Dong myth of migration not only enhances these preoccupied site qualities but even makes them culturally and politically empowering. As with their origins, there are many scenarios of Dong migration. Without going into details, the basic migration route most relevant to Dong sites is the one relating to the myth that they lived previously in Wuzhou of Guangxi province (Figure 2.2). Because Wuzhou was overpopulated, particularly by the Han, or because natural disasters occurred, such as drought, the Miao and the Dong decided to migrate to the upper reaches of the rivers (Yang and Wu 1981, 110). The Miao, a hardworking people, went to remote, thickly forested mountains to get *nanmu*, a high-quality hardwood, which they used to make boats. The Dong, by contrast, simply made their boats from nearby maple. Together they started their migration journey on an auspicious day. The Miao's *nanmu* boat went faster than the Dong's maple boat. One day

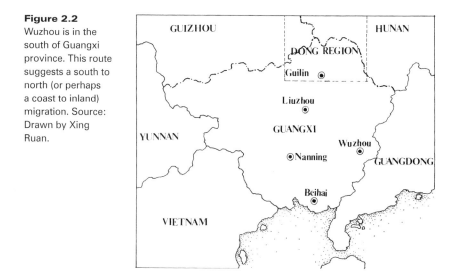

Figure 2.2
Wuzhou is in the south of Guangxi province. This route suggests a south to north (or perhaps a coast to inland) migration. Source: Drawn by Xing Ruan.

they stopped to have lunch together, and the Miao kindly suggested that they swap boats with the Dong, allowing the Dong to go ahead and leave straw signs for the Miao to follow. Unfortunately, the straw signs at a river junction were moved to the other side of the riverbank by some wild pigs. Wind blew the straw signs to the mountain slope. The Miao, thinking that the Dong had gone into the mountains, landed and tried to follow them. They failed to find the Dong, however, and eventually settled on mountain highlands. The Dong kept travelling to the upper reaches and finally settled in the mountain river valleys.

The choice of site in the Dong migration allegory culturally and politically distinguishes the Dong from the Han and the Miao. One of the implications of Dong migrations is obviously that both the Dong and the Miao were somehow driven to the upper reaches and high mountains by the Han. The distinction of the upper versus the lower reaches is how the Dong have henceforth been differentiated from the Han. In relation to the Miao, the mountain river valley versus highland distinction is not only a geographic one: the Dong view themselves as socially and culturally superior to the Miao.[6]

From Wuzhou to the present Dong region—the cross-border area of Guizhou, Guangxi, and Hunan provinces—the migration route is roughly from south to north. Based on the architectural and other material cultural features, or perhaps linguistic affiliations, one possible assumption is that the Dong once lived along the coastal margins of Asia. If they did, they probably have forgotten their migration from the south and even seem to have forgotten their migration from the coast to Wuzhou. Nevertheless, water-associated analogies and nautical images are very much part of the Dong's site and settlement. A widely held belief among the Dong is that a settlement has to be backed by thick forest, because a village is the boat and the forest is the water that bears the boat. As an extension of this analogy, the drum tower is often seen as the "mast and sail" of the village boat.[7] Another interesting water-associated analogy for the settlement is the "fish nest" in the water. The Dong's own name for themselves, Gaeml, also literally means "fish nest." (Other nautical images, such as "coil," are discussed later in this chapter.)

Dong sites and settlements can be generally classified as "mountain types" and "plain types." The mountain type of settlement usually is a village that is built on the terraced mountain slope facing the river and roughly aligned south. The flat land is thus left for rice paddies and fishponds. Ma'an, analyzed later in this chapter, is a typical example in this regard (Figure 2.3). This type of Dong settlement usually has a stunningly picturesque skyline (Figure 2.4). In large mountain river valleys, Dong settlements are sometimes built on flat land along the riversides. In Zhaoxin in Liping of Guizhou, probably the biggest "plain type" village, some seven hundred households along the two sides of the river create a high-density Dong settlement (Figure 2.5).

Figure 2.3 The settlement pattern of Ma'an village in the Sanjiang region, Guangxi province, showing houses built on a terraced mountain slope as well as flat land for rice paddies and fishponds. Source: Drawn by Xing Ruan.

Figure 2.4 The skyline dominated by the drum tower of Longtu village in the Congjiang region, Guizhou province. Source: Photograph by Xing Ruan, 1993.

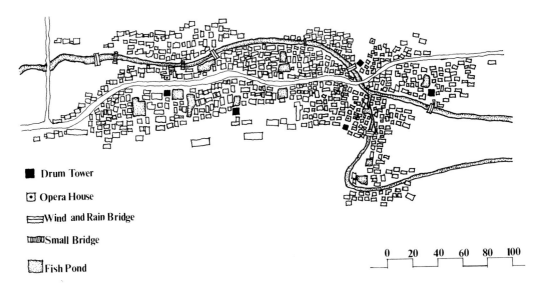

■ Drum Tower

⊡ Opera House

≋Wind and Rain Bridge

▥Small Bridge

▦Fish Pond

0   20   40   60   80   100

Figure 2.5 The plan of Zhaoxin village in the Liping region, Guizhou province, showing the village built on flat land. The drawing also indicates that there are five drum towers and a number of wind-and-rain bridges scattered within the settlement. Source: Drawn by Xing Ruan.

Settlement Pattern

A sketchy picture of Dong architectonics and settlement has been painted in Chapter 1 with a focus on the cultural activities that are staged by the built world. Before we look into the interactive relationship between ritual and the settlement of the Dong, this section examines in greater detail the roles of architectonic elements—in particular their strategic positions within the Dong settlement pattern.

SAX ALTAR

The Sax altar is not always a visible formal structure in a Dong settlement. Sometimes it is even hidden to outsiders.[8] It is a public place for only the Dong themselves, rather than for outsiders. It is also a place for special occasions rather than for daily activities. Even the most elaborate and visible Sax altar is just a simple roofed shelter. This type of Sax "temple" usually is found in areas with considerable Han influence, like Chezhai of the Rongjiang region in Guizhou province (Figure 2.6).

A village may have more than one Sax temple. Seemingly they are randomly scattered within the settlement and often merge into the housing blocks without attracting visitors' attention; only locals know where they are. These temples are usually locked, and people are allowed to enter only when rituals are performed. An altar, constructed with white stones and often with an umbrella inserted in the top, is in the temple.

Figure 2.6 One of the Sax altars in Chezhai village of the Rongjiang region, Guizhou province, is housed in a simple temple. Despite the roofed shelter, the Sax is further "protected" by an umbrella. Source: Photograph by Xing Ruan, 1992.

Figure 2.7 The Sax altar of Gaozeng village in the Congjiang region, Guizhou province, is enclosed within a compound located near the drum tower. Source: Photograph by Xing Ruan, 1993.

Figure 2.8 The Sax altar in Longtu village of the Congjiang region is enclosed within gable walls that are curved at the top. The curves resemble the roofs of the drum towers and wind-and-rain bridges in the same region, which are quite possibly serpent-related. Source: Photograph by Xing Ruan, 1992.

Another type of Sax altar is a compound enclosed within walls but without a roof. These compounds are usually adjacent to the drum tower. The Sax altar in Gaozhen of the Congjiang region in Guizhou province is typical of this type (Figure 2.7). A small boxwood tree is planted on top of the altar, apparently in place of the paper umbrella of the indoor altars (see Figure 1.5). The compound altars occasionally have very striking forms, such as the Sax altars in the Longtu area of the Congjiang region, Guizhou, which are enclosed with curved gable walls, possibly in the form of a serpent or Naga, as it is known in Southeast Asia (Figure 2.8). (This point is discussed further in Chapter 4.)

Figure 2.9 The Sax altar of Dudong village in the Sanjiang region, Guangxi province. The Chinese script on the background building reads: "Long Live the Communist Party!" This is indeed an ironic juxtaposition between the meaning of a text and a quite different instrumental role played by an architectonic element. Source: Photograph by Xing Ruan, 1992.

The most common form of Sax altar is a small round hillock constructed of earth and covered by a layer of stones. A boxwood (or cypress) tree, an umbrella, and sometimes twelve or twenty-four small pieces of wood or stone crown the top to stand as guards for the Sax. These open altars are also relatively hidden and scattered within the settlement. There are, however, exceptions: the Sax altar in Dudong in the Sanjiang region is right at the center of a semienclosed open space, separated from the drum tower square by only a few steps (Figure 2.9). Although this Sax altar is visually hidden, it is spatially very close to the drum tower. Similar Sax altars are found in Zengchong of the Congjiang region (see Figure 1.6).

A unique Sax altar is in Pingrui in the Congjiang region. The drum tower and the opera house are opposite each other, defining the center square, and the Sax altar is almost on the central axis of the square (Figure 2.10). Here the significance of the Sax altar and its relationship with the drum tower and the square is explicitly expressed. The Sax altar in Mapang in the Sanjiang region is another case of visible formal expression. It too is close to the drum tower and the square (Figure 2.11). In most Dong settlements, however, the presence of the Sax altar may be obscure. In some instances, huge old trees at the front or back of the settlement are regarded as Sax altars. According to Zou Hongcang, in some Dong villages giant old trees at the front or rear of the settlement are respected as "king trees." The Dong believe that the Sax

Figure 2.10 The Sax altar is placed at the center of the drum tower square in Pingrui village, which indicates the connection between the Sax altar and the drum tower. Congjiang region of Guizhou province. Source: Photograph by Xing Ruan, 1993.

Figure 2.11 The Sax altar of Mapang village in the Sanjiang region, Guangxi province. Visible in its location, this is the only large-scale Sax altar in a cubic form that I found in my fieldwork. It is also "inhabitable," with steps for people to climb on. Source: Photograph by Xing Ruan, 1992.

lives in the king tree; they usually hold the Sax ceremonies in front this tree.[9] Zou believes that this is
a combination of ancestor ceremony and holy tree
worship.

DRUM TOWER AND OPERA STAGE

Within the Dong settlement the drum tower is
visually the most outstanding and physically the
most dominant formal structure.[10] In most cases,
the drum tower occupies the central area of the
settlement—often defining and forming a drum
tower square or open space. Commonly, housing
and an opera stage also help enclose this drum
tower square.

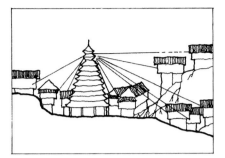

Figure 2.12 Diagrammatic section of a
mountain-river-valley Dong village showing
that the drum tower is sited where it can be
seen from every household in the settlement.
Source: Drawn by Xing Ruan.

In the spatial disposition of a Dong settlement, one of the most important principles states that the drum tower's top pavilion must be seen from
every house in the village (Figure 2.12). In reality, however, this can only
be achieved symbolically. Though it is all too easy to be impressed by the
sheer height and dominance of the drum tower, this nevertheless is more
than a primordial awareness of an architectural vanity—by sharing a view
of the drum tower, each house, and hence every Dong, is empowered to be
a member of their society. This is not dissimilar to a "borrowed view" in a
Chinese garden where visual access to a pagoda in the distance, for example,
endows the garden with a symbolic ownership of the view.

For settlements located on the plains, the drum tower normally occupies
the physical center of the site with housing wrapping around the tower and
along the nearby river valley. Such a pattern usually results in an expressive
nautical image with the village viewed as the boat while the drum tower serves
as its mast and sail. Examples of this type of settlement are all concentrated
in the Dong regions of Guizhou province, such as the settlement of Gaozhen
in Congjiang (Figure 2.13) or even the complicated Zhaoxin settlement in the
Liping region with its five drum towers (see Figure 2.5). Because the sites are
flat and the villages are often large, a drum tower has to be very high so that
it can be seen from every house (Figure 2.14).

In settlements located in the mountains, the drum tower does not necessarily occupy the physical center of the site but is located at a topographic
focal point. With the houses on the slopes of the surrounding mountains, for
example, the drum tower of Gaobu village in the Tongdao region of Hunan
province is built on the lowest point of the site at the edge of the village (Figure 2.15). Ma'an's drum tower is another thoughtfully chosen topographic
focal point, a subject to be discussed in detail later. A third position for the
drum tower is at the front or entry of a village where it is constructed as a

Figure 2.13 Viewed from above, Dong villages along the two sides of the mountain river valley are regarded as "boats," with the drum towers as "sail and mast." Gaozeng village, Congjiang region, Guizhou province. Source: Photograph by Xing Ruan, 1993.

Figure 2.14
The drum tower of Gaoqian village in the Congjiang region, with fifteen eaves, is the highest in the whole Dong region. Source: Feng Yuzhao and Wu Zhenguang (1985).

Figure 2.15 Elevation of Gaobu village in the Tongdao region in Hunan province showing the location of the drum tower as the lowest point yet a focal point of the whole settlement. Source: Drawn by Xing Ruan.

Figure 2.16 The drum tower of Zaimao village in the Sanjiang region, Guangxi province, a combination of gate and drum tower, stands at the village's edge. Source: Photograph by Xing Ruan, 1992.

freestanding object in an open area, sometimes with an opera stage opposite it. In this instance, the drum tower also serves as the village gate (Figure 2.16).

The Dong opera stage is simply a pile-built structure with an open front. The drum tower square, in most cases, is also the opera stage square.[11] The central square defined and enclosed by the drum tower, opera stage, and housing in the village of Guandong of the Sanjiang region is such a shared square (Figure 2.17). The sequence of open spaces, and the resulting quasi-spatial axis, is commonly generated by the drum tower and opera stage. Baxie village in the Sanjiang region is another example (Figure 2.18).

More elaborated opera stages have their own squares where each becomes a focal point for the village. Hence, in addition to the drum tower square, a settlement may have a number of open spaces. A distinctive example is the opera stage of Pingpu village in the Sanjiang region, where the opera stage is located at the immediate intersection of the two main roads (Figure 2.19).

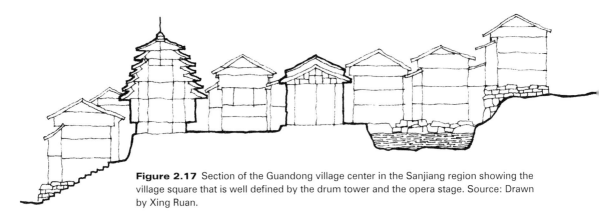

Figure 2.17 Section of the Guandong village center in the Sanjiang region showing the village square that is well defined by the drum tower and the opera stage. Source: Drawn by Xing Ruan.

Figure 2.18 In Baxie village of the Sanjiang region, a clear spatial sequence is formed through a juxtaposition of opera stage, drum tower, and other public shelters. Source: Photograph by Xing Ruan, 1992.

VILLAGE GATE

In today's Dong regions, not all settlements have gates. Particularly in Guizhou, the village gate is sometimes a zone defined by a huge tree (Figure 2.20). Regardless of whether there is a real gate or just a vaguely defined zone, Dong villages have fronts and backs and are seen as "heads and tails," and these must be claimed and identified through a gate. In an anthropomorphic manner, the Dong see the upper reach of the river that goes through the settlement as the "head," while the lower reach is the "tail." The gate identifies the "head" of the village. The Dong village gate is a symbol of the Dong settlement of a place, their bodily relationships with the site, and their migration origins, rather than simply a physical boundary for defensive purposes.

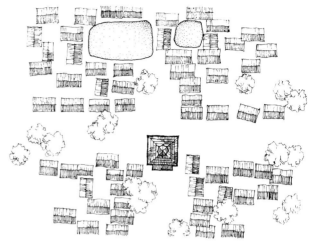

Figure 2.19 The opera stage is located right at the center of an intersection in Pingpu village, Sanjiang region, Guangxi province. Source: Drawn by Xing Ruan after Li Changjie et al. (1990, 109).

Gates do, however, serve functional and social purposes. The village gate, for example, is a ritualistic performance place for greeting and bidding farewell to visitors. The Dong are well known for their hospitality, and these gate rituals are an essential aspect of their daily social activities (Figure 2.21).

Figure 2.20 In Pingrui village of the Congjiang region, Guizhou province, the village "gate" is a zone defined by two huge trees. Source: Photograph by Xing Ruan, 1993.

Figure 2.21 One of the gate rituals is greeting guests. The horizontal pole is the symbolic gate before guests are welcomed to the village. Congjiang region, Guizhou province. Source: Courtesy of Wu Quanxin (1993).

The Dong village gates combine indigenous with foreign elements. The village gate of Liangzhai in the Sanjiang region, for example, is a typical Han-influenced gate that clearly distinguishes the outside and inside of the village (Figure 2.22). As an ordering element, this gate begins the spatial sequence linking to the center of the settlement where the drum tower and its square are located.

The types and styles of gates are sometimes freely improvised by the Dong. The gate of Yanzhai village in the Sanjiang region is a freestanding pile pavilion loft on the side of the stream (Figure 2.23). This gate does not constitute a boundary for the settlement; it only serves as an identifying device that claims the "head" of the village, the upper reach of the stream. The gate of Baxie village, also in the Sanjiang region, is another well-crafted, freestanding pavilion (Figure 2.24). The method of construction, particularly the use of *dougong* (eave brackets) in supporting the upper roof, echoes the style of the drum tower and the opera stage at the center of the settlement (Figure 2.25). The use of *dougong* in major public structures in Baxie marks a sophisticated architectural spatial sequence and is one of the most distinctive among Dong settlements. For some steep, riverside settlements, the gate not only claims the "head" of the village but also functions as a "pass" for the mountain river valley itself. The gates of Huangchao and Pingliu villages are examples (Figure 2.26).

It appears that the mountain village gates are much more elaborate than those of the plains settlements. The gate of Gaozeng village in the Congjiang region, an enlarged "pavilion" with dragons on the roof ridge, demonstrates a kind of celebration seldom found in plains villages (Figure 2.27). The gate of Xindi village in the Congjiang region is another example: a combination of a gate and three pavilions, it serves not only as a point of passage or transition but also as a roadside pavilion for resting and social interaction (Figure 2.28).

Figure 2.22 The village gate of Liangzai in the Sanjiang region is like a Han village gate. Source: Li Changjie et al. (1990, 321).

WIND-AND-RAIN BRIDGE

While the Dong settlements are vertically dominated by their drum towers, the wind-and-rain bridges offer a powerful, horizontal balance. An ethnic identity and a sense of their own place aside, the juxtaposition of mountain river valleys and towering structures as well as roofed bridges does give a striking picturesqueness to a Dong settlement (Figure 2.29): mountains and valleys are claimed mainly by drum towers, either as the highest formal structures or as the topographic focal points of the valleys, while the rivers are claimed by wind-and-rain bridges.

Despite style variations, the formal structure and construction of Dong wind-and-rain bridges are consistent across the Dong regions. Compositionally and structurally, a wind-and-rain bridge is constructed with four parts (Figure 2.30): roof, inhabitable body (usually an open corridor plus some semi-enclosed shrines or temples underneath pavilion roofs), log-constructed cantilever, and stone piers. Except for the stone piers, the entire bridge is constructed of timber, with horizontal cantilevers of several spans over the river. Each pier is crowned by pavilions of many-tiered roofs, linked by tiled roofs, making the entire bridge a

Figure 2.23 The Yanzhai village gate in the Sanjiang region claims the "head," the river's upper reach, of the settlement. Source: Photograph by Xing Ruan, 1992.

Figure 2.24 The Baxie village gate is a freestanding, well-crafted pavilion. Sanjiang region, Guangxi province. Source: Photograph by Xing Ruan, 1989.

covered walk. All the elements are bound together by mortise and tenon construction. Following the same structure and construction system, Dong wind-and-rain bridges sometimes can be developed into a spatially intricate composition. An interesting example is the Batuan bridge in the Sanjiang region where the corridor inhabited by humans is separated from an animal walkway at two different levels (Figures 2.31–2.32).

Wind-and-rain bridges not only connect two sides of a river but also, in most cases, connect the outside world to the village. Wind-and-rain bridges often are located at the "head" of villages, in the upper reaches of rivers, or at the "tail" of villages, in the lower reaches. As mentioned earlier, the bridge also is considered to have *fengshui* power that, in particular, protects the wealth of the village from running away through the river. Very often the "tail" of a village, at the lower reaches of the river, is said to be "locked" by the wind-and-rain bridges. I shall return to this point later in the chapter.

The Dong usually inhabit their sites with zoomorphic images: the sites are viewed as incarnations of animal deities. Bridges in the central part of the settlement, particularly that part considered to be the "belly" of the site, are to be avoided since it is believed that, if the center is touched by bridges, fire or pestilence will enter the village. Yet in certain circumstances, wind-and-rain bridges do get built at the center of settlements, where "dragon's veins" of their zoomorphic sites have to be connected by the bridges. The "dragon's veins" are those topographic features considered to have features of the animal deities. In these cases, the bridges do not have to cross rivers but are used to bridge the "dragon's veins" (Figure 2.33). The Huilong bridge, literally "curling dragon bridge," of Pingtan village in the Tongdao region of Hunan province is a case of the potent use of a bridge in relation to the "dragon's veins." Some 80 meters long and 4 meters wide and built in 1921,

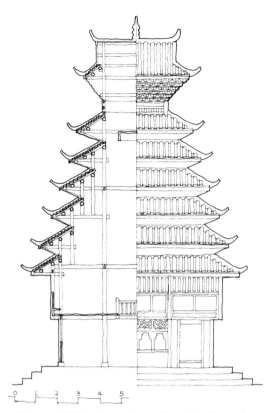

Figure 2.25 Section and elevation of the Baxie village drum tower in the Sanjiang region showing the top pavilion supported by *dougong* (eave brackets), which echoes the village gate in Baxie. Source: Drawn by Xing Ruan after Li Changjie et al. (1990, 165).

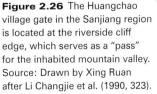

Figure 2.26 The Huangchao village gate in the Sanjiang region is located at the riverside cliff edge, which serves as a "pass" for the inhabited mountain valley. Source: Drawn by Xing Ruan after Li Changjie et al. (1990, 323).

Figure 2.27 The elaborate gate of Gaozeng village in the Congjiang region, Guizhou province, clearly addresses the entry of the mountain river. Source: Photograph by Xing Ruan, 1993.

Figure 2.28 The Xindi village gate of the Congjiang region is a combination of gate, roadside pavilion, and wind-and-rain bridge. Source: Photograph by Xing Ruan, 1993.

Figure 2.29 Dong settlements are usually intermingled with Miao and Zhuang settlements. A Dong settlement is distinguished from the others by its composite juxtaposition of wind-and-rain bridge and drum tower. The center of Xiazhai village of the Xindi area in the Congjiang region, Guizhou province. Source: Photograph by Xing Ruan, 1993.

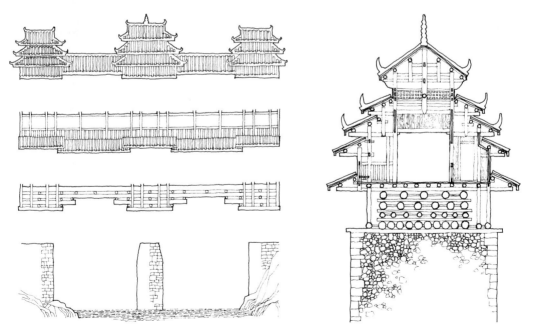

Figure 2.30 Elevation and section of a typical wind-and-rain bridge showing the formal structure and composition. Source: Drawn by Xing Ruan after Li Changjie et al. (1990, 208 and 212).

Figure 2.31 The wind-and-rain bridge of Batuan village in the Sanjiang region of Guangxi province. Source: Photograph by Xing Ruan, 1989.

the whole bridge is curved to focus the center of the village (Figure 2.34). In terms of its relationship with the whole settlement, particularly with the "village's heart" and the drum tower square, the *fengshui* power of this bridge protects and "locks" the village.

PAVILIONS, WELL SHELTERS, AND SHRINES

In addition to the drum tower, square, opera stage, and wind-and-rain bridges, the Dong also have pavilions, well shelters, and shrines that together form their consummate public space system.

Pavilions are called "cool pavilions" in that they are quite literally located in ventilated positions and are used mainly for summer social occasions. Although most of the Dong public places serve quasi-religious purposes, the "cool pavilions" are quintessentially profane. The pavilion of Mapang village in the Sanjiang region is one example: located at the intersection of roads and a stream, the Mapang pavilion is worthy of its name as a "cool pavilion" (Figure 2.35). Ventilation is enhanced by the intersection and an open space that includes a pond on one side (Figure 2.36). Like other Dong architecture, however, there is substantial variation in the location of these pavilions. Some are located on the roadside, for instance, or in the fields.

A different type of pavilion within Dong settlements is the well shelter. Well shelters in general are often found among southern ethnic groups, particularly among the Tai linguistic groups. For the Dai in Xishuangbanna, well shelters are significant and architecturally crafted constructions within the settlements (Figure 2.37). There, for example, fetching the water is ritualistically celebrated during their annual Water Splashing Festival in spring. Dong wells, however, are not real wells; they are usually ponds of water gathered from small streams. Simple pavilion structures are built to roof the "wells." Often there are seats in well shelters for weary travelers to rest and drink cold spring water (Figure 2.38).

Shrines scattered throughout the Dong settlements are quite often Tudi (earth god) shrines. The Dong build miniatures of Han temples along the roadside or in open spaces around the drum tower (see Figure 1.8). These shrines, which are not at all sacred, are about 1 meter high on average. Often these shrines are carved stone miniatures of Han temples. Sometimes they are simply constructed with stone slabs as a box, with one side open, forming a space in which incense is burnt. In a rather pragmatic manner, the Dong burn incense to worship Tudi when they need him.[12] Occasionally other temples, such as a mountain god temple, can be seen within the settlements. The Dong burn incense to ask for blessings from these gods: for example, they worship their mountain god before hunting or water buffalo fighting. The mountain god temple is often situated outside the village; the one in the village of Batuan in the Sanjiang region, for example, is on the riverbank across from the village and adjacent to the wind-and-rain bridge (Figure 2.39).

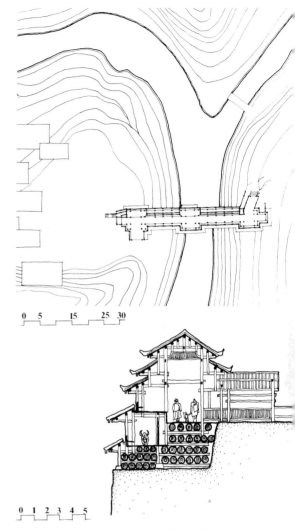

Figure 2.32 Plan and section of Batuan bridge showing two separate levels: one for humans and the other for animals. Source: Drawn by Xing Ruan.

Figure 2.33 One of the wind-and-rain bridges in Zhaoxin village of the Liping region, Guizhou province, is in the center of the settlement, perhaps to bridge the "dragon's veins." Source: Photograph by Xing Ruan, 1993.

STORAGE, HOUSING, AND GRAVEYARD

Spring plowing, summer weeding, autumn reaping, and winter storing are the basic agriculture cycle of the Dong. The primary architectural expression of this rice farming lifestyle is the store, which is made up of a granary and *heliang*, a timber frame for drying paddies. The granary is a simplified pile-type building (Figure 2.40), while the *heliang* is a freestanding timber framework with horizontal bars (Figure 2.41); sometimes the two are combined together (Figure 2.42).

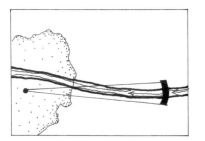

Figure 2.34 Diagram showing the relationship between the curved Huilong bridge and the settlement center. Source: Drawn by Xing Ruan.

Rice paddy farming is the locus of Dong life. Not surprisingly, therefore, rice is one of the most precious commodities of the Dong. The amount of rice stored indicates a family's wealth and its social status. For this reason, a granary has to be specially protected. Because of its timber structure and high density, fire is the fatal disaster that could easily destroy not only the granaries but the whole village. Unfortunately, fire does erupt from time to time.

For relatively large, "plain type" settlements, the store is in a specially designated zone separated from the housing (Figure 2.43). The granary and *heliang* are often located at the "heads" or "tails" of settlements. To protect them from fire and rats, they are either adjacent to a river or simply built over fishponds. In autumn, the dried yellow rice paddies tied on *heliang* paint a colorful picture (Figure 2.44). This kind of clustered and segregated storage is not found in Guangxi province. Compared with the Dong in Guizhou province, the Dong in Guangxi are more modern: due to the proximity

Figure 2.35 The "cool pavilion" of Mapang village in the Sanjiang region, Guangxi province. Source: Photograph by Xing Ruan, 1992.

to cities, they avail themselves of more convenient transport. Storing rice is no longer a significant part of their agricultural life. Houses are relatively large in Guangxi. Quite often some of the frameworks of houses are left open to be used for drying rice paddies (Figure 2.45). On steep sites and in narrow valley villages, individual granaries are scattered within the village or built over fishponds detached from the housing. Granaries in the village of Gaozeng in the Congjiang region are disposed in this way (Figure 2.43).

The Dong public places are physically, visually, and symbolically linked together with a series of nodes, such as the drum tower, Sax altar, wind-and-rain bridge, and gates. Housing, by contrast, is less differentiated and less identifiable, becoming essentially a context and a mass background to this nodal structure. Dong housing contributes to the spatial character of Dong settlements, particularly through its articulation and the circulation space formed by this articulation. What distinguishes Dong housing from most traditional Han housing is its pile-built type that contrasts with the land-based courtyard type. This pile-built type produces housing with an open and outward orientation. As a consequence, the spatial disposition of a Dong settlement is public, and it supports a gregarious social character, especially in relation to its elaborate public space system.

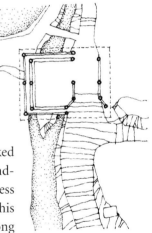

Figure 2.36 Plan of the Mapang village "cool pavilion" showing the intersection of roads and a stream. Source: Drawn by Xing Ruan after Li Changjie et al. (1990, 329).

The social space of Dong housing is semipublic. A large amount of the space in the elevated first floor of a Dong house, sometimes even half of the first floor, is taken up by an open porch (Figure 2.46). The density and attachment

Figure 2.37
Well shelters take a variety of forms in Dai settlements in Xishuangbanna, Yunnan province. This one is like a Dai pagoda. Source: Photograph by Xing Ruan, 1989.

Figure 2.38 A newly constructed well shelter in Dudong village in the Sanjiang region, Guangxi province. The shelter not only marks the stream but also provides seats for weary travelers. Source: Photograph by Xing Ruan, 1992.

of houses produces a continuous edge of porches that is distinctly semipublic in their character and use and serves as an in-between zone for social inter-action between families. This aboveground porch space also makes possible a continuous arcade-like space on the ground level. The most ordered "street colonnade" is formed where a row of houses are attached to each other along a riverbank. Very few large, plain-based Dong settlements, such as Zhaoxin village in the Liping region, can afford to have this articulated "urban space"

Figure 2.39 Mountain gods in a temple near Batuan village in the Sanjiang region, Guangxi province. Source: Photograph by Xing Ruan, 1992.

(Figure 2.47). Most Dong settlements, however, are built on rugged sites. For this reason, the ground spaces for storage and stock barns are flexible while the upper first levels are basically modularized. To connect the space on the first level, overbridging is often used (Figure 2.48).

The counterpart to Dong housing in the settlement is the graveyard: the houses for the dead. Every Dong village has its own grave mountain where, it is believed, their ancestors reside. The graveyard often has a close proximity to the living zone; sometimes they even overlap, with the pile foundation of a house built on the graveyard (Figure 2.49). The Dong, like the Han and others, hold that this world and the netherworld are not much different from each other. While the body dies in this world, the soul is still alive and returns to the hometown, the netherworld. For the Dong, like the Han and certain minority groups, the netherworld is worldly: the dead need food and clothing; they need to spend money; and, of course, they need houses and villages as well. A Dong folk song describes the hometown of the soul as a place called Gaos Sinl Nyoc Nyanh, where people also play *lusheng*, dance, and sing hand in hand in a circle. In the netherworld there is enough food and clothing so they do not need to grow rice and cotton. The netherworld, therefore, is thought to be a paradise, a home to return to. In contrast to their timber houses, the graves are constructed with stones and seem to be more permanent. Each gravestone is carved as a house gate or a miniature house, almost all in a Han house type and style (Figure 2.50).

Figure 2.40 A freestanding granary at the outskirts of Pingrui village of the Congjiang region, Guizhou province. Source: Photograph by Xing Ruan, 1993.

Figure 2.41 The *heliang,* the freestanding timber framework for drying rice paddies, in Binmei village of the Congjiang region, Guizhou province. Source: Photograph by Xing Ruan, 1993.

Settlement Made Legible

The physical and spatial disposition of a Dong settlement and its architectural elements alone are not legible illustrations of myths. Dong myths become knowable in an allegorical sense during the ritual acts that are shaped by the pattern of a settlement. Dong myths are not necessarily original; quite often they are not. Rather, in recurrent ritual acts in Dong settlements, their myths are transformed and reinvented. Accordingly the myths become constitutive rather than merely narrative, symbolic rather than semiotic, for they become the way the Dong inhabit and make their settlements. The myths are thus told through architecture and the pattern of a settlement.

In a Dong settlement, the density of Dong housing supports an elaborate system of public places. The density of a Dong settlement falls in between a walled Han city and the open Dai settlement in southern China, and this density is also justified by the myth of their migration. Dong folk songs of migration mention the Han city when describing the selection of the sites. One such song states:

> Miao ancestors loved to climb high mountains;
> they chose to settle there for generations.
> Han ancestors were fond of the plain;
> there they built city walls and multistory buildings.
> Our Dong ancestors did not want highlands and
> plains;
> they purposely chose happy mountain river valleys.
> [Yang and Wu 1981]

Another folk song describes how the Dong ancestors were driven to migrate by the Han. Quite coincidentally, as discussed earlier, one of the arguments from the Republican period (1912–1949) explaining Dong origins proposed that they were the living ancient Han who invaded today's Dong regions and finally were assimilated by the Miao. The Han influence on Dong architecture and settlement is palpable. But what is of interest is the way in which those aspects of the Han urban structure adopted by the Dong were transformed into Dong settlements and, moreover, how this adoption works for them in their inhabiting and making.

Figure 2.42 This granary in Zengchong village of the Congjiang region is a combination of *heliang* and pile-built building. Source: Photograph by Xing Ruan, 1993.

The monumentality of the public structures, as well as their physical and visual connections, are what distinguish Dong settlements from those of other minority groups, including the other Tai linguistic groups in southern China. Compared with Dong settlements, the settlements of these other groups, such as the Dai villages in Xishuangbanna (Figure 2.51), are quite loose in their structure. For example, the Buddhist temples of Dai villages are additive rather than an integral element: they neither dominate a village nor construct its hierarchy but simply coexist with the earlier, organic, animistic order of the village. The village's "heart" or *zhaiwan* is often in a hidden place. The symbolic structure lacks the powerful sense of architectural making that Dong villages possess. This is realized particularly when their rituals are performed. One of the causes for this loose structure is that Dai houses are freestanding, detached blocks within their settlements. Each freestanding house is inhabited by a two-generation, nuclear family, the basic unit of Dai society. Dai housing does not have the density to support the public structures to nearly the extent of Dong settlements. Thus the ritual routes and the symbolic structure are not as decisively architecturally claimed. This type of open structure is carried into the urban structure. Even now, many Thai cities lack a dense articulation of buildings (Figure 2.52),[13] except in the Chinese territories, which are formed by dense and street-oriented shop/houses.

Like other Tai linguistic groups, the two-generation, nuclear family of the Dong is still the basic unit of society. But, as discussed earlier, even extended families do not necessarily live in separate or scattered housing units; usually three generations, including married brothers and their children, live in the same house, or adjacent houses are closely connected to each other by bridges between porches (see Figure 2.48). Each family unit is, however, identified; for example, a small family must have its own fire pit room to

Figure 2.43 In Gaozeng village of the Congjiang region, pile-built granaries are grouped and separated from the village. Source: Photograph by Xing Ruan, 1993.

Figure 2.44 Autumn scene of a Dong village with dried rice paddies hanging on *heliang.* Source: Courtesy of Wu Quanxin (1993).

Figure 2.45 A house in Ma'an village of the Sanjiang region. Some frameworks of the house are left unfilled for drying rice paddies. Source: Photograph by Xing Ruan, 1989.

indicate its presence where many small families share a big house. In this way, Dong houses serve as a socially and physically articulated mass with many outward-oriented edges of the housing connecting back into public structures (see Figure 2.47).

But this picturesque settlement does more for the Dong, once again, than offering them a degree of vanity that they may be able to show off to others living in the same region. It also gains them a deep affinity with their place. The workings of the Dong settlement are achieved through an understanding of the meanings of its architectural elements and its structure. This understanding is both a mental and a bodily experience that is made tangible via rituals in the settlement.

SAX RITUAL AND THE CLAIMING OF SETTLEMENT PATTERN

The Sax ritual is perhaps the most architecturally formulated act of Dong settlement. On the one hand, it claims the power of the abstract formal structure; on the other hand, it makes a symbolic journey to the past possible, particularly to the Dong myths. In this way, architectonic ritual shaped by the

Figure 2.46 Typical Dong house in Guangdong village of the Sanjiang region, Guangxi province, showing the semipublic porch space. Source: Li Changjie et al. (1990, 421).

Figure 2.47 Riverside "colonnade" in Zhaoxin village of the Liping region, Guizhou province. Only in large villages do the connected house porches give a street feel. Source: Photograph by Xing Ruan, 1993.

settlement pattern, and the ritualistic posture of the settlement, shed light on each other.

In Dong society, there are three kinds of Sax ritual operating at different scales: reconstructing, commemorating, and entertaining Sax. Reconstructing a Sax altar, which occurs only occasionally, is the most solemn event. At most it happens every two or three decades, but the Dong hold it to be the event of a century or at least a defining event during their own lives. Since Sax has the power to control diseases and retain water, the soul of Sax is thought to have escaped from the settlement if pestilence and drought occur in the village. At such times, a Sax altar is sometimes replaced with a new one through an elaborate ritual. The annual Sax memorial ceremony is another grand-scale event in which every villager is expected to participate. The third kind of Sax ritual is literally entertaining Sax. In the past, this entertainment was usually performed when the Dong dispatched troops. Now it usually entails a small-scale Sax ceremony before water buffalo fighting or a group visit to other villages. Let me now focus on how the formal structure of the ritual, which is determined by the settlement pattern, makes the settlement a meaningful posture for the Dong.[14]

Figure 2.48 Dong houses are sometimes connected through overbridging. Mapang village of the Sanjiang region, Guangxi province. Source: Li Changjie et al. (1990, 385).

An eminent shaman or a *nyens laox,* the chief, who is a revered old man, must coordinate the reconstruction of a Sax altar. Auspicious dates are believed to fall in the third month of the Chinese lunar calendar. Since the reason for this reconstruction is that Sax's soul has returned to a place called Longl Dangc Keik, where she was buried, the first step in the reconstruction is to make a trip to Longl Dangc Keik to invite back the soul of Sax. Longl Dangc Keik is located at the border of the Congjiang and the Liping regions. The Dong never clarified whether this is the place from where the Dong migrated, or if it was a stop where Sax died in their long migration journey.[15] In some Dong villages, fetching soil and water from Longl Dangc Keik is a real action involving a round trip of more than 50 kilometers for villages in the Guizhou Dong region. A team of three young men, led by the Sax caretaker holding an umbrella, must leave and return to the village in one day without stopping. Neither umbrella, soil, nor water must touch the ground on the way back to their settlement; otherwise Sax's soul will escape and the process must be reenacted. If a village is too far away from Longl Dangc Keik, inviting Sax's soul back to the settlement can be performed symbolically. In this case, villagers just go somewhere nearby to get soil and water.

Figure 2.49 Grave mountain of Baxie village of the Sanjiang region, Guangxi province, showing a proximate relationship between the graveyard and the village. Source: Photograph by Xing Ruan, 1989.

Regardless of whether it is a real action or a symbolic performance, the ritual of greeting the team with the soul of Sax is the key to the first step. The villagers assemble in the drum tower, waiting for the arrival of the team. Young people then play *lusheng* and beat brass gongs at the gate when the team approaches the settlement. The team is stopped outside the gate, and the villagers ask: "Where do you come from?" The team answers: "We come from Longl Dangc Keik." The villagers then ask: "What are you doing here?" The team answers: "We heard this is a good place and people are kind; we come here to share parents, brothers, and sisters with you. Will you allow us to join you?" The villagers answer together: "Yes!" After that, the soil, the water, and the team are escorted to the drum tower by villagers

Figure 2.50 A Dong gravestone made as a miniature of a Han house, Bingmei village, Congjiang region of Guangxi province. Source: Photograph by Xing Ruan, 1993.

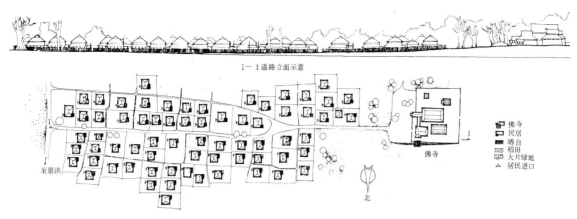

i—I道路立面示意

至景洪

佛寺

北

佛寺
民居
晒台
稻田
大片绿地
居民进口

Figure 2.51 Elevation and plan of Manmai village in the Xishuangbanna region, Yunnan province. The Buddhist temple is a self-defined compound at the western edge of the settlement; the village is loose in its structure. Source: Yunnan Sheng Sheji Yuan (1986, 218).

and *lusheng* playing. The "melody of the ancestors" is then played three times by *lusheng* in front of the drum tower; the soil and water are then installed in the Sax caretaker's home waiting for the time of reconstruction.

Despite its variations, this part of the ritual is almost certainly an imagined reconstruction of Dong migration. During this particular part of the ritual of settlement, a journey to the past is made tangible in an allegorical way. Architecturally, the settlement begins to be claimed through various kinds of inhabitation—for example, the drum tower as the center of the settlement in relation to the gate. Thus the drum tower is inhabited as the destination of the journey in which Sax's soul is brought back to the settlement. Furthermore, for the Dong the spatial relationship of gate/drum tower is symbolically and

Figure 2.52
A typical Thai city streetscape in northern Thailand, which is not unlike a Dai village in Yunnan in terms of its open structure. Source: Photograph by Xing Ruan, 1994.

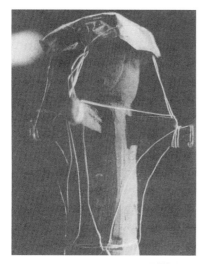

Figure 2.53 The Sax statue of Zhanli village in the Congjiang region, Guizhou province. Source: *Echo* (1991, 32:31).

meaningfully transformed from an outside/inside spatial relationship into concrete migration/settlement, ancestor/us, and past/present relationships.

Offerings are prepared before the construction of a new Sax altar. Usually they include three umbrellas, a small amount of soil from the courtyard of the local county government, and a bottle of water from where two rivers join together. Other offerings include a Sax statue (Figure 2.53), weapons, tools of production, and kitchen utensils, among other items. Not surprisingly, most of these offerings are considered to make Sax more empowering. In the Dong region, Sax is widely acknowledged as both a heroine and the leader of production, and these rituals and offerings are intended to propitiate these beliefs.

The day before the ritual, the old Sax altar is refurbished and made ready for Sax's statue, for the soil and water from Longl Dangc Keik, as well as for the other offerings. Most of the Sax altars, as described earlier, are actually round, tomblike hillocks. In the early morning on the day of the ritual, all the villagers awake and extinguish the fire in their home fire pits. From that point onwards, villagers are not allowed to do any housework and all daily routines are temporarily stopped. At the same time, the settlement must be shut to outsiders by closing the village gate. This again is often only a symbolic act, because most Dong settlements do not have any physical boundaries, and in many cases the gates serve only as shelters. A few young men usually guard the settlement at the gate with rifles. Roadblocks are set up for settlements that do not have gates.

The ritual route begins at the drum tower. Young men congregate there and then proceed to the Sax caretaker's house. Sax's statue, soil, and water are then taken to the altar accompanied by young men playing *lusheng* and beating brass gongs. People already waiting at the altar then fire iron cannons three times to welcome Sax; young men walk around the altar while playing their *lusheng*. After that, all the participants move away from the altar except the master builder and his assistants. Once the altar is sealed, in other words, Sax's statue and other offerings are buried, the round hillock is constructed with stones, and people move back to the altar and fire iron cannons to celebrate. The master builder then decorates the altar surface with usually twelve or twenty-four white stone pieces;[16] umbrellas are also set up; and a small boxwood tree is sometimes planted. The next step is "calling back the spirit of Sax." The master builder and his assistants chant and sing praises of Sax; the content of these songs is mainly Sax stories. Finally, a fire lit at the altar is taken to the fire pit in the drum tower. One by one, the villagers go to the drum tower to obtain live cinders to light the fires in their fire pits at home. Life now returns to normal, but the ritual is yet to be completed.

The most intriguing aspect in this part of the ritual is the role that fire plays: fire claims meaningful relationships between houses, the Sax altar, and the drum tower. As we already know, in each family the fire in their fire pit is regarded as the genesis of the family as well as the memorial tablet of its ancestors. Sax, as the Dong's grandmother, is of course the female ancestor. The Dong may have forgotten the male ancestor worship in terms of the drum tower's archetype (which I discuss in Chapter 3). Nevertheless, the ancestor worship and rebirth are architecturally reified through a spatial sequence: extinguishing the fire in the house, lighting the fire at the Sax altar, moving the fire to the drum tower fire pit, obtaining live cinders from the drum tower, and finally relighting the fire in the house. In the process of inhabiting and making their settlement pattern, a story, though tacit in meaning, is told. Even at an abstract level, the relationship between the Sax altar and the drum tower can be objectified, through the Sax ritual, as one that is hidden and sacred while the other is open, public, and profane.

The reconstruction of an altar has to be completed before noon. In the afternoon, the ritual continues as a parade in the settlement. The formal structure of the settlement, dominated by the drum tower but grounded by the Sax altar, is therefore turned into a theater. The procession starts at the drum tower square as an assembly of young men, dressed up young women, and children. The first stop is at the Sax altar, where the procession circles the altar three times. Then the parade sets out into the settlement, following a roughly coiled route. During the parade, *lusheng* are played, brass gongs are beaten, young men stop at the gate and road intersections to fire off shots. The whole scene appears to mimic going off to battle. The parade ends as a *duoye* at the Sax altar.[17] Finally the *duoye* moves to the drum tower and continues until dark. The *duoye,* following a coil dance pattern, at this moment almost reaches a carnival performance (Figure 2.54). A rich banquet is held in the drum tower the same evening.

On the second day of the ritual, chicken bone divination is performed to test whether Sax is well settled and the altar is soundly built. Once the divination indicates good results, a pig must be slaughtered in the evening in the drum tower for the final celebration. On the third day, the Sax caretaker and the *nyens laox* go to the altar to offer rice wine, meat, and tea to Sax. They then shut the altar compound. Usually people are not allowed to approach the Sax altar except on ceremony days. At the same time, the village gate is reopened, which indicates that the whole settlement is reopened, and people recommence their daily routines.

The formal structure of a settlement pattern and the disposition of its architectural elements can be recognized in several ways. Visual links and

Figure 2.54 The Dong *duoye* was performed in front of the drum tower after the Sax ritual on 23 January 1993. The whole performance was conducted as continuous clockwise and counterclockwise movements that might be seen as a coil in form. Source: Photograph by Xing Ruan, 1993.

map reading are obvious means for visitors. But towns and settlements are also cognitive as meaning-laden mental structures. To understand the pattern of a town, or a settlement, requires both mental and bodily engagement from the inhabitants, often in a collective process of making and inhabiting this formal structure—that is, rituals. Another level of understanding, a figurative imagining, often helps form an intimate affinity with the settlement pattern. One example in the Sax ritual is the coil structure, one of the water-associated images cited earlier (Sumet 1988), which can be easily identified in Dong architecture and artifacts. Nautical images are widely transformed into artifacts (Figure 2.55), architecture, and settlements among minority groups in southern China and Southeast Asia, as well as among the Pacific people (Sumet 1988).

What is surprising is that these nautical images, if they indeed are the remains or evidence of an Asian coastal origin of the Dong, have been retained as a kind of recurrent motif throughout the settlement and its architecture. The Dong may not be able to (or perhaps do not have to) understand the meaning of these transformed coils in their rituals and architecture as they relate to their origins. In other words, the Dong do not relate coil images in their architecture to the nautical symbolism of a coil, or the drum tower to a mast, and a settlement to a boat, in a one-to-one linguistic pairing. In fact, these recurrent coil images are handed down and retained as materialized

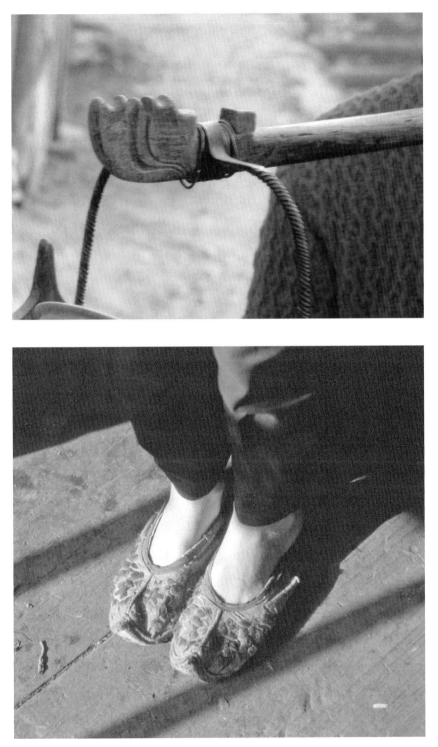

Figure 2.55 Some Dong forms—shoulder poles *(top)* and embroidered shoes *(bottom)*, for example—may be seen as nautical images. Source: Photograph by Xing Ruan, 1993.

transformations in architecture and ritual. They may not be decipherable signs to the Dong, but they remind the Dong of a figurative and bodily engagement with their built world.

FENGSHUI AND DONG SETTLEMENT

If the Sax ritual is a journey to the past through the settlement, the *fengshui* connotation of Dong settlements is a journey to a different culture. *Fengshui* is a Han term for what is generally known as geomancy in English. It is basically a protocol that advises people how to choose a site, decide orientations, and plan layouts in order to determine constructions of *yangzhai* (yang house, living house) and *yinzhai* (yin house, tomb, or graveyard). To explore the Dong's use of *fengshui* in their settlements, let me begin with its key applications in architecture for the Han.

Fengshui in Chinese literally means wind and water, both of which flow. *Qi,* the cosmic breath or energy, also flows. There are two types of *qi:* one is *shengqi,* which is auspicious and brings life; the other is *xieqi* or *xiongqi,* which is ominous and brings death. One important rule of *fengshui* is *changfeng deshui*—that is, avoiding wind and collecting water. It seems that wind and water are taken as the media of *qi.* Wind is considered to be ominous and water auspicious.[18] Furthermore, topographic features, particularly mountains that assume certain postures *(shi),* are also considered to have *qi.* Consequently, mountains are imagined to have been embodied with mythical animal deities. In *fengshui,* four popular animals are commonly associated with colors and orientations: *qinglong* (blue dragon, east, left), *baihu* (white tiger, west, right), *zhuque* (red bird, south, front), and *xuanwu* (black tortoise, north, back).

According to the general *fengshui* doctrines, particularly those of southeastern China, the ideal sites for settlement can be abstracted into two patterns:

- For sites in mountain river valleys, a settlement should rest on the mountain slope, with water wrapping around in the front and facing the "screens" (mountains in the distance) (Figure 2.56).
- For sites on plains, a settlement should rest on the water, that is, a settlement is usually linear with its back to the river and its front along the street.

The pattern of facing the water with the mountains behind must be on a south-north axis. Most Dong

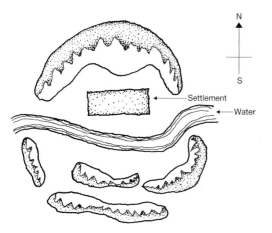

Figure 2.56 An ideal mountain-river-valley *fengshui* pattern showing the settlement protected by a mountain in the north and with a river and distant "screen" mountains in the south. Source: Drawn by Xing Ruan.

Figure 2.57 A close view of the Pingyan wind-and-rain bridge in Ma'an village, Sanjiang region, Guangxi province. Source: Photograph by Xing Ruan, 1992.

settlements do fall into this pattern. Naturally this pattern absorbs southern sunlight and avoids northerly winds. This may appear as just a coincidence with *fengshui*, but a key component of a Dong settlement pattern suggests that the Dong have incorporated Han *fengshui*.

Other than a quintessential Dong structure, the wind-and-rain bridge also serves a *fengshui* purpose (Figure 2.57). In a Han settlement, the *longmai* (mountains as dragon veins) on which the settlement rests have to be wriggly like a flying dragon that can generate the *shengqi* for the settlement. The Dong, who appear to have accepted this rule, nevertheless apply the *fengshui* protocol flexibly: *longmai* can be created, as mentioned earlier, by connecting the mountains with wind-and-rain bridges in a settlement. These bridges, sometimes in the central part of a settlement, do not necessarily cross a river but simply offer shelter to the villagers.

Both the Han and the Dong consider water to be wealth that has to be collected and protected from running away. In Han settlements, there are usually

Figure 2.58 The watercourse in a Han village is "locked" by a combination of temple, pavilion, bridge, gate, and large *fengshui* trees. Source: Drawn by Xing Ruan after He Xiaoxin (1990, 87).

two ways to achieve these aims. The first one is simply collecting water by creating a pond either in front of the settlement or at its center. The second strategy involves constructing a watercourse to "lock" the wealth from running away. The watercourse in a Han settlement is often at the lower reach of the river or stream that wraps around the southern front of the settlement. A simple strategy could be just a small bridge; a complicated one could be a grouping of bridge, temple, tower, gate, pavilion, and trees (Figure 2.58). Within a Dong settlement, certain well-preserved huge trees at the head of the village are called *fengshui* trees. These trees do not seem to serve a *fengshui* purpose; rather, they are spiritual trees for Dong ceremonies. The wind-and-rain bridges, either at the head or the tail of a village, can be seen as a transformed Han watercourse. The bridge, gate, pavilion, and temple are, in the case of Dong wind-and-rain bridges, combined into an elaborate formal structure that serves not only as the power to protect the Dong's wealth from running away, but also as a central part of their own poetic use (Figure 2.59).

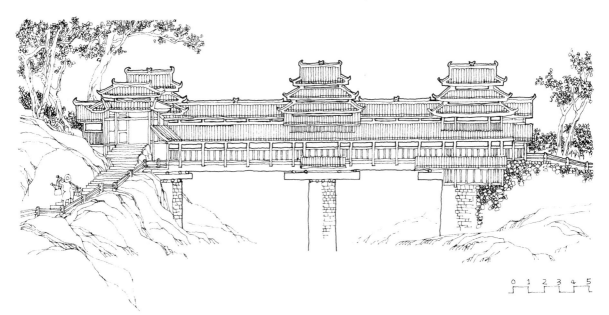

Figure 2.59 Elevation of the Batuan wind-and-rain bridge in the Sanjiang region, Guangxi province, which can be seen as a combination of temple, pavilion, bridge, gate, and *fengshui* tree in one composite structure. Source: Drawn by Xing Ruan after Li Changjie et al. (1990, 221).

Figurative Imagining: The Settlement of Ma'an in Chengyang

Ma'an is a Dong *zhai,* a hamlet that belongs to Chengyang village in the Sanjiang region, Guangxi province. Compared with other Dong villages, Ma'an is relatively small. During my second fieldwork visit in Ma'an (January 1993), I measured and sketched approximately one hundred houses within the settlement. Each house has an average two or three fire pit rooms, indicating that they each accommodate two or three small families.

Set along the lower reaches of the Lingxi River, the site of Ma'an, like other *zhai* of Chengyang, is a typical mountain river valley in the Dong region (Figure 2.60). The site is considered to be particularly zoomorphic by the Dong in this region and therefore auspicious. One myth of Ma'an holds that the site is the incarnation of a mythical horse. Legend has it that two of the Dong ancestors travelled to this area a long time ago. One, called Cheng, came from the south and rode a red horse; the other, Yang, came from the north and rode a white water buffalo. They met at a featureless site and stopped to have a chat. The red horse went down to the lower reaches, and the white buffalo went to the upper reaches. Then they sat down. As Cheng and Yang were talking to each other, the red horse and the white buffalo were turned into mountains—resulting in a beautiful mountain river valley with green hills and clear waters. After their farewells, Cheng and Yang realized they could no longer continue their journey. They then thought this to be a sign from the gods and concluded that these two mythical animals were incarnations of deities. They decided to bring their families there to settle on these two mythical animals. Later the whole village was called Chengyang. Ma'an, which rests on the "red horse," literally is a saddle (Xu et al. 1992, 14–17).

Another widely acknowledged myth of the site is that of "two dragons playing with a pearl," a familiar Han morphology of a *fengshui* site. The mountain to the north is considered to be one "dragon," the mountain on the west side of the Lingxi River is the other "dragon," and the small hill on which the settlement rests is the "pearl." The topography and orientation of the Ma'an village site do form an auspicious *fengshui* pattern. Probably because the mountains at the back of the settlement do not constitute a continuous, enclosed *fengshui* barrier, the Chengyang bridge is used to connect the "dragon veins" (Figure 2.61). As a result, the whole settlement is convincingly "locked" by the combination of the Chengyang bridge at the lower reaches and the Pingyan bridge at the upper reaches (see Figure 2.60).

In fact the Chengyang bridge and the Pingyan bridge belong to the whole Chengyang village along the Lingxi River. Not surprisingly, the Chengyang

Figure 2.60 Plan of Ma'an village in the Sanjiang region showing the elevated first level of every house in the settlement. Source: Drawn by Dongmin Zhao and Xing Ruan.

Figure 2.61 Image of the Chengyang wind-and-rain bridge in Ma'an village showing the connection of "dragon veins" (mountains). Source: Photograph by Xing Ruan, 1992.

bridge located at the lowest reaches of the eight villages along the river is the grandest and most elaborate. It thus serves as the most powerful lock (Figure 2.62). Similarly, the Pingyan bridge serves as the lock for the settlement at its upper reaches. Viewed from their *fengshui* capacity, it is obvious that not only the lengths but also the levels of grandeur and the intricacy of craftwork increase in three bridges, including a small bridge at the upper reaches, in the Chengyang area, stretching from the upper to lower reaches (Figure 2.63).

These three bridges connect the villages along the Lingxi River. The Chengyang bridge is in fact a composite assemblage of gate, temple, pavilion, and bridge. But it first serves as the gate for the settlements along the river, particularly for Ma'an village. The settlement of Ma'an is visually identified by the Chengyang bridge and by its drum tower. The Ma'an drum tower does not occupy the highest or the most central position in the settlement; rather, it is situated on a very convincing topographic focal point. Villagers in Ma'an often claim that the view of their village from the Chengyang bridge is one of the most picturesque among all the Dong settlements in the region (Figure 2.64). The drum tower can be seen from anywhere inside or outside the village (Figure 2.65).

Figure 2.62 The Chengyang wind-and-rain bridge, the most elaborate Dong bridge, viewed from Ma'an village.
Source: Photograph by Xing Ruan, 1992.

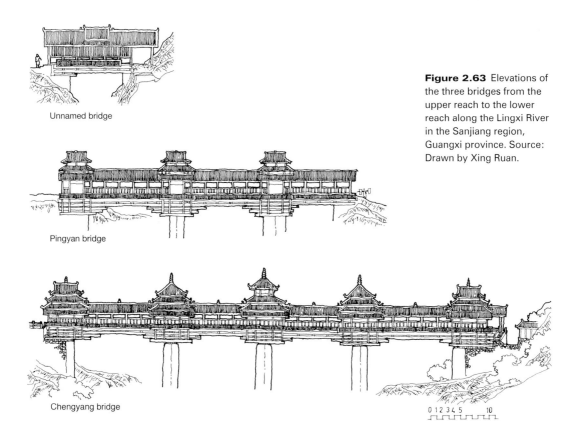

Unnamed bridge

Pingyan bridge

Chengyang bridge

Figure 2.63 Elevations of the three bridges from the upper reach to the lower reach along the Lingxi River in the Sanjiang region, Guangxi province. Source: Drawn by Xing Ruan.

0 1 2 3 4 5   10

Figure 2.64 Picturesque skyline of Ma'an village viewed from the Chengyang bridge.
Source: Li Changjie et al. (1990, 263).

Figure 2.65 Located at a topographic focal point, the Ma'an drum tower can be viewed from anywhere inside and outside the settlement. Source: Photograph by Xing Ruan, 1992.

Figure 2.66 The Ma'an square viewed from the opera stage. The central square of Ma'an village is architecturally defined by the drum tower, housing, and opera stage. Source: Photograph by Xing Ruan, 1992.

Figure 2.67 Ma'an village and its drum tower viewed from the north. Source: Photograph by Xing Ruan, 1992.

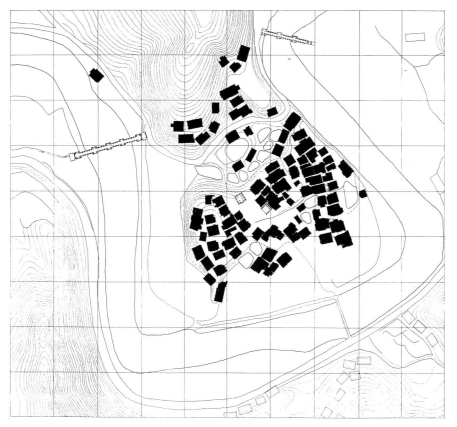

Figure 2.68 Figure-and-ground of Ma'an village showing the footprints of public structures. Source: Drawn by Xing Ruan.

The central square of Ma'an is well defined by the drum tower, opera stage, and housing (Figure 2.66). The square itself is a terrace that opens at its north side. The drum tower and the square can therefore be viewed at a distance from the north (Figure 2.67). The density and uniformity of the housing do form a continuous mass and hence a supportive background for the powerful public structures: bridges, drum tower, and opera stage (Figure 2.68).

There is no Sax altar or temple in Ma'an. Ruins of Sax altars are found in the villages along the Lingxi River, however, suggesting that Sax ceremonies used to exist in these locations and, perhaps, that some small *zhai* shared one Sax altar. The ritual performance of *duoye* is alive and well in this region. The *duoye* at Ma'an retains the form and pattern described earlier, including dancing clockwise and counterclockwise in front of the drum tower to form a coil. No evidence suggests that the *duoye* at Ma'an is in any way related to the Sax ceremony, however, and there are a number of signs that it does not. At Ma'an, for example, the *duoye* is performed during festivals or on any

Figure 2.69
A *duoye* in Ma'an village performed for tourists. Source: Photograph by Xing Ruan, 1992.

other special occasion, but today the *duoye* is more commonly performed in order to entertain tourists (Figure 2.69). From Sax ceremony to tourist entertainment, the contents of the *duoye* no doubt have been totally changed. Nevertheless, as a ritual, the *duoye* still plays its critical role in claiming a meaningful relationship with the settlement pattern in the process of inhabiting and making. Although the rituals in Ma'an are no longer related to Sax ceremony, in entertaining the tourists they could well retell the stories of the figurative site of their settlement both to visitors and to themselves while ensuring that the *fengshui* capacity of their bridges is still enacted. Using the *duoye* to entertain tourists may seem to differentiate the Dong through their architecture and settlement from the contexts of the majority Han and other minority groups. (Some other minority groups, the Miao for example, entertain tourists in a similar way.) At the same time, the *duoye* serves as a means of self-reassurance in that it consolidates the pattern of their settlement as the hearth of their own world.

3

CHORAL SYMBOLIZATION
The Social Life of Public Structures

In *The Unbearable Lightness of Being,* Milan Kundera could not reconcile beauty in the European sense with that of New York. Despite his distaste for New York's "unintentional beauty," Franz, Kundera's character, admits that it sparkles "with a sudden wondrous poetry." Yet, although intriguing, the beauty of New York frightens him; it is an alien world (Kundera 1984, 101–102). The frightening aspect, in fact, is the vertical New York—the skyline, which is set against the premeditated beauty of a Gothic cathedral. Joseph Rykwert, making explicit the neglected city skyline, quotes Montgomery Schuyler in his book on ancient cities (1988): "It was not an architectural vision, but it does, most tremendously, look like business." In his book on cities of the twenty-first century, Rykwert makes similar remarks (2000, 18 and 189).

Verticality may well be a common trait for premodern people, where a stratified cosmos is necessary to complement a confined horizon (Tuan 1974, 132). In other words, it is sheer height that heightens awareness. But the New York skyline, or any other towering silhouette of a city center in the twenty-first century, other than occasionally providing tourists with a viewing platform, does very little to expand its citizens' horizon. Two questions should be asked: Does the New York skyline actually animate business? And can verticality become an architectural vision, beautiful as well as instrumental?

In a village settlement in southern China, a public structure, such as a "council shed" or, in its fullest elaboration, a Dong drum tower, would serve both purposes in that they define the village skyline and are also instrumental in organizing village life. But it serves, first and foremost, as the hearth of a village settlement. Given that the minority groups in southern China have been subject to the historical and political fabrications of the majority Han, a hearth, in a broader sense, is a necessary instrument for these groups in order to create the warmth, as well as the security, of their home in the context of an overarching Han cosmos (Tuan 1996). Public structures in villages, typically, are honored. This is not because, as the formally dominant structure in the settlement, they look like a sign of honor; rather, the honor is a consequence of the social authority that the public structures have been afforded through the processes of their *workings*—inhabiting and making. An old Dong saying holds that "the drum tower governs" *(gulou wei zheng)*. This indicates that the honor of the drum tower is itself productive: it not only has the instrumental capacity to structure society, but it also gives form to the Dong's rich and intricate cultural practices. That honor is, therefore, a formative force in organizing a way of life and making visible the hearth as home and identity. But before visible verticality was developed, the seed of such a village structure had already foreshadowed an architectural vision.

From Village Heart to Hearth

The drum tower is widely referred to as the village heart by the Dong. For both the Han and the southern minorities, the heart plays a symbolic role as the seat of life. The belief is that the physical heart dies when the body dies, but the soul, as the surrogate of the heart, "lives for a long time after death and is much concerned about those it leaves behind—on the condition that they make proper sacrifice to it" (Eberhard 1986, 260). As noted earlier, when founding a new village, once the boundary is defined, the Dong first erect the drum tower; usually the trunk of a fir tree is set up and the real drum tower is built afterwards. At the same time, the location of the Sax altar must also be defined. Only then do the villagers start building their own houses.

As in Dong villages, the "village heart" exists in the villages of China's southern minorities and Southeast Asia as both the spiritual and physical center.[1] Most of these village hearts take the form of tree trunks or carved wood pillars. The heart of a village does not have to be the physical center of the settlement. The spiritual center for the Akha in Thailand is usually a holy tree near the settlement chosen by the village chief before the remainder of the village is built. Because the soul of the god is believed to have taken the form of a holy tree, this tree is regarded to be the house of the soul. When the holy tree is identified, the chief must pray in front of it for the god's permission to build their village there and must plead for the protection of his villagers. The next step is to construct the entry and exit gates. Once they are completed, the villagers then go to the holy tree to pay their respects. They build a small temple for the god near the holy tree, using a fence to define the sacred place (Figure 3.1). Then they present offerings to the god. At this point, the village's heart is formed and the villagers can start building their own houses (Yang Changming 1990, 116).

In southwestern China, a variety of village hearts are found among the minorities. The Hani in Xishuangbanna, for example, have a founding ritual for their villages that essentially involves finding the central location for the village heart. The village priest throws iron filings together with an egg on the ground, with the result that the place where the egg breaks is considered to be the site of the village heart. At this location, a wooden pillar is then erected to serve as the village heart. For the Dai, also in Xishuangbanna and one of the six Tai linguistic groups in southern China, a village is literally analogized as the human body. Here the hearts of most villages are defined as the physical centers. Although these village hearts take different forms, in most cases they are pillars or variations of pillars (Figure 3.2). Some do appear, however, as shrines or even as altars.

Such hearts of villages are commonly seen as the souls of their ancestors. For the Bulang of Yunnan, for example, the gods at the center of the village are the male and female ancestors. Occasionally the village pillars are carved to look like male and female ancestors with explicit gender features. In these cultures, the souls of the ancestors are considered to still be alive, so they have to be fed by the villagers. One of the offerings, for instance, is the sacrifice of water buffaloes practiced extensively in Austronesian cultures.[2]

Perhaps the most potent way of founding a village heart is the use of fire rather than physical structures. When the Yeche, a branch of the Hani who live in the Red River valley of southern Yunnan, build their village, the first step is to light a fire at the center of the new site in recognition of its significance as the heart of the village. The villagers gather around the fire pit and chant: "This is the very place that can bring us harvests and prosperity!" Regardless of how long it takes, this fire must be carefully kept alive until every house in the village is completed.

A wooden pillar may remain discreet in the village settlement; certainly it does not make the hearth a visible structure. An "invisible" site from an extinguished fire would be undecipherable for an outsider. Participation in the founding ritual—as the Romans did in antiquity (Rykwert 1988)—and the recurrent performance of these rituals would thus ensure the legibility of the village heart and hence its power. The village heart, for its instrumental capacity in founding the settlement and its potential role in guiding the villagers' lives, indeed deserves the presence and should be monumentalized as a reminder, as well as enshrinement, of the rituals. A Dong drum tower is such an example: as a village heart, it is intricately made and vertically monumentalized, and it indeed mobilizes an architectural vision. Yet almost

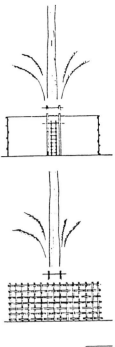

Figure 3.1 The Akha in Thailand identify their holy tree by enclosing it with a fence. Source: Yang Changming (1990, 116).

Figure 3.2 Two pillarlike village "hearts" in the Xishuangbanna region of Yunnan province. Source: Photograph by Xing Ruan, 1986.

all of these village heart precedents can be found in the drum tower complex. Visually the drum tower in the Dong settlement is a giant, celebrated village pillar. From a structural point of view, the single-column "tree structure," presumably one of the early types of Dong drum tower, can be seen as the prototype of the drum tower structure.

As we already know, an analogy for the drum tower, widely recognized by the Dong, is the China fir; a forest of China fir is regarded as the water to bear the village "boat." Hence the fir is thought of as a holy tree by the Dong. The Dong believe that the village's prosperity must be protected in the shade of a giant umbrella, which can only be a fir tree. A Dong legend has it that, in the past, the Dong grew a large fir tree at the center of the village. The village chief always stood under the fir to gather villagers in an emergency.

A surviving case is found in Shudong village in the Liping region of Guizhou province.[3] This seven-eave drum tower, built in 1927, has an exterior that appears similar to two other drum towers in the same village. It is, in fact, quite different, for the interior has only one load-bearing column, right at the center, with the overall structure balanced with eight peripheral columns (Figure 3.3). Because of this particular structure, the fire pit has to be, inevitably, off center; in this case, it is located in a corner. The previous drum tower fell apart, and it is believed to be the third single-column drum tower built on the same site. A single case does not necessarily warrant proof of this drum tower being the prototype. It could well be a new fabrication from the Dong that is influenced by, so to speak, the "cultural textualization" of anthropologists. The strong fir tree analogy, nonetheless, still exists in the Dong region. Villagers believe that the *zhai* previously had a large fir tree, as an umbrella, to cast shade for the whole settlement. This fir tree died after many years. Their ancestors then decided to imitate the fir tree and built a gigantic "umbrella" for the village. According to mythology, this is how the first single-column drum tower was invented.

Following this line of speculation, one of the reasons for the transformation from a single load-bearing column structure to four or six load-bearing columns is that the fire pit was introduced to the drum tower. The centrality of the fire pit, essential for making the hearth, led to a "hollow pillar" idea defined by the four load-bearing columns and covered by the multi-eave roof shelter. As a potent metaphor for male ancestor ceremony, the central fire pit explains what the drum tower inhabitation is fundamentally about (Figure 3.4). The significance of fire in relation to ancestor ceremony can be best understood through the drum tower. It appears that the Dong only remember their female ancestor, Sax. As discussed in Chapter 2, the annual ceremony devoted to Sax is one of the most celebrated rituals performed by the Dong. Sax has her own altar in the village. Yet some ritual fragments involved in the Sax ceremony, and in relation to certain other customs, seem to suggest that the drum tower plays a role as the counterpart to the Sax altar within the settlement.

The way of living together under the clan's surname is thought of as the historical remains of Dong patriarchy. Strictly speaking, a drum tower signifies a clan's surname. The number of drum towers in a village indicates the number of clan groups living there. In Zhaoxin village of Liping county in Guizhou province, for example, five drum towers signify the five clan groups in this village (Figure 3.5). With increasing migration, however, people with different clan surnames intermixed. As a consequence, the tradition of a

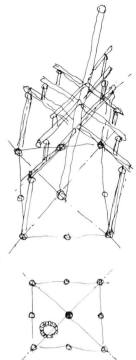

Figure 3.3 Speculative structural diagrams of the single-column drum tower. Source: Sketch drawn by Xing Ruan.

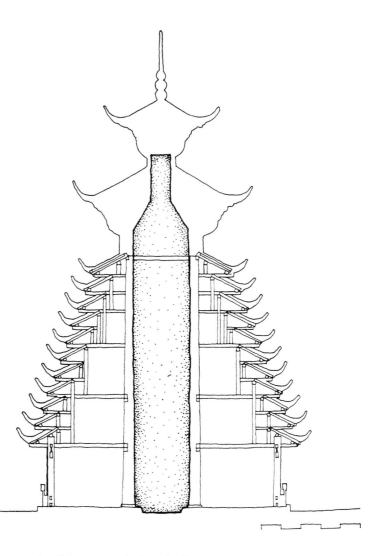

Figure 3.4 Section of the Zengchong village drum tower indicating that the internal space is a "hollow pillar" designed for the fire pit. Source: Drawn by Xing Ruan.

drum tower signifying a particular clan's surname has been lost in some Dong areas.

The Dong generally appear to have forgotten the significance of their drum tower in terms of its association with the village pillar, male ancestor, and their patriarchy. But the ritual of fetching live cinders from the drum tower during the Sax ceremony is an important and carefully maintained act. As described in the previous chapter, during the ritual the fire is kindled in the fire pit of the drum tower, and from there every family must fetch live cinders to light their own family fires and, symbolically, perpetuate their ancestry.

The Dong at times serve offerings to the drum tower, although the ritual and the offerings are different from those during the Sax ceremony. For instance, the Dong tie water buffalo horns to one of the drum tower columns

(Figure 3.6).[4] As part of their custom of holding water buffalo fights between villages, the defeated buffaloes must be slaughtered, the meat shared by all villagers, and the horn tied to a column in the drum tower. Dong water buffalo fighting is, metaphorically, a masculine game with male-oriented symbolization—similar to the significance of fire and the clan surname. Given the difference in form of female and male ancestors in the Sax altar and the drum tower, it is quite possible that the drum tower serves as a phallic analogy. But either the Dong do not consciously realize this or the morphological connotation alone simply does not evoke much meaning to them. The Dong, however, do become aware of the power of the drum tower through rituals and inhabitation; in this way the drum tower's role in structuring the masculine aspects of Dong society is realized and indeed empowered.

The transformation from village pillar to drum tower is by no means an unconscious process. Every step of the transformation is taken on the basis of

Figure 3.5 In Zhaoxin village, Congjiang region of Guizhou province, the number of drum towers signifies the number of clan groups within the settlement. Source: Photograph by Xing Ruan, 1993.

Figure 3.6 A water buffalo horn, perhaps an offering, is tied to one of the four load-bearing columns in the drum tower in Xiaohuang village, Congjiang region of Guizhou province. Source: Photograph by Xing Ruan, 1993.

the previous type, simultaneously as acculturation as well as invention. This process of transformation, displacements notwithstanding, produces tacit yet rich drum tower analogies. Whether hypothetical or not, the transformation described here is one possible story of the Dong drum tower's "choral" or "polyphonic" allegories.

The umbrella/fir tree analogy implies another scenario that relates the village pillar to the drum tower transformation. The shade cast by the "umbrella" is in fact an architecturally defined space that, in functional terms, probably serves as a shelter for public gatherings. This is confirmed in the description of the Dong legend, noted earlier, that the village chief usually stood under the "fir tree" to call people together. Naturally the "fir tree" was a man-made shelter serving the purpose of an imaginary gigantic umbrella. This shelter, which served as a public meetinghouse, might have existed before the village pillar/village heart was transformed into the shelter of the drum tower. The Dong's own name for the drum tower, "*beengc,*" suggests a possible early, log-constructed shelter. The "*dangc wagx,*" or "*dangc kah,*" simply means a meeting place for the public. The houselike drum tower is even found today in villages where the old towers were burnt or destroyed by accidents. I shall return to this type later.

A bronze cowrie-shell container (dated 200–100 BC) found at Shizhaishan in Yunnan province reveals an integral combination of a shelter, a pillar, and a sacrifice ritual (Figure 3.7). The scene on the lid of this container is a complex of images and forms. Some interesting similarities can be drawn between this scene and the Dong drum tower. The pile-built, saddle-roof shelter on the container is the focal point and dominates the whole scene. The platform is raised above the ground with pillars at its four corners. Two pillars, one at each end of the platform, support the saddle roof, and the platform is open without any enclosing walls. From an architectural point of view, the similarities between the Dong and the tribes living in the Dian Lake region in Yunnan province more than two thousand years ago are apparent. It seems, for instance, just as in Dong tradition, that this freestanding open shelter could have served as the "umbrella" for this particular gathering. Even the saddle roof could be regarded as an early type of gable-and-hip roof similar to that used by the Dong (Figure 3.8).

Two prominent pillars are at the rear of the scene. One pillar has two coiled snakes wrapped around it. The huge snake at the base of the pillar is devouring a man. The other pillar is a slablike tablet that has a naked man tied to it who is evidently about to be sacrificed (Figure 3.9).[5] Although no human sacrifice has been found among the Dong, holding buffalo fights and tying the horns of slaughtered buffalo to the drum tower column are undoubtedly sacrifice-related rituals. In this particular scene, a slaughtered ox is lying on the ground and other animals are about to be sacrificed. From a variety of material sources we can assume that buffalo sacrifice was, and still is, an important ritual among some cultures in southern China and Southeast Asia and, moreover, that human sacrifice and animal sacrifice might have coexisted previously. The hanging buffalo head, for example, and even the buffalo-head ridge gable and roof, as seen in the Shizhaishan bronzes, exist in many cultures of Southeast Asia (Figure 3.10).

The verticality and the intimate connection with the earth in the Dong drum tower are achieved through its architectural artifice—particularly the "hollow pillar" defined by the four center load-bearing columns and the sunken fire pit (see Figure 3.5). Snake or dragon analogies and motifs also appear on the drum tower. Curiously, a distinction between snake and Han dragon is not clearly drawn by the Dong; in their communal lives they may have adopted this isomorphism or in fact still view it as a snake. In any case, the tiles and multi-eave roofs of Dong buildings—described as a "bright and beautiful scaly covering" by Kuang Lu in the Ming dynasty—have a "coiled" corner at each eave that is evidently another snake/dragon feature (Figure 3.11). More explicitly, snakes/dragons are occasionally added to the roof ridges of the drum tower or can even be found in the tower (Figure 3.12; see also Figure 2.27).[6]

The comparison between this Shizhaishan ritual setting and Dong drum tower suggests that the complex components of the Shizhaishan structure might possibly be condensed into one Dong drum tower. In other words,

Figure 3.7 Ceremonial shelter model on the lid of a cowrie container showing a ritual sacrifice. Shizhaishan bronze dated 200–100 BC. Source: Drawn by Xing Ruan from the photograph in *The Chinese Bronzes of Yunnan* (Rawson 1983, 31).

Figure 3.8 House in Ma'an village in the Sanjiang region, Guangxi province. The roof is typical of the gable-and-hip form across the whole Dong region. Source: Photograph by Xing Ruan, 1992.

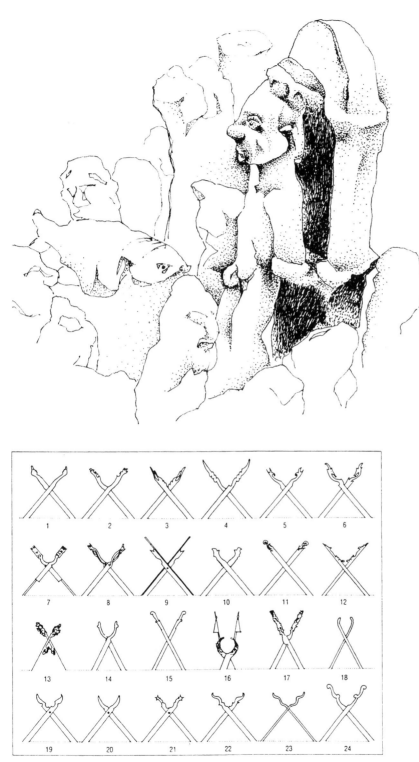

Figure 3.9 Close view of the Shizhaishan bronze cowrie-shell container showing a human figure tied to a pillar and about to be sacrificed. Source: Drawn by Xing Ruan from the photograph in *The Chinese Bronzes of Yunnan* (Rawson 1983, 33).

Figure 3.10 Various gable horns from Southeast Asia; all assume the form of a buffalo head. Source: Domenig (1980, 20).

Figure 3.11a and b Many drum tower eaves are curved with distinctive snake or dragon features. Dong drum towers from *(top)* Zengchong village, Congjiang region in Guizhou province; *(bottom)* Mapang village, Sanjiang region in Guangxi province. Source: Photographs by Xing Ruan, 1993 and 1992.

Figure 3.12 A wood carved snake/dragon found in the Gaozeng village drum tower, Congjiang region of Guizhou province. Presumably it is used as one of the long benches surrounding the central fire pit. Source: Photograph by Xing Ruan, 1993.

the architectural complex of the drum tower is powerful enough to structure and absorb these rituals—regardless of whether they are ceremonies to swear oaths of alliance or allegiance or whether they are sacrificial rituals to the earth god to ensure a good harvest. Moreover the sunshade shelter, which may have served as a critical step for the Dong in their transformation from the village pillar to the drum tower complex as a ritualized meeting place, is also present in the Shizhaishan example. A Dong drum tower, an architectural artifice, is a village heart turned into hearth.

Naming and Tacit Analogies

Despite the preceding speculations, the origin of the Dong drum tower, which can readily be dated back several thousand years, is still out of reach. The original conditions and meanings may bear little significance to the Dong themselves. Indeed architecture, as I have argued, reproduces the condition that gives rise to it historically, but it never is the same as the original conditions. The Dong drum tower, "travelling" from the past to the present, or even from one place to another, is regarded as such a historical memory. The textualizations imposed by the Han and others intertwine with their own imagination, which has enriched its current working conditions. The following are living myths that are still associated with Dong drum tower.

NAMING OF THE DRUM TOWER

For the Dong, history is more a memorable moment than a time procession. Because they did not have a written language to record their history into a clear chronology, Dong history never became a mere accumulation of intellectual information but instead became a dense assemblage of past/present relations. When the drum tower was invented or first appeared is an issue that does not matter much to them since time itself is regarded as something vague. Because of the honor of the drum tower, there is good reason to believe that it was generated before Dong settlements were founded or at least was formed at the same time. Even today, when rebuilding a Dong village after a fire, or when migrating to a new place, the first thing to be constructed is a drum tower.

Hypotheses from Dong scholars regarding the dating of the invention of the drum tower range from the Qin and Han dynasties (221 BC–AD 220) (Wu and Chen 1985) to the Tang and Song dynasties (618–1279) (Shi Ruopin 1984; Huang Caigui 1983) to the Ming dynasty (1368–1644) (Zhang Min 1986). Regardless of their assumed necessity, these hypotheses are questionable. First, as I have argued, the Dong and their culture are by and large not textualized; yet these hypotheses are mainly based on Han Chinese historical texts. Second, it can be argued that the drum tower itself is a Han Chinese concept. In Chinese, drum towers are called *gulou*, in which *gu* means drum and *lou* means a multistory building with upper-level floors and rooms. The Dong usually call the drum tower *louc*, but they also use other Dong names. One important difference between the Chinese and Dong etymology is that the Dong omit all references to the drum. The Dong *louc* seems to equate to the Chinese *lou* but is pronounced with a slightly different tone. As a building type, the Dong drum tower is more a tower than a *lou*.

The following discussion of the Han drum tower is based on literary evidence as well as unearthed material artifacts. As a form of history, the text has, to a great extent, served as a dominant power to form peoples' belief but not necessarily their habitus. In this sense, for the Han, the use of the drum tower as a warning device for defensive purposes is a commonly accepted belief. But whether or not the Han drum tower is also

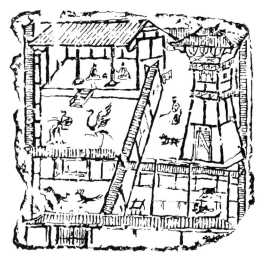

Figure 3.13 A Han-dynasty brick engraved with a house image showing a watchtower in the compound. Chendu in Sichuan province. Source: Liu Dunzhen (1978, 51).

Figure 3.14 Han-dynasty clay models of various "watchtowers." Source: Liu Dunzhen (1978, 74).

a pretextual myth is not my concern here. I am only discussing this Han concept in the naming of this particular type of Dong architecture and its paradoxical "social life" for both the Dong and the Han.

Premodern Han Chinese architecture, with the exception of Buddhist towers, is horizontal in tendency. The earliest evidence of multistory buildings or towers appeared in the Han dynasty (206 BC–AD 220). Unearthed Han bricks with engraved images on their surfaces from Sichuan province show that a tower was usually placed at the back of the compound (Figure 3.13). The names of these towers—such as *guan* (watch) or *wang lou* (watchtower)—explicitly indicate that they were built for defensive purposes. These towers may also have been used to store treasure (Liu Dunzhen 1978, 52). The unearthed clay models of watchtowers from the Han dynasty are in fact Chinese *lou* (Figure 3.14) with upper, inhabitable floors. How these watchtowers worked as warning devices or whether they contained drums is still not clear.[7]

The "drum *lou*" and "bell *lou*" in premodern Han cities were not towers but multistory buildings. Their locations in cities were off center. The historically recorded drum towers in villages were in the Northern Wei dynasty (386–534). Because of bandits, the governor Li Cong of Yanzhou in Shandong province developed the idea of a tower with a drum hung in it as a warning device. He then instructed every village to build such a drum tower. Although the form and location of the drum tower were not described, they may have served purposes similar to the watchtowers from the Han dynasty (Zhang Min 1986, 92–94).

In terms of inhabitation, the Dong drum tower is far more complicated than a simple warning device. In today's Dong region, while drums are still hung in the top drum lofts in Guizhou, most drum towers in Guangxi do not have drums. In the Dong area of Guangxi, a man walks around the village

Figure 3.15 The top drum pavilion of the Xindi village drum tower is supported by *dougong*. Congjiang region of Guizhou province. Source: Photograph by Xing Ruan, 1993.

beating a gong to solicit the villagers' attention.[8] For the Dong, a drum tower can exist without a drum in it; and while drums have a long history in this region,[9] hanging them in towers may be a borrowed custom. According to Zhang Min (1985, 40–46), "drum tower" in fact is a Chinese term derived in translation and transliteration from the Chinese *"gulou,"* or drum tower. The custom of hanging a drum in this tower and calling it a drum tower in the Dong area happened only in the Ming dynasty (1368–1644). Yet this specific type of architecture existed in Dong society long before it was called a drum tower and before the drum beating custom evolved in the tower.

Either the idea of the Han drum tower was politically imposed on the Dong in the Ming dynasty, or the Dong adopted it due to their admiration of Han culture—not an atypical minority response to the majority Han. It is this paradoxical fate of the drum tower that affords the Dong warmth and centrality as a hearth of their own; in the meantime it makes an ethnic identity not only visible but accepted by themselves and the Han alike. Whatever the reason, the name of the drum tower does not matter much to the Dong. In today's Dong region, the use of the drum tower as a warning device, in a Han Chinese way, is even lost in some places.

Formal and structural similarities between the top pavilion of the Han-dynasty watchtowers and the top drum pavilion of Dong drum towers are evident (Figure 3.15). The *dougong* (eave bracket set) is accepted as a distinctive and sophisticated Han building technique. There is no evidence to show that the southern minority groups, or the Southeast Asian and Pacific peoples, ever used this technique in their architecture. Among the Dong, the use of *dougong* is also limited to the top of drum pavilions in the drum towers and a few village gates in Guizhou.[10] The dense *dougong*, supporting the top pavilion, causes a sudden change in the smoothly curved, multi-eave roof profile, enhancing the drum pavilion as an elevated top. No single piece of existing Han wooden architecture, the oldest of which can be dated back to the Tang dynasty (618–907), demonstrates this particular enhancement of a tower top. It appears, therefore, that the Han lost this specific technique some time between the Han and Tang dynasties. It probably has been alive for many thousands of years in Dong architecture, however, possibly as early as the Han dynasty.

In addition to the *gulou*, the Dong themselves have a number of other names for their drum towers. In the Chejiang area of the Rongjiang region, drum towers are called *beengc*, which in the Dong language means "building by piling up." This particular name seems to refer to a specific drum tower building technique utilizing log construction. Although the overall structural frame of the drum tower in this area is a combination of pillar-and-beam and pillar-and-transverse-tie-beam, log construction still can be seen at the top. Particularly for those drum towers that have pavilion lofts at the top, log construction is often used with *dougong* to support the overhanging pavilion roof. Log construction is also one of the most important building techniques for Dong wind-and-rain bridges, where piled up logs form a horizontal cantilever between the stone pier and timber bridge (Figure 3.16 a and b). From the name and this type of construction, it is quite possible that the early drum tower was not a tower but a log-constructed shelter.

In terms of language affiliation and migration, the Dong, as well as other Tai linguistic groups and minority groups in southern China, have been related to Austronesian cultures in Southeast Asia and the South Pacific region. A variety of material evidence can be found to support this proposition. Images engraved on the side of a bronze drum found at Shizhaishan, Yunnan, for example, show sheaves of grain being stored in granaries built with piled up, cross-log construction (Figure 3.17). This bronze drum dates to the second or first century BC. According to Roxana Waterson, cross-log foundation can be found extensively distributed throughout Southeast Asia and may even be encountered in Papua New Guinea. Waterson (1990, 24) states: "The discovery at Shih-Zhai-Shan (Shizhaishan) seems to indicate that this manner of building may have coexisted with pile building in the Austronesian world from a very early date."

The name *beengc* suggests a number of possibilities for early Dong drum towers. First, it suggests that this type of architecture existed long before the Han Chinese drum tower and, moreover, served purposes other than a warning device. As we have seen, the custom of hanging a drum in a tower occurred perhaps in the Ming dynasty. Second, most Dong buildings today

Figure 3.16 a and b The log-constructed horizontal cantilever of *(top)* the Wangdong village bridge, Congjiang region of Guizhou province; *(bottom)* the Chengyang bridge of Ma'an village, Sanjiang region of Guangxi province. Source: Photographs by Xing Ruan, 1993 and 1992.

are on pile foundations. However, a structure might be built with piled logs so that it could be celebrated and distinguished in relation to other pile buildings. Third, the coexistence of a pile foundation and cross-log construction suggests a possible link between the Dong and other minority cultures in southern China as well as Austronesian cultures in Southeast Asia and the South Pacific region.

Another frequently mentioned name for the drum tower is *luo han lou*. This is a Han Chinese transliteration from the Dong *louc lagx hank*. Young men are called *lagx hank* in the Dong language. A Ming-dynasty scholar, Kuang Lu, who travelled in Guangxi province, described *luo han lou* in his book *Chi Ya* as follows:

> This single-column tower is constructed by depressing a huge trunk into the earth. The height is about 100 chi.[11] Tiles with five colors are baked to cover it; they look like a bright and beautiful scaly covering. In this tower, young men sing to their hearts' content, drinking as much as they like until late at night, and then sleep in it. People are very proud of this tower.[12]

The custom described by Kuang Lu is still alive in Dong society. The drum tower becomes *louc lagx hank* when young men host girls from other villages and they sing antiphonally together in it. On ordinary days, young men often gather in the drum tower to learn Dong folk songs; sometimes they sleep near the fire pit in the tower at night. This custom, once again, is not related to the drum.

The Dong drum tower is also called *dangc wagx*, or *dangc kah*, both meaning a meeting place for the public. The Dong still use these names to refer to a kind of drum tower that looks like a house. As already indicated, it is usually built when an old drum tower burns down by accident and villagers cannot afford to build a new one. The Dong do need a drum tower, but not necessarily as a warning device. Insofar as the naming of the Dong drum tower suggests the purposes it once served, from this we can quite safely assume that the Dong drum tower has never been what one of its names indicates. The paradoxical naming—drum tower—does help create a Dong identity desired by the Han. But in the meantime, notwithstanding its use unrelated to the name, it is a necessity for the Dong to find themselves the warmth of a hearth and a legitimate place in the context of an overarching Han cosmos.

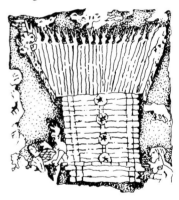

Figure 3.17 A barn built with cross-log construction engraved on a Shizhaishan bronze drum. Source: Drawn by Xing Ruan after Liu Dunzhen (1978, 70).

WATER ANALOGIES

In addition to the analogies of village heart and drum tower naming, Dong architecture involves a series of analogies that are tacitly associated with water—tacit in the sense that these analogies are not always evoked in the process of making and inhabiting architecture. Although not necessarily active all the time, this "debris" of the past, argues Victor Turner, is an essential ingredient of culture: "The culture of any society at any moment is more like the debris, or 'fall-out,' of past ideological systems, than it is itself a system, a coherent whole" (1974, 14). The allegorical process of making and inhabiting architecture is that the debris, or stories of the past as we may call them, may generate other stories that cause poetic displacements and, ultimately, cultural renewal.

To some extent, the following analysis is triggered by a broad and rather speculative hypothesis of "water-based" cultures and their migrations advanced by Sumet (1988). According to Sumet, what he calls water-based people lived along coastal areas, typically creating pile-built structures. These distinctive structures, as well as other water-based cultural architectonics, were then retained by some of those groups as they migrated to the interior of the mainland. The purpose of this analysis, however, is not to use Dong architecture as material evidence to prove cultural origins or migrations of any sort, as Sumet attempted in his book *Naga: Cultural Origins in Siam and the West Pacific* (1988). Even if they do appear to be an "authentic knowledge" that deserves to be pursued, generally speaking prehistoric cultural origins are out of reach. Future archaeological and ethnographic evidence may shed new light on this water-based hypothesis. Yet even if such notions of cultural origins are proved to be contemporary fabrications, consequences of cultural textualization, the issue is to examine an impact of cultural fabrication on the renewal of material cultures.

Dong legends remind us that their migrations from coastal areas to the interior were made possible through sea and river travel and, moreover, that they are a displaced people. One of the most interesting features of their material culture is, as discussed earlier, the extensive use of the boat image.[13] This image can be found in items ranging from household utensils to the house itself and even the whole settlement. A prevalent belief among the Dong, and among other water-based cultures, is that souls will cross the sea and return to the paradise of their ancestors after death. The boat image is believed to be related to this belief (Yang Changming 1990, 80–87).

Since the Dong see their settlement as boat and the forest as sea, very often drum towers are seen as important components of the boat, although these components are attributed to drum towers in arbitrary ways. Zhaoxin village in the Liping region of Guizhou province is an example of this point. Zhaoxin is set in a large mountain river valley that was historically described as "Dong Brook" (see Figure 2.5). The heights of the five drum towers located there were purposely decided according to their exact positions on the "boat." At the center of the "hull," the two drum towers, with eleven and thirteen

Figure 3.18 One of the five drum towers located in the central area of Zhaoxin village in the Liping region, Guizhou province. This is the only flat, gable-and-hip roof among the five drum towers, which is claimed to symbolically roof the "cabin" of the whole village "boat." Two birds stand on the roof ridge. Source: Photograph by Xing Ruan, 1993.

eaves, are among the highest. These two drum towers are thus referred to as the mast and sail. Another drum tower that also forms part of the center of the hull has nine eaves ending with a gable-and-hip roof (Figure 3.18). The only flat roof against the other four pyramidal roofs in Zhaoxin, it symbolically encloses the center of the hull as the boat's "cabin." To enable the boat to sail fast, the drum tower at the "bow" is the lowest, with seven eaves, and the drum tower at the "stern" has to be high with eleven eaves. This is how the Dong commonly see their villages: as boats with the drum towers as masts and sails.

Two bird figures occupy the roof ridges of drum towers with gable-and-hip roofs, as seen in Figure 3.18. The Dong consider these two birds to be the two cormorants for the boat of Zhaoxin. A variety of other birds also occupy the roofs of both Dong drum towers and wind-and-rain bridges (Figure 3.19). Sailing was dangerous for these water-based people, and their fate was unpredictable; birds, thought to be immune from this danger, were seen as bearers of the gods and hence were related to the boat and to sailing safety.

These boat images, or nautical images in general, may well have been juxtaposed with other water symbols to give rise to some of the Dong's favorite cultural architectonics and motifs. At the micro level of the drum tower, besides the additive snake/dragon motifs, the distinctive curved corners of the drum tower eaves appear to be a combination of snake/dragon coils and boat images (Figure 3.20). (The coil was discussed in relation to the Dong

Figure 3.19 Two birds standing on the roof of a wind-and-rain bridge, Zhaoxin village of the Liping region in Guizhou province. Source: Photograph by Xing Ruan, 1993.

Figure 3.20 Curved eave corners of the Dazhai drum tower appear to be a combination of coil and boat. Wangdong village, Congjiang region in Guizhou province. Source: Photograph by Xing Ruan, 1993.

Figure 3.21 The Naga balustrade at the Khmer temple of Khao Phnom Rung, eastern Thailand. Source: Drawn by Xing Ruan from the photograph in Sumet (1988, 16).

settlement ritual and dance in Chapter 2.) What must be emphasized here is that this coil/boat image not only occurs in architecture but is present in many aspects of the Dong's daily life—in their silver jewelry, hunting rifles, shoulder poles, shoes, musical instruments, and so on (see Figure 2.55).

Similar examples are mentioned by Sumet in relation to other Southeast Asian cultural groups (1988, 16–25). According to Sumet the Naga motif, which in Sanskrit means serpent, is an aquatic symbol that extensively permeates the daily life of people on the Asian coast in various mutated forms. And in the Pacific region, including inland areas, the serpentine coil has been used in house carving and in boat motifs since prehistoric times (Figure 3.21). Although, as stated, I do not intend to prove Dong origin on the basis of these similarities, they do indicate cultural homologies between the Dong and the Asian coastal region. Without using any textual evidence, material cultural artifacts (especially architecture) provide us with a direct view of cultures including their transformations. Even if the Dong did migrate to the interior of the mainland and their physical conditions were totally changed, these similarities show a cultural consistency in that these water-associated analogies are still playing significant roles in the making of Dong's architectural allegories.

Type and Artifice

The workings of the Dong drum tower—its productive and instrumental capacity—lie in its spatial disposition. This is best classified, architecturally,

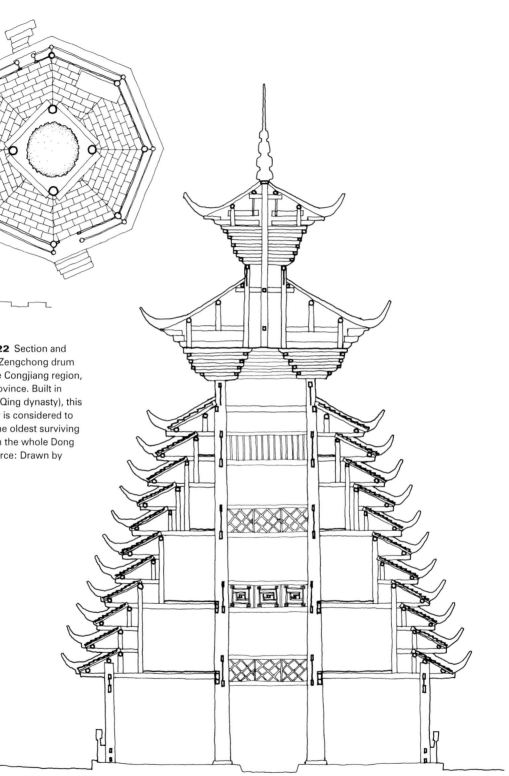

Figure 3.22 Section and plan of the Zengchong drum tower in the Congjiang region, Guizhou province. Built in 1672 (early Qing dynasty), this drum tower is considered to be one of the oldest surviving examples in the whole Dong region. Source: Drawn by Xing Ruan.

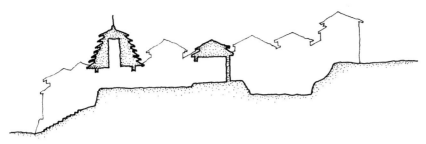

Figure 3.23 A Dong village square defined by opera stage and drum tower showing the spatial flow from inside the drum tower to the outside square. Source: Drawn by Xing Ruan

as a type through the plan and the section. A type, therefore, exercises and transforms power via its specific spatial disposition. To understand this "canalization" of power, as Foucault puts it (1984), through the drum tower in animating Dong social life, let us first examine the drum tower's architectural type.

In most cases, the Dong drum tower (Figure 3.22) is a multi-eave, timber frame structure. The number of eaves is always uneven, ranging from three to fifteen, while the plans range from square or hexagonal to octagonal but always with an even number of sides and, hence, always concentric. The average height of the drum tower is about 20 meters. Four (sometimes six or eight) load-bearing columns run from the ground to support the roof and, commonly, also a loft with a hanging drum. The roof forms, which are very diverse, include overhanging gables, gable-and-hip forms, and pyramidal forms. Most drum towers do not have upper-level floors. The ground-level main hall, where the primary inhabitation occurs, is often without a sense of enclosure and sometimes is totally open. In such cases, the actual space flows from the top of the roof to the edge of the housing, with the housing contributing directly to the definition of the drum tower square (Figure 3.23).

The square plan of a drum tower, due to its load-bearing columns, becomes a nine-square grid. Such an order explains the spatial disposition and the basic construction of this timber frame structure (Figure 3.24). The four load-bearing columns give form to the central core, within which, on the ground, is centered a fire pit. In addition to the four columns, twelve peripheral columns define another layer of space that wraps around the central area. The construction is a combination of pillar-and-beam, pillar-and-transverse-tie-beam, and logs, producing a stepped-back silhouette towards the top of the roof. The pyramidal roof is structured by a central *lei gong* (king post) supported by a beam and truss. In some drum towers, the stepped-back timber frame structure ends as a pyramidal roof, which becomes the final of the multi-eave roofs rather than a separated and elevated pavilion loft enhanced by *dougong* (eave brackets). While this nine-square grid can be

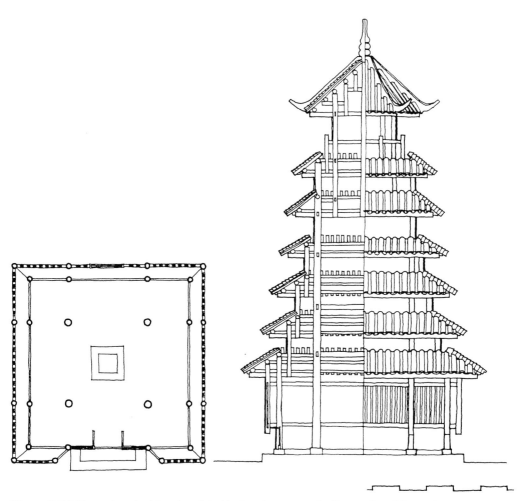

Figure 3.24 Plan and section/elevation of the Hualian drum tower, Sanjiang region of Guangxi province, showing the formal structure of a nine-square-grid drum tower. Source: Drawn by Xing Ruan.

seen as the prototype of the drum tower's formal structure, there are in fact a number of structural and formal variations.

ELEVATED PILE-BUILT DRUM TOWER

One variation is a drum tower elevated above the ground, which in the Dong language is called *yang jongk*, literally meaning an elevated house or, more accurately, a tall building added to a pile-built house. The basic construction and structure are similar to the ordinary pile-built house. According to the site, the pile foundation raises the building at least partially, but sometimes entirely, above the ground (Figure 3.25 a and b). The main hall is likewise elevated on the first level.

A sloping site is not necessarily the reason for an elevated drum tower. More likely, this type is related to the Dong's pile-built housing. Pile-built drum towers of the village Pindeng in the Longsheng region are all built on flat ground. One of them in Pindeng is sandwiched between the two rows of pile-built housing (Figure 3.26). The main hall is thus elevated on the first level, with a staircase leading to it from the street, to give way to the paved street underneath. This second level is immediately linked to the inhabited level of the housing, producing an effect whereby the elevated drum tower square seems to extend directly to the covered porches of the housing one story above ground level.

LAND-BASED DRUM TOWER

While the principles of structure and construction are exactly the same as for the elevated drum tower, the land-based drum tower, due to the primacy of the fire pit, is the predominant type. In the Dong language this structural form is called *dih louc,* which literally means a multi-eave, land-based tower. The land-based drum tower has more plan variations than the elevated type and, structurally, is more intricately assembled. This high level of craft sophistication, which

Figure 3.25 a and b In Heli village of the Sanjiang region, Guangxi province, the inhabited level of one drum tower *(top)* is elevated above the ground *(bottom).* Source: Photograph by Xing Ruan, 1992.

helps create the distinctive Dong drum tower silhouette and village skyline, directly contributes to an aesthetic admiration of it, both for the Dong and others (Figure 3.27). I shall elaborate this point later; but first let me examine the nuances of the drum towers. Even similar construction and structural techniques have not produced replicas. For example, features such as the proportions and styles of drum towers in Guizhou differ significantly from those in Guangxi province in a number of respects, with,

Figure 3.26 The drum tower in Pindeng village, Longsheng region of Guangxi province, is located at an intersection. The main hall of the drum tower is raised above the paved street and connects with the porches of the surrounding housing. Source: Li Changjie et al. (1990, 161).

Figure 3.27 The density of the eaves usually creates a distinctive drum tower silhouette. Drum tower in Gaozeng village, Congjiang region of Guizhou province. Source: Photograph by Xing Ruan, 1993.

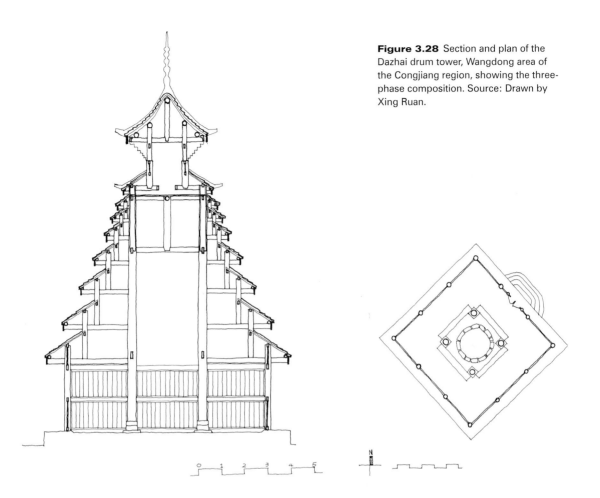

Figure 3.28 Section and plan of the Dazhai drum tower, Wangdong area of the Congjiang region, showing the three-phase composition. Source: Drawn by Xing Ruan.

importantly, different architectural as well as cultural connotations. Among these features are the following.

The pavilion loft. The pavilion loft is one distinctive feature of the drum towers in Guizhou province. The land-based drum towers in this region generally have a three-phase composition: the ground-level (and very often open) main hall as the base; the dense multi-eave body; and the top pavilion loft (Figure 3.28). Because the drum is housed in it, this loft is also called the drum pavilion. The pavilion loft has, as well, its own three-phase structural composition: a timber grid fenestration enclosing the floor area; a dense *dougong* (bracket set) support for the pyramidal roof; and a spire element at the peak known as the *baoding*, a variation of the Buddhist pagoda top. The *baoding* runs through from the interior central *leigong* post (or small king post) to the top of the exterior. Usually the *baoding* is made of an iron bar with glazed ceramic bottles strung together.

An example of a pavilion loft drum tower, built in the early Qing dynasty (1672), is in Zengchong village in the Congjiang region (Figure 3.29). Four

Figure 3.29 The drum tower in Zengchong village has a double-eave pavilion loft. Congjiang region in Guizhou province. Source: Photograph by Xing Ruan, 1993.

Figure 3.30 The top pavilion loft of the Baxie drum tower is a gable-and-hip roof. Baxie village, Sanjiang region, Guangxi province. Source: Photograph by Xing Ruan, 1989.

load-bearing columns and eight peripheral columns support a total of thirteen eaves and a much celebrated, double-eave pavilion loft, producing a strong visual identity (see Figure 3.22). Most pavilion lofts have pyramidal roofs, although overhanging gable roofs or gable-and-hip roofs are occasionally used (Figure 3.30).

An open shelter. The drum tower, in Guizhou in particular, is an open shelter. Neither the multi-eave body of the drum tower nor the ground-level main hall has enclosing walls; except for the pavilion loft, the other parts of the tower are left open. Because of the densely overlapping eaves, protection from sun and rain and ventilation for the fire pit smoke are ensured. Some drum towers have sills on the ground level to define the main hall; the area above the sill is left open and without windows.

Multi-eave without floors. The drum tower is, in fact, a multistory tower-like pavilion rather than a tower.[14] It is tall and sometimes has as many as fifteen eaves; yet except for the top pavilion, it does not have floors. Occasionally a single log ladder, near one of the load-bearing columns, connects the ground level and the top pavilion loft in which the drum is sometimes housed (Figure 3.31).

Some drum towers in Guangxi do not have pavilion lofts. The stepped-back structural frame and the densely overlapped eaves result in a smoothly curved profile. The Mapang village drum tower (Figure 3.32) in the Sanjiang region is one example. Initially built in the late Qing dynasty, it was reconstructed in 1943 by a local craftsman, Lei Wen-xin. This four load-bearing column and twelve peripheral column frame structure is about 10

meters high; its nine eaves end as a gable-and-hip roof. The drum is placed on the main framework simply because there is no pavilion loft at the top (Figure 3.33). Although totally different in their proportions, these drum towers are similar in their structure and construction.

MEETING HALL DRUM TOWER

This type of drum tower is similar to a house, but it is built directly on the ground and can be a modest replacement for a drum tower if it is accidentally burnt down and the villagers cannot afford to build a new one. The Dong call this type *dange wagv*, a public meeting hall (Figure 3.34), which may be combined with a drum tower structure to form a "drum tower complex." The Yanzhai drum tower in Linxi of the Sanjiang region consists of one elevated pile-built structure and one meeting hall (Figure 3.35). The relatively enclosed hall is a winter drum tower that contains the fire pit; the open hall is a summer drum tower with a shrine facing the gate. Each hall has its own structure and roof—one an overhanging gable roof, the other a multi-eave, gable-and-hip roof—yet the two halls are internally connected to each other. The overall complex also serves as the gateway to the village from the lower riverbank (Figure 3.36).

LOU DRUM TOWER

Although, strictly speaking, very few drum towers in the Dong region can be classified as *lou*, the Dong usually call their drum towers simply *lou*, a Chinese word that has a different meaning than "tower" in a Western sense. Rather, it refers to the upper story of a private house containing rooms for

Figure 3.32 Front elevation of the Mapang drum tower, which has no pavilion loft. Sanjiang region in Guizhou province. Source: Photograph by Xing Ruan, 1992.

Figure 3.33 Since there is no top pavilion, the drum of the Mapang drum tower is placed on the main structural framework. Source: Photograph by Xing Ruan, 1992.

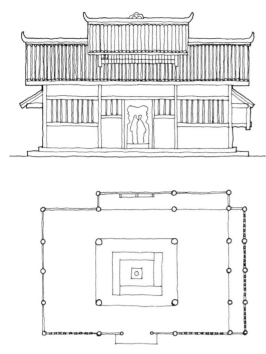

Figure 3.34 A meeting hall drum tower in Liangzhai village, Sanjiang region of Guangxi province. Source: Drawn by Xing Ruan after Li Changjie et al. (1990, 191).

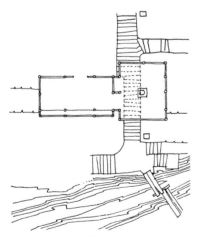

Figure 3.35 Plan of the Yanzhai drum tower (in Linxi of the Sanjiang region) showing two meeting halls, one for summer and one for winter with a fire pit. Source: Li Changjie et al. (1990, 187).

family use. Except for the top pavilion loft, most drum towers do not have upper-level floors and rooms.

Exceptional cases can be found where the Dong simply adopted a Chinese *lou* as their drum tower. The Chezhai village drum tower in the Rongjiang region, originally built in 1877, is a real *lou* (Figure 3.37). The present drum tower has three eaves and three floors. The two upper levels are basically used as lookouts, the ground level forming a raised Dong opera stage enclosed on three sides and open at the front. Unlike other drum towers, here the top, the pyramidal roof, and the other two eaves of the Chezhai drum tower are curved in a manner similar to southern Han architecture (Figure 3.38). The Baxie village drum tower in the Sanjiang region, probably another example of a *lou* (Figure 3.39), has an upper level accessed through a staircase. Here a small void is cut into the floor to articulate the two levels, with the fire pit at the ground level seemingly working for the two inhabitable halls.

As an architectural type, the Dong drum tower is the culmination of the Dong's building craft and is invested with much loving care, skill, and playful creation. It not only showcases an artifice of their material culture but also arouses an aesthetic admiration for the drum tower. The fact that the Dong and other minority groups in southern China, as well as the Han and Westerners, consider the drum tower beautiful and the Dong villages visually attractive is largely due to the admiration of technical artifice. Alfred Gell, emphasizing the *workings* of art, sees art as a "technology of enchantment," which is the very essence of aesthetic appreciation (Gell 1999, 159–186). Here the skyline, the visual aspect of an architectural vision, also contributes to the *workings* of architecture in its social life, which I shall fully elaborate in discussing the inhabiting and making of a drum tower.

Choral Symbolization

The historical sediments of the drum tower described here are by no means understood or made knowable to the Dong through a "reading" with their minds alone; this occurs through

Figure 3.36 Elevation of the Yanzhai drum tower showing the connection between the lower-level riverbank and the upper-level drum tower square. Source: Drawn by Xing Ruan after Li Changjie et al. (1990, 187).

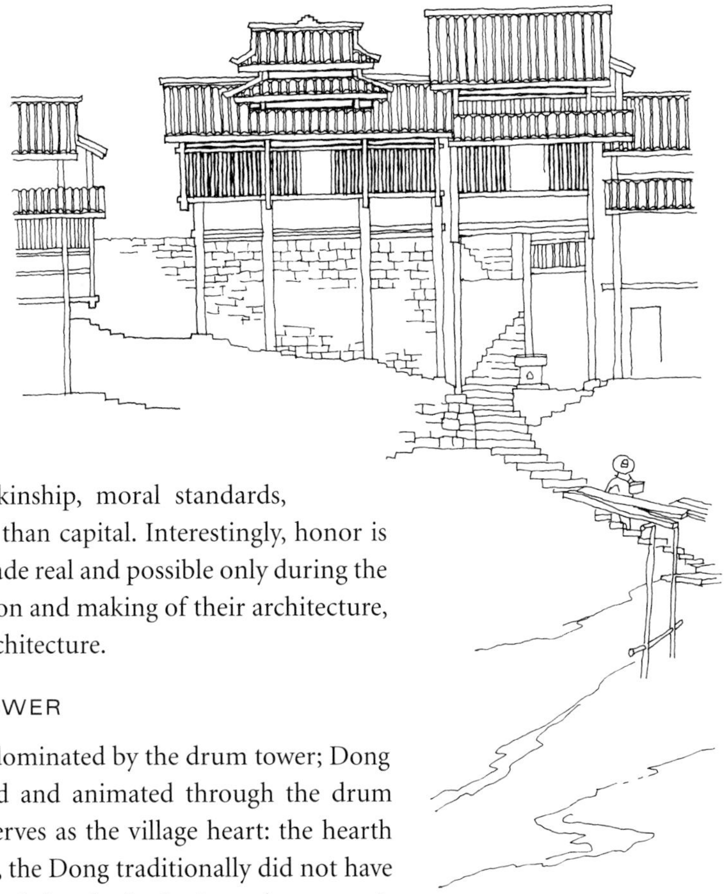

a reading with their bodies as well. This reading is what I refer to as the inhabiting and making of architecture. Like other rural societies, Dong society is structured through the instrumental power of honor—rank, status, kinship, moral standards, customary law, tradition—rather than capital. Interestingly, honor is inscribed in architecture and is made real and possible only during the processes of the Dong's inhabitation and making of their architecture, in other words, the *workings* of architecture.

INHABITING THE DRUM TOWER

A Dong settlement is, physically, dominated by the drum tower; Dong society is, symbolically, organized and animated through the drum tower, which, more specifically, serves as the village heart: the hearth of the Dong. As already described, the Dong traditionally did not have an administrative hierarchy. Instead they had a basic settlement unit called a *zhai,* which, strictly speaking, was settled only by those with the same surname. As previously speculated, the drum tower may be related to the tradition of the village pillar and male ancestor ceremony, so the drum tower itself signified this clan's surname. Usually two or three, sometimes even five, *zhai* occupy a mountain river valley to form a village. The relationships, status, rank, and hierarchy among the *zhai* were realized through the making of drum towers. A typical example is Gaozeng village in the Congjiang region of Guizhou province in which the village is formed by three *zhai*. The earliest clan, called Yang, that settled in this valley has the highest drum tower, which is referred to as "father." Another, the Wu clan, who settled this area after the Yang clan, has a slightly lower drum tower named "mother." The third *zhai* is a group that split off from the two groups to form their own social unit. Their *zhai* has the lowest drum tower, which is termed "son" (see Figure 2.13). Zhaoxin village is another example: here the power hierarchies among the five *zhai* are explicitly materialized through the heights, styles, and locations of the five drum towers of that gigantic village boat.

A *zhai* with a drum tower can therefore be regarded as the basic unit of Dong society in which two or three chiefs, usually the elderly and most

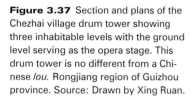

Figure 3.37 Section and plans of the Chezhai village drum tower showing three inhabitable levels with the ground level serving as the opera stage. This drum tower is no different from a Chinese *lou.* Rongjiang region of Guizhou province. Source: Drawn by Xing Ruan.

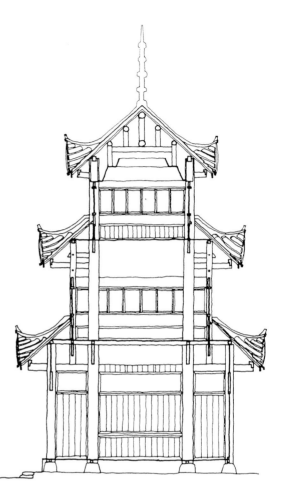

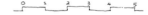

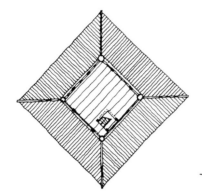

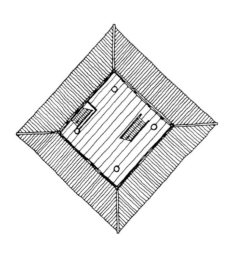

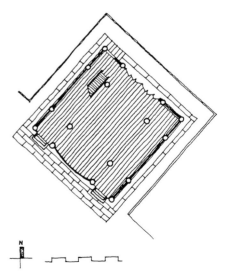

Figure 3.38 The Chezhai village drum tower, pyramidal with curved eaves, looks like southern Han architecture. Rongjiang region of Guizhou province. Source: Photograph by Xing Ruan, 1992.

highly respected members, called *nyens laox* or *yangp laox* govern. For the purpose of governing the *zhai,* the *zhai*'s drum tower serves as the council house in which every item of customary law is made and executed by these chiefs. Once a *zhai*'s customary law is formulated or revised, a stone tablet engraved with the content of this law must be set up in the drum tower. Since the text is in Chinese, the Dong traditionally were not able to read the stone tablet. This, however, is not important, for the customary law is also conveyed within the community as chants that can be recited. Sometimes even a piece of stone without any text, called a *jinl bial,* is used.

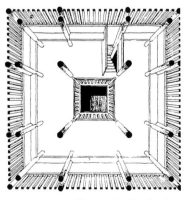

Figure 3.39 First level of the Baxie drum tower showing the connection to the ground level. Source: Li Changjie et al. (1990, 165).

What matters most to the Dong is that the drum tower has been symbolically endowed with the power of customary law, that this is the case from the moment the stone tablet is established, and that the law is made public in the drum tower. In the drum tower of Zengchong village, for example, there are two stone tablets of customary law: one was set up during the time of Emperor Kangxi in the Qing dynasty (1672); the other was set up during the time of Emperor Guangxu in the late Qing dynasty (Figure 3.40). The stone tablet (erected in 1897 during the Qing dynasty) found in Mapang village in the Sanjiang region is on one side of the drum tower square. It has two sides, one engraved with the Dong customary law for Mapang village, the other engraved with a permit validating this law by the local Han Chinese county government. But this juxtaposition, through the paradoxical role of the drum as both the hearth for the Dong and the representation of their ethnicity in the Han cosmos, strengthens rather than weakens the instrumental capacity of this particular architecture in Dong society.

Customary law is also called small-*kuanx* regulation. As a military alliance, for example, the *kuanx* links the *zhai* to their village and links villages to a larger Dong region. The content of Dong customary law covers many aspects of Dong life: family, marriage, land, house and property, forests, safety, and protocols of proper social conduct between young men and women. Thus almost every aspect of Dong life and society is disposed through the use of the drum tower. As the incarnation of Dong customary law, it provides identification and authenticity simply through the action of inhabiting it.

Enforcing customary law, a crucial part of the drum tower's inhabitation, both empowers the drum tower and makes the meanings of the drum tower

Figure 3.40 Two stone tablets engraved with customary laws in the drum tower of Zengchong village, Congjiang region in Guizhou province. Source: Photograph by Xing Ruan, 1993.

knowable to the Dong. In the past, anyone who broke customary law was penalized publicly in the drum tower. Legend has it that in 1947 a bandit was even executed in the drum tower of Jingou village in the Congjiang region of Guizhou province.[15] In the Dong area of Guangxi, one who seriously violated customary law could be expelled from the *zhai* by way of an action taken in the drum tower. In this case, the chief took an iron rake from the home of the person who had violated the law and then nailed it onto a column of the drum tower in the presence of all villagers. The iron rake, an object believed to expel the soul once it is driven into the column of the drum tower, symbolically expelled this member from the clan and village forever. Even his soul will not be allowed to return to his home village after his death. The remains of this custom still can be seen today as witnessed by the six preserved iron rakes fastened to the columns of the Pingzhai village drum tower in the Sanjiang region.

Small disputes beyond customary law are usually settled by the mutual agreement of both parties to ask an elderly person from their own clan to be the referee and help them reach a settlement. But some disputes, particularly those relating to marriage, land, and forest, must be submitted to "drum tower arbitration." In these cases, only the *nyens laox* can be the referees. With the hearings held in the drum tower in the presence of the public, drum tower arbitration becomes an ultimate form of resolution in Dong society. As long as a settlement is reached, no one is allowed to appeal; and anyone bold enough to reject the drum tower arbitration will be utterly isolated.

Although the drum tower operates as the "council shed," in the sense of governing the village, making the law, and executing it, the drum tower itself is not a sacred place. Rather, it is primarily a public meeting place. In Dong society, almost all collective activities—decision making, ritual performances, entertainment congregations, and so forth—are disposed, and more importantly animated, through the drum tower. Drum beating serves as the basic means to call villagers to gather at the drum tower. Different drumbeats convey different messages, and villagers readily can distinguish between good news and warning alarms. In the Congjiang region in Guizhou province, drumbeats are still used today. Nine drumbeats, along with the firing of three small iron cannons, signal the welcoming of guests from other villages.[16] Yet, particularly in the Guangxi area, most drum towers do not have drums so that the drum tower caretaker, who in the past was called the *kuanx leg,* must beat a brass gong while walking around the village to solicit villagers' attention. Drum tower decisions cover almost all other public activities from economic to military affairs: choosing an auspicious day for transplanting rice seedlings; collective hunting, fishing, and distributing goods and supplies; controlling prices;[17] and deciding on major constructions such as dams, irrigation works, roads, and bridges.

Ritual performance is a central part of the drum tower inhabitation. The Sax ceremony, described in Chapter 2, is one of the most significant drum tower rituals. These rituals range from memorial ceremonies for ancestors, village history, migrations, and Dong historical heroes to name giving, funerals, and welcoming and bidding farewell to guests from other villages. Most memorial ceremonies are similar to the Sax ceremony and are performed in a particular disposition that relates to the drum tower. As previously noted, the Dong, hand in hand, sing and dance in a circle or form a parade as described by the Song-dynasty writer Lu You. In the past, this could have been a daily routine of the Dong.[18] Today, however, it is performed only periodically at the Sax ceremony, at other memorial ceremonies, and at festivals.

The *duoye* ceremony, which is highly communal, musical, and very visual, conveys an almost carnivallike atmosphere. Young women are dressed in their finest woven and embroidered clothing, adorned with handmade silver bangles (Figure 3.41), while young men usually are made up with chicken feathers. They congregate in the drum tower or at the drum tower square, dancing and singing hand in hand, not only in a circle but also in coils (see Figure 2.54). At the beginning of the *duoye,* the coil dance pattern is usually repeated clockwise and counterclockwise several times in front of the drum tower. In terms of the water connotations of the coil, the drum tower is naturally referenced as the mast in this ritual performance. In the late 1980s, a *duoye* was performed on a temporary platform supported by floating boats at the village of Binmei in the Congjiang region. Interestingly, two masts, painted red, were used as the drum tower surrogates for the purposes of that *duoye.*[19] This event was unlikely to have used nautical images coincidentally but was indeed a fundamental expression of Dong's nautical imaginings. After the *duoye,* just like the Sax ceremony, a parade departs from the drum tower. Led with *lusheng* playing and brass gong beating, the procession follows the boundary of the *zhai* as the processional route. Finally, they return to the drum tower to continue the performance of the *duoye.*

Regardless of the content of the ceremony, the *duoye* is recurrently performed primarily to ensure the instrumental role of the drum tower in Dong society; in other words, the *duoye* can be seen as a ritualistic enchantment of the drum tower. Hence the fact that the drum tower is referred to correlatively and simultaneously as an analogy, or incarnation, of ancestors, historical heroes, the holy tree, the village heart, and the mast of the village boat is important to the Dong. Architectural symbolization, rather than simply symbolism, thus becomes possible when the drum tower's technical artifice as well as its visual verticality in the settlement are transformed into allegorical power that disposes and animates the inhabitations—very often they are rituals—of it.

The honor of the drum tower itself is also expressed in a number of other

Figure 3.41
Young girls after
duoye. Longtu village,
Congjiang region,
Guizhou province.
Source: Photograph
by Xing Ruan, 1993.

drum tower rituals such as funerals. In the village of Zhaoxin in the Liping region, people who die at sixty years of age or older are routinely given a drum tower funeral. If the deceased person is younger than sixty but highly respected in the local society, a drum tower funeral may be awarded. This is indeed a process of symbolic capital transformation in which the honor of the architecture is symbolically transformed into the status of a person in the society through a drum tower funeral.

Name giving is another drum tower ritual in Dong society. In the village of Zhaoxin, a one-month-old baby must be carried to the drum tower where a ritual is performed in which a *nyens laox* takes the responsibility of giving a name to this new member of Dong society. After the name-giving ritual, this baby becomes entitled to claim back his mother's dowry from the grandmother. This new member is thus formally initiated into the society through the drum tower ritual (Huang 1986, 225–236). In the Congjiang region, the name-giving ritual in the drum tower is also the rite of passage for young boys. Boys are usually called by children's pet names before they reach the age of thirteen. To initiate the name-giving ritual, a boy must take some meat and rice wine to the drum tower and ask his maternal uncle to give him a nickname that portrays his character—such as Jinkao (clever), Waliang (smart), Jungua (strong), Jinpang (tall), Wadu (short), and so on (Shi Tingzhang 1985, 115–119). After the boy is given a nickname in the drum tower, people no longer call him by his pet name. Thus he is symbolically transformed into adulthood.

In the past, drum beating and the drum tower served important military purposes. In the event of an emergency, the drum tower became the command post for the *kuanx* army. The *kuanx* army personnel were ordinary male farmers in peacetime. Before dispatching troops to join a large *kuanx* military group, the small *kuanx* army assembled at the drum tower in each *zhai* to swear oaths of allegiance, to offer tea to Sax, and to pray for victory. The *kuanx* army also assumed responsibility for the safety of their *zhai*. When bandits insulted the village or people were robbed, the drum tower caretaker *(kuanx leg)* beat the drum three times or fired two iron cannons to call the *kuanx* army together to expel the bandits. Every year before the New Year, the *kuanx* army also escorted villagers to the local town fair.

In addition to these special occasions, the everyday inhabitation of the drum tower plays an equally important role in Dong life. The drum tower serves numerous other practical functions, such as providing shade in summer and fire in winter. It also lends an important aspect of cultural continuity to Dong life. For example, an almost daily routine that is ritualistically held in the drum tower is the telling of stories by the elders to their youngsters after daily work ceases—an activity called "telling the ancient stories" *(baigu)*. The content of these stories is always Dong ancestors, migration, historic heroes, and the like. This is an important means whereby Dong history is passed to younger generations. In fact, the process is not entirely repetitive or prescriptive but commonly involves new interpretations and new myths reproduced from old ones. Most important, the drum tower is filled with a sense of history, and hence an assumed power of authenticity, during the processes of its daily inhabitation.

Singing and antiphony in the drum tower are sometimes used as a different form of both ritualistic and ordinary storytelling. The Dong love singing: as an old Dong saying goes, "rice nourishes the body, songs nourish the heart." Seemingly all folk songs, which are one form of their oral literature, tell stories of the Dong's past. Dong youngsters, particularly girls, are compulsorily trained to sing folk songs in the drum tower when they reach the age of thirteen. These training sessions work in exactly the same way as the drum tower storytelling, with elders supervising the learning of the songs.

At certain festivals, an elaborate and highly ritualistic polyphonic chorus, called *al laox,* is commonly held in the drum tower. Boys and girls are segregated and sit on benches around the fire pit in the drum tower to sing antiphonally (see Figure 1.16). The *al laox,* no doubt the climax of their folk song custom, is shared with other villagers, further charting the Dong's poetic inhabitation of their drum tower. As previously noted, drum tower antiphony also is the traditional way for young people to become acquainted for purposes of courtship and marriage. Both special occasions and daily activities in the drum tower inform and teach the Dong, as well as others, what Dong culture and society are about. Architecture in this way becomes allegorical—narrative as well as didactic.

MAKING THE DRUM TOWER

A drum tower combines the three basic Dong social organizations—*kuanx, zhai,* and clan—into a cultural and social whole. The symbolization of the drum tower is, however, made possible in both the inhabiting and the making processes. The Dong view their village as authentic only if it has a drum tower, even if the drum tower is not an "authentic" one. The making of the drum tower is, therefore, the most important event in a Dong community. Every member of the village, either physically or symbolically, is involved in the making processes—not only because all families in the village share the construction cost but primarily because the making of the drum tower is a collective event that is perceived to be intimately tied to the village's future and to the Dong's fate.

A drum tower can last hundreds of years; equally, it can be destroyed, very often burnt down by fire, in a matter of minutes. Rebuilding a drum tower does occur from time to time in Dong society. Most of the Dong drum towers seen today were reconstructed in the 1980s because of the damage caused by the Cultural Revolution between 1966 and 1976. The contribution of building materials by villagers is the first step in the process of making a drum tower. Every family contributes some of their stored timber to the construction project; the amount depends on their financial resources. Generally, participating in the making process is much more important than the amount of material a family contributes to the construction. Even so, this is not a process shared equally among the households. The four load-bearing columns, for example, must be donated by the most prestigious family in the village. If this prestigious family is on the decline, however, another family may be awarded the right to donate the columns or provide the money to buy them. Sometimes a neighboring village that is considered to be consanguineous will contribute one of the four load-bearing columns or the four benches around the fire pit. Contributors must also prepare sacrificial offerings for the building ritual.

The action of contributing to the making of the drum tower can be seen as a symbolization of being a Dong or being identified as a Dong by others. In 1993, a new drum tower was built in Sanjiang town, the capital of the Sanjiang Dong Nationality Autonomous County. Like many of the Chinese county towns, Sanjiang itself is very uneventful, consisting mainly of undistinguished brick and concrete buildings. But the demography is culturally rich, consisting of Han, Zhuang, Miao, and the majority Dong. The increasing number of tourists prompted the county government to decide to build a Dong drum tower and give the town a visible Dong identity. For the same purpose, a museum of Dong culture and history was built at one side of the drum tower square. Rather than being a replica of a traditional drum tower,

Figure 3.42 The new drum tower of Sanjiang town is a hybrid of drum tower, wind-and-rain bridge, and opera stage. Sanjiang Dong Nationality Autonomous County, Guangxi province. Source: Photograph by Xing Ruan, 1992.

as a tourist attraction the new drum tower, designed and built by a local builder, is a combination of drum tower, wind-and-rain bridge, and Dong opera stage (Figure 3.42). Even though the new tower no longer serves the role of drum tower in a village, the urbanized Dong in Sanjiang donated money to its construction. Parents even donated on behalf of their newly born children so their names would appear on the list of donors. This list is engraved on several stone tablets erected at the edge of the drum tower square. Having an involvement in making the drum tower effectively identifies the Dong and distinguishes them from other people in the town. As an architectural type, this hybrid drum tower has everything to do with tourism. Nevertheless, the cultural consistency of being Dong and being a Dong drum tower—and the cultural renewal in terms of a new type and new ways of inhabiting it—are interestingly mediated by the drum tower's role as Dong's hearth as well as its capacity in engaging the bigger cosmos.

Before a drum tower is built, the honor of the drum tower is symbolically predisposed. The meanings of the four load-bearing columns, or their association with the prestigious families, are examples of this point. The significance of these columns, and hence of the drum tower, is further enhanced in a series of ritualistic acts during the process of preparing them. The load-bearing columns usually are chosen by a hereditary donating family from a China fir woodland near the village. A pig is slaughtered and shared by young men before the trees are chopped down. The Dong believe that the tree trunks must not be laid down before they are erected as columns. When the trees are cut, therefore, they are carefully supported and then carried to the site to be put on stands where they are ready to be worked (Figure 3.43).

The local builders are ordinarily farmers who have a hereditary right to be builders and have become skilled craftsmen through experience gained in building houses. Drum tower builders have the highest reputation and are held in awe and veneration in Dong society because it is the builder who makes the honor of the drum tower real and tangible. Dong buildings are carefully prefabricated with mortise joint construction well before the drum tower is to be assembled. Mistakes are not allowed in the measurement of these components—the length or height of the columns or beams; the position or dimensions of the tenons and mortises of the components—otherwise it is difficult, even impossible, to assemble the whole framework.

The Dong do not work with drawings, although some builders use an unscaled working model, made of reeds, to show the framework of the drum tower. The most skilled builders, however, never do this. With the design of the framework and the dimensions of components in mind, they use a long piece of bamboo to record the dimensions and position of tenons and mortises of almost every component of a drum tower—all at a 1:1 scale. This piece of bamboo, fully inscribed with signs and dimensions, becomes the "magic wand" to produce the drum tower. To make a component precisely, the chief builder uses a roll of linen thread soaked with ink and the bamboo ruler to

Figure 3.43 Tree trunks being worked into columns on stands. Ma'an village, Sanjiang region, Guangxi province. Source: Photograph by Xing Ruan, 1992.

mark the dimensions on it. This technique is called *tanmo,* which literally means "flicking ink." The chief builder first fixes the two ends of the thread where he wants to print an ink line; he then holds the center of thread, carefully keeping it vertical to the timber surface; finally, he releases it, thereby marking an ink line on the timber.

Tanmo is a mythical moment in making the drum tower. Every ink line made by *tanmo* is considered to have a bearing on the fortune of the Dong. The first ink line on one of the main columns is particularly important. Before this line is printed, the villagers must offer the chief builder three pickled fish, a basket of cooked glutinous rice, a bucket of raw rice, and a red paper wrapper with one to three pieces of Chinese paper money in it. Villagers also must pray for blessing from the gods. Since this first ink line is also believed to have an impact on the affairs of young men and women, these concerns too form part of this ritualistic *tanmo* performance. When executing the *tanmo,* the chief builder swings the thread to left and right, keeping the balance between young men and women, before carefully releasing it.

Once all the components are fabricated, assembling the drum tower, particularly erecting the four load-bearing columns, becomes another mythical moment in the ritual performance. An auspicious date is chosen by the *nyens laox* and several young men are asked to help the chief builder. These young men must come from families in which the parents, brothers, and sisters are all alive and no family members died by accident. Setting upright the four load-bearing columns must occur at midnight. During that evening, the children of single-child families must stay in the village. These seemingly odd rules may reify the drum tower's analogies as male ancestor, as phallic symbol, as family genesis, and the like. All the participants must remain silent, and the chief builder uses only gestures to coordinate the construction. Once the four load-bearing columns are set up, the silence is broken by firing iron guns and firecrackers. The villagers then awaken and congregate at the drum tower square, and the raising of the major beam is performed as a public ritual. A red cock, rice wine, pickled fish, and Dong cloth are offered to the gods. Villagers listen to the chief builder's chants. Every word has to be appropriate and auspicious, because these chants are considered to have a bearing on the Dong's destiny and any offense to the drum tower as a result of the builder's chants poses a threat to the builder's life.

On the morning following the assembly of the drum tower framework, the neighboring villagers usually bring presents—sometimes including the four benches around the drum tower fire pit—to commemorate the erection of the new drum tower. A three-day celebration is then held where, among other things, the Dong are taught what the drum tower is about. When the whole construction is completed, a *duoye* is performed at the drum tower square. The process of making the drum tower then comes to an end.

Instead of being a symbol, or a sign in a linguistic sense, the Dong drum tower is symbolic capital fully inscribed with the vicissitudes of Dong history and their status quo. Instead of reading the drum tower with their minds alone, the Dong inhabit and make the tower with both their bodies and minds. Involved in these actions, "stories" are evoked and made cognitive. Like allegories, the meanings of these drum tower stories are tacit. Consequently, they are symbolically transferred into honor and enchanted as choral symbolic power to dispose the Dong's cultural practice. In the process of making, as well as inhabiting, a Dong drum tower thus works in a beautiful way for both the Dong and others and indeed becomes legible to them.

Politics and Poetics: The Drum Tower of Ma'an in Chengyang

If I have conveyed an undertone of romanticizing the Dong drum tower, this is not to suggest that the cultures of minority groups in southern China are unaffected by the global sociopolitical context. On the contrary, it is this romanticism, both from the minority group and from the Han, that affords the Dong drum tower a special role in cultural renewal that is firmly, and strategically, rooted in this global context of the Han cosmos. The following case study of the Ma'an drum tower reveals the politics as well as poetics of establishing a new drum tower.

The location of the drum tower in Ma'an village in relation to its settlement has been analyzed in Chapter 2. The formal structure of the Ma'an drum tower is a typical nine-square grid. Like other drum towers in Guangxi, the Ma'an drum tower does not have a pavilion loft: the four load-bearing columns support the top pyramidal roof right from the ground. A central space is formed, but the fire pit is curiously off center (Figure 3.44). This off-

Figure 3.44 Elevation and plan of the Ma'an drum tower, Sanjiang region of Guangxi province, showing the off-center fire pit. Source: Fieldwork sketch by Xing Ruan, 1993

center fire pit is no accident; it suggests a different rationale, and a specificity in its making and inhabiting, from other drum towers.

A stone tablet in the Ma'an drum tower is engraved with a Chinese text that describes its reconstruction. The local primary school teacher, Chen Nengjun, wrote this text in quasi-classical Chinese style. Apart from the fact that it is a brief record of the history of the Ma'an drum tower, the whole text is full of laudatory rhetoric praising the "wise policy" of China's central government in the 1980s. In many ways, it is quite similar to the stone tablet of the Mapang drum tower mentioned earlier. Although the content is completely different, it still can be seen as a strategic engagement with the Han ruling power; at the same time, from the moment of the building ritual, the drum tower has been symbolically endowed with a sense of authenticity by the act of erecting this stone tablet.

The authenticity of the newly built drum tower is reinvented, and it is different from the traditional one. Yet the text engraved on the stone tablet serves as a mask to be read by outsiders. According to that text, the Ma'an drum tower was reconstructed in 1985. Prior to that, the village had two drum towers, one built in 1926 and the other in 1944. The last drum tower was destroyed during the Cultural Revolution. The renovation of the Chengyang bridge, funded by the central government, prompted the Dong of Ma'an to think about the reconstruction of their drum tower. They finally decided to raise the funds themselves and complete the construction of this new drum tower by the end of 1985. The text also states that both the wind-and-rain bridge and the drum tower are well known as identifiers of Dong nationality; moreover, the wind-and-rain bridge offers protection from the elements and convenient transportation, while the drum tower provides a place for social gatherings. This is true, of course, but constitutes only part of the picture. Two other reasons for this reconstruction are the drum tower's appeal to tourists and its capital value. These are equally important reasons behind the reconstruction. In its effect, the drum tower is still empowering; but the off-center fire pit explicitly speaks of a radical displacement from its traditional honor to its new authenticity.

The master builder of Ma'an, Wu Chenfang, served as a government tax officer in Sanjiang county before he retired to his home village. Not only was he one of the advocates of reconstruction, but he also coordinated the fund raising as well as the design and the actual building process.[20] While he believes that this reconstruction is an authentic replica of a traditional Dong drum tower, he also understands his own, as well as other people's, rationales for this reconstruction. It was he who persuaded the Ma'an people to accept a new seven-eave tower instead of their old five-eave one. When asked why he dared to change tradition, his response was that the new height follows a traditional Dong protocol: since the village had grown larger, the new drum tower obviously had to be bigger and higher to make sure that every home in Ma'an could see it. In actuality, however, the site of the Ma'an drum tower was already a topographic focal point that could be seen from anywhere inside or outside the settlement, and so it was unnecessary to construct a higher drum tower.

If a smaller drum tower would have sufficed, what is the real reason for the new design? The most apparent reason seems to be that it was constructed to complement the adjacent Chengyang bridge, which was becoming an increasingly popular tourist attraction. Compared with other Dong villages in this area, the smaller tower would not have stood out, which would have been unacceptable for image reasons.

Quite surprisingly, the radical distortion of a traditional Dong drum tower—the off-center fire pit—did not arouse controversy among the villagers. Apparently it was such a spontaneous change that the master builder did not even mention it, and the Dong in Ma'an do not seem to care. As we shall see in Chapter 5, the Ma'an drum tower does not serve the traditional ceremonies for ancestors and Sax, so the fire pit is no longer symbolically significant. Yet this tangible architectural decentralization indicates, symbolically, the transformation from its traditional honor to its capital value. If the drum tower in Ma'an is still meaningful and still empowering as the village's heart, albeit with its new meaning of authenticity, it is in the name of tradition, not in its contemporary expression, that it is so. The drum tower in Ma'an is the Dong's hearth, but it also finds itself a place in the bigger world.

4

TYPE, MYTH, AND HETEROGENEITY
Pile-Built Dwellings

In 1926, the Swiss-born French architect Le Corbusier, together with his part-
ner Pierre Jeanneret, published the famous "five points" for new architecture,
which have become some of the key criteria for defining modern architecture
in the twentieth century. The five points are piles *(piloti),* roof garden *(les
toits-jardins),* free plan *(le plan libre),* free facade *(la façade libre),* and long
window *(la fenêtre en longueur).* Among them, the most curious is *piloti.*
Why do buildings have to be raised above the ground on piles? Corbusier
elaborated this particular point with another five points. According to him
(Vogt 1998, 9), the pile system makes the following possible:

- Cleaning of the dwellings
- Separation of traffic into pedestrian and car zones
- Restitution of the built-up ground and public ground to the
  inhabitants
- An awning *(abri)* that gives protection from sun and rain and
  also shelters children at play
- Abolition of the facade: there is no longer front or back to
  the house

A revealing manifesto of these five points is Villa Savoye in Poissy,
designed by Corbusier and built between 1929 and 1931 (Figure 4.1). But
another Corbusier-designed pile-built building, the unbuilt house on the

Côte d'Azur from the group of Maisons Citrohan, may prompt one to question his pragmatic reasoning (Figure 4.2). This house appears to be a more spontaneous pile-built type, if not a lyric one, as it is a house raised above the water. Adolf Vogt describes this house "as if it were born from water" (1998, 9). Vogt's studies on Corbusier's childhood education have shown that his obsession with *piloti* is due to the discovery of lake dwellings, reconstructed by Ferdinand Keller, on the Lake of Zurich in 1854 (Figure 4.3). In 1896, the nine-year-old Corbusier had a textbook that included the story of lake dwellings and images of reconstructed pile-built houses. Vogt also discovered that Keller's reconstruction of Swiss lake dwellings was in fact based on Louis-Antoine Sainson's illustrations of the Pacific pile-built and water-based dwellings described in the travel reports of Jules S. C. Dumont d'Urville. Sainson, of course, did not see those Pacific buildings firsthand.

Regardless of the real reasons for Corbusier's reinvention of *piloti*, which are most likely out of reach to us, this story suggests first that Pacific pile-built dwellings are the prototypes for the reconstruction of the Swiss lake dwellings and, second, that pile-built dwellings are water-based. Water alone, however, does not justify the incredibly wide distribution of pile-built dwellings from the coastal areas of the Pacific to inland areas of Asia. This chapter is concerned with the figurative yet universal meaning of pile-built dwellings. It discusses in detail the instrumental role of pile-built dwellings, as an architectural type and against the background of Han dwellings, in framing the domestic life found among the numerous minority groups in southern China in order to examine the intricate and complex relationships between type, myth, and heterogeneity.

Type and Reason

As discussed in the previous chapter, an architectural type can be loosely defined as a specific spatial disposition, which often suggests a particular way of inhabitation. In this sense, pile-built dwellings, which are elevated above the ground, can be seen as an architectural type in contrast to dwellings built directly on the ground. Whatever the archaeological origins of the Swiss lake dwellings, pile-built dwellings are still widely found throughout Asia. There are various names for this dwelling type in the English-speaking world, including stilt or pile housing and elevated housing, all of which include a load-bearing wooden structure. In Japanese, the term literally means "high-floor housing." This type of dwelling is named *ganlan* in Chinese, a term that first appeared in Chinese literature of the Wei and Jin dynasties (220–420) as a transliterated word from the languages of the indigenous people (Wu Zhide 1989, 1). The present meaning of *ganlan* in Chinese is a type of dwelling with an integrated wooden framing system in which the floors are raised

Figure 4.1 Le Corbusier's Villa Savoye in Poissy, France, is a manifesto of his "five points" for modern architecture. 1929–1931. Source: Photograph by Xing Ruan, 1994.

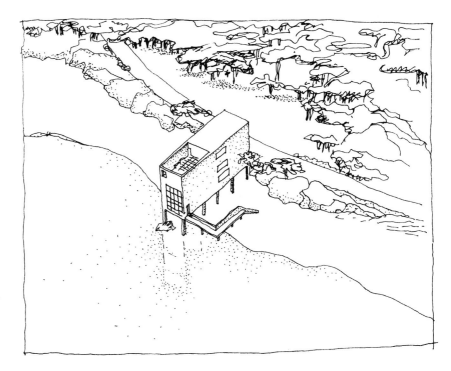

Figure 4.2
Le Corbusier's
design for a house
on the Côte d'Azur
developed from the
Citrohan type. The
"pile-built" structure
appears to be gener-
ated by the water
site. 1921. Source:
Drawn by Xing Ruan
after Vogt (1998, 11).

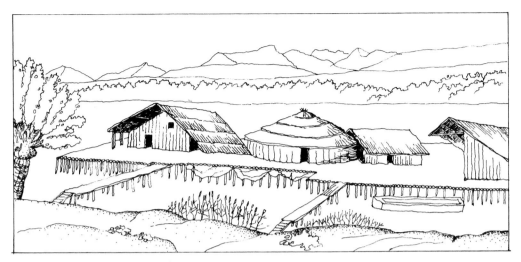

Figure 4.3 This reconstruction of lake dwellings on the Lake of Zurich was based on the pile-built structures in the Pacific region. Source: Drawn by Xing Ruan after Vogt (1998, 228).

above the ground to provide living space, while the space beneath, the ground floor, is for animals and storage. Among the numerous Tai linguistic groups in southern China, including the Zhuang, Buyi, Dai, Dong, Shui, and Li, their appellations for housing of this type are very similar to the Chinese *ganlan*.

In China, pile-built dwellings are widely distributed in the southwest, south, and southeast of both the continent and the islands. Archaeological findings from Zhejiang, Jiangsu, Hubei, Hunan, Jiangxi, Fujian, Guangdong, Guangxi, Guizhou, Sichuan, and Yunnan provinces all demonstrate the existence of pile-built housing in China from the Neolithic period through to the Qin and Han dynasties (221 BC–AD 220). Indeed, the components of sophisticated mortise and tenon joinery used in the construction of pile-built houses were found at the archaeological site of the Hemudu culture (5000–3000 BC) in Zhejiang province. From the evidence of the site and building components found there, one particular house at Hemudu is deduced to have been 25 meters wide and 7 meters deep, with a 1.3-meter-deep porch at the front. Another example can be seen in the bronze models of pile-built houses and shelters unearthed from Shizhaishan in Jining, Yunnan province, that date to the Eastern Han dynasty (25–220).

There are three types of elevated dwelling in China. One is called *diaojiaolou*, which is only half a *ganlan* structure built on a hillside site; examples are found on terraced slopes in Sichuan province as well as among the Dong in Guizhou, Guangxi, and Hunan provinces. A second type is *ganlan*, mainly referring to pile-built houses constructed on level sites with the first floor completely raised above the ground; typical examples are found in the houses of the Dai in Yunnan province. The third elevated type, *tutanshi*, is in fact not constructed using a pile foundation but the floor is raised above the ground using an earthen foundation so that the ground floor can be still used for storage; a few examples are found in Yunnan province. The distribution of these three elevated types within China, and their associations with different minority groups, are indicated in the accompanying table.

Elevated Dwellings in China

diaojiaolou

> HAN: Chongqing and southern Sichuan; mountain areas of Zhejiang
>
> MIAO: southeastern Guizhou
>
> DONG: southeastern Guizhou, northern Guangxi, southern Hunan
>
> LISU: Nujiang of Yunnan
>
> WA: Ximeng of Yunnan
>
> YAO: northern Guangxi
>
> NU: Nujiang of Yunnan
>
> BENGLONG (DE'ANG): Dehong of Yunnan

ganlan

> DAI: Dehong and Xishuangbanna of Yunnan
>
> HANI: Xishuangbanna of Yunnan
>
> JINPO: Dehong of Yunnan
>
> ZHUANG: Longshen, Debao, Jinxi, and Longzhou of Guangxi
>
> LISU: Nujiang of Yunnan
>
> LAHU: Menghai of Yunnan
>
> NU: Nujiang of Yunnan
>
> DONG: southeastern Guizhou and northern Guangxi
>
> BUYI: southern Guizhou
>
> SHUI: southern Guizhou
>
> LI: Hainan Island
>
> BENGLONG (DE'ANG): Dehong of Yunnan
>
> MIAO: southeastern Guizhou
>
> BLANG: Menghai of Yunnan
>
> GAOSHAN: Taiwan
>
> WA: Ximeng of Yunnan
>
> HANI: Honghe, Yuanyang, and Luchun of Yunnan

tutanshi

> MAONAN: northern Guangxi

Conventional definitions of ethnicity—with implications regarding cultural affinities—are often based on language affiliation. As can be seen from the table, however, different linguistic groups share the pile-built dwelling type yet there are no logical relationships between the language affiliations of

Figure 4.4
Distribution of pile-built dwellings in East Asia, Southeast Asia, and the Pacific region. Source: Drawn by Xing Ruan after Yang Changming (1990, 33).

ethnic groups and their domestic architectural types. One of the issues raised in this chapter is that ethnicity is indeed a cultural construct that is not determined merely, or even necessarily, by language affiliation to the same extent as the way people dwell or live their lives. In the context of China, distinctive architectural types afford minority groups the warmth of home within the Han world. Compared with language, which is, to a great extent, a political tool in colonization, architecture serves as a more primordial cultural construct within which most cultural practices are staged. This is particularly so in southern China, where minority nationalities, as the Han call them, are not only minorities but are also perceived, psychologically rather than physically, to be remote and inaccessible to the majority of Han.

From a different point of view, it may well be that whatever link one finds between architecture and language is accidental. As previously mentioned, pile-built dwellings are an extensively shared type—widely dispersed spatially and temporally well beyond China, including mainland and insular Southeast Asia, as well as Micronesia, Melanesia, and even Polynesia (Figure 4.4). Roxana Waterson notes an "independence" between architecture and language similar to that we have noted in China: "Even in New Guinea, whose languages and cultures largely differ markedly from those of island

Southeast Asia, we find many remarkable similarities in architectural style" (1990, 4). These similarities include a number of pile-built, saddle-roof ceremonial houses, as recorded by Domenig (1980). Waterson believes that language provides one of the most important clues to the underlying historical and cultural ties between peoples. The world's largest language family, the Austronesian, stretches more than halfway round the world's circumference, from its westernmost point of distribution, Madagascar, to the easternmost, Easter Island, encompassing the whole of island Southeast Asia, Micronesia, and Polynesia, as well as parts of the Malay Peninsula, southern Vietnam, Taiwan, and coastal pockets of New Guinea (Waterson 1990, 12). Even the Japanese language, which is classified as belonging to the Altaic family, is considered by Japanese linguists to possess an ancient substratum of Austronesian (Domenig 1980, 80). While the Austronesian language family does not include mainland Southeast Asia and southern China (the Dong and the Dai, for example, belong to the Sino-Tibetan family), these regions and Austronesian cultures nevertheless share many architectural features, including the pile-built dwelling type.

Despite the language differentiation, many southern Han Chinese and southern China's minority groups share not only the pile-built dwelling type but also other cultural practices, customs, and rituals with mainland Southeast Asia and the Pacific region. If China, as a nation, is a political construct formed first in the Qin dynasty (221–206 BC) through the unification of different languages by Emperor Qinshihuangdi, and if the Chinese culture, reductively perceived, can be loosely associated with its Huang He (Yellow River) valley origin, then the southern China of the Yangzi River basin and further south was not during the Qin dynasty culturally "Chinese" (Han). In fact, it was not until the subsequent Han period (206 BC–AD 220) that the peoples of southern China began to be strongly influenced by a unified northern China. For some southern Chinese—particularly the numerous minority groups found within the southern region—this influence was by no means a complete assimilation except perhaps in terms of political colonization and language assimilation. Architecture, such as the pile-built dwelling type and the particular inhabitations associated with it, was actively involved in the construction of ethnicity and cultural renewal of minority groups throughout southern China, as well as in finding its legitimately recognized places by the Han.

The extensive distribution of pile-built housing makes it difficult to explain conclusively why and how this architectural type was invented. Motivated by a migration theory of south to north— a migration from the Asian coastal areas and the Pacific to the interior mainland—Sumet (1988, 83) believes that "the real reason

Figure 4.5 A "nest box" in a tree, the Chinese *chaoju*. Source: Drawn by Xing Ruan after Yang Changming (1990, 57).

behind all this lies in the amphibious and equatorial origin of the house." He argues that the obvious rationale for pile-built housing does not explain why, for example, in Burma the same wooden house is sometimes raised and sometimes placed completely on the ground in the same locale—or why a tropical house on piles should find itself in the middle latitudes at 35 degrees north, an essential part of traditional Japanese architecture, to the misery of its occupants winter after winter. Furthermore, such a rationale does not explain opposite examples: why do rice-farming Chinese in the northern portions of the tropical Malay Peninsula still live in land-based dwellings that their ancestors brought with them from China? In the end, Sumet's theory remains dubious or, at least, highly speculative. Other possibilities in fact exist. For example, with the same migration theory but a different direction, such as the old idea of distinct waves of migration from the mainland into Southeast Asia, a completely different picture of the origin of pile-built dwellings can be constructed.

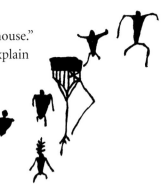

Figure 4.6 Tree house from the cliff painting in Cangyuan, Yunnan province, which is believed to date back to the Neolithic period. Source: Drawn by Xing Ruan.

Some Chinese scholars, for instance, have postulated a theory of *chaoju*, or nest dwellings, encompassing two types: the first is a "nest" structure built on the ground; the second is a "nest box" inserted among the branches of a huge tree (Figure 4.5).[1] This second nest dwelling is in fact a universal type of primitive hut, a tree house that was reconstructed by Marc-Antoine Laugier and seen by him as the guide to understanding the essential components of an order of architecture (Rykwert 1981). Within China, however, this type of tree house can be found extensively—for example, explicitly in cliff paintings in Cangyuan, Yunnan province, which are believed to date back to the late Neolithic period (Figure 4.6). Moreover, the early Chinese pictograph of "nest dwelling" is a hut supported by two trees (Figure 4.7). Even today in northern and southern China, temporary tree dwellings are still used in the fields for purposes of resting and supervision during busy farming seasons. From a structural point of view, it may be convincing to interpret the pile foundation as a transformation from the tree house. But in terms of its extremely wide distribution and its many topographically and climatically inappropriate adoptions, the nest dwelling, or the tree house, offers no better explanation than that of an amphibious and equatorial origin.

Figure 4.7 Chinese pictograph of a "nest dwelling" showing a small hut supported by two trees.

Another utility-based argument for the origin of the pile-built dwelling is the "rice cultivation theory" advocated by Japanese scholars (Duan Xiaoming 1985). This explanation is not dissimilar to Sumet's amphibious origin, mentioned earlier, since the dwelling was first raised above the wet rice paddies in order to protect the fire pit and cooking utensils. Hence a further argument—due to the remarkable similarities between the Japanese and Chinese archaeological evidence, as well as living examples—is that the Wazoku, or

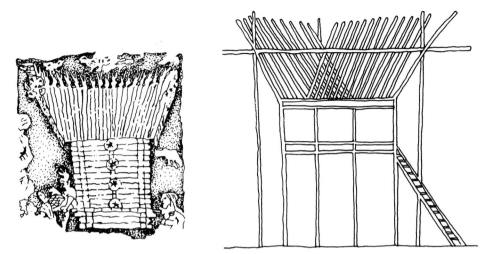

Figure 4.8 Engraved image of a granary from a Shizhaishan bronze drum *(left)* and a Japanese barn incised on a Kagawa prefecture bronze *(right)* showing similarities between the two structures. Source: Drawn by Xing Ruan after Liu Dunzhen (1978, 70) and Duan Xiaoming (1985, 12).

ancient Japanese, are migrant people who fled to Japan, via the Yangzi River in China, from their homeland in Yunnan. For example, the granary images engraved on the sides of a Shizhaishan drum, dated between the second and first centuries BC, are often compared with a Japanese barn incised on a bronze from Kagawa prefecture dated to the first and second centuries AD (Figure 4.8). One can be skeptical about this argument, of course, for many minority groups, Jingpo in Yunnan for example, build their pile-built dwellings on mountainous high land that is often far from the wet rice paddies.

Type and Myth

A cosmological model offers an explanation for the pile-built dwelling that is related to neither the water nor the tree house thesis. In the three-tiered cosmos, for example, one layer is placed on top of the other, resulting in the coexistence of three worlds that can be associated with the three levels of a pile-built structure: the sacred upper world, abode of gods; the middle world, inhabited by humans; and the netherworld, abode of animals and lower deities (Wessing 1984; Dall 1982; Waterson 1990). While similar three-tiered cosmological models can be found in many cultures—for example, among the Han—those cultures did not develop pile-built structures. Among the Dong and the Dai peoples in southern China, who favor pile-built dwellings, they do not appear to associate cosmological meanings with the three-level cosmos.

Although the existence of an architectural type such as the pile-built dwelling is not necessarily related to pragmatic reason, the type itself could serve as a convenient cultural vessel for meaning. Of the two pile-built structures found on bronzes in Shizhaishan in Yunnan province, one is a model of a ceremonial shelter on the lid of a cowrie container (discussed in relation to the Dong drum tower in Chapter 3) and the other is an engraved image of a barn on the side of a bronze drum (Figure 3.7; see also Figure 4.8). They indicate a few formal features: saddle-back roofs that are often associated with boats and birds (although birds are sometimes found on roof ridges) and crossed roof finials that may suggest buffalo horns. The engraved pile-built dwellings on Dong Son bronze drums, from the bronze culture in northern Vietnam (ca. 600 BC–first century AD), share incredible similarities with the Shizhaishan bronzes (Figure 4.9). The mutual influence between the Shizhaishan bronzes and the Dong Son drums, whether due to trade or migration, is not of concern here.

Figure 4.9 Image of the pile-built dwelling from Dong Son drums that looks like the granary structure found on Shizhaishan bronze drums. Source: Yang Changming (1990, 83).

Saddle-back roofs are not as widely found in southern China among the minorities as they are in Southeast Asia and the Pacific region. A living example of the type is the Jingpo pile-built long house in Yunnan province (Figure 4.10). Most of the pile-built dwellings are crowned with gable-and-hip roofs, such as those of the Dong and the Dai (Figure 3.8; Figure 4.11). A linear reconstruction of technical evolution may suggest that a simple sloping roof structure has been developed into the gable-and-hip type because of protection from rain, structural strength, and the economical use of material (Figure 4.12). Various types of saddle-back roof, however, represent the different stages of this evolution (Yang Changming 1990, 90). The striking structural affinities between the Shizhaishan ceremonial shelter and the Dong and Dai roofs should prove their architectural kinship. The symbolic connotations of saddle-back roof structures are likewise common in ethnic southern China, Southeast Asia, and the Pacific region.

The saddle-back roof in Southeast Asia, its curved roof ridge and pointed ends in particular, may have been exaggerated by anthropologists as being associated with boat symbolism (Waterson 1990, 20–23); the common belief is that a boat house would enable spirits to return to their homeland. Although most of the pile-built dwellings in ethnic southern China are not saddle-back structures, the Dong, as previously mentioned, see their entire village as a boat and see the forest as water that bears the village boat; the drum tower is naturally referred to as "mast" or "sail" (Figure 4.13).

A large, saddle-back roof structure with its highly curved roof ridge, such as a Toba house or a Toraja house in Indonesia and those found on the Dong Son drums, may look like a bird taking off from the ground. In fact, the pointed ends of the Dong Son saddle-back roof images are bird heads, and birds stand on the roof ridges (Figure 4.9). Bird ornaments are seen on the roof ridges of Dong houses and public structures such as bridges and drum towers (Figure 3.19). Many of the Dong groups deck themselves with feathers at ceremonies and ritual performances. The Dong, as mentioned earlier, believe that since birds are free from the potential dangers of sailing, they are the bearers of gods and hence are related to the village boat and its safe voyaging.

Another symbolic connotation of the soaring saddle-back roof and its "open scissors" gable finials is buffalo horns. Waterson (1990) has examined a series of examples in Southeast Asia ranging from a real buffalo head as the gable ornament to hornlike gable finials. A buffalo head is found hanging below the gable finial on the Shizhaishan ceremonial shelter. Living examples of hornlike gable ornaments can still be seen in some of the pile-built dwellings in Yunnan province. Among the Dong, defeated water buffaloes are sacrificed after a fight and buffalo horns are usually tied to a column in the drum tower. Buffalo horns represent might and power for the Dong; in Southeast Asia they are connected more with wealth.

The various shades of symbolic connotation between saddle-back and gable-and-hip roofs makes one wonder whether the architectonic myth of

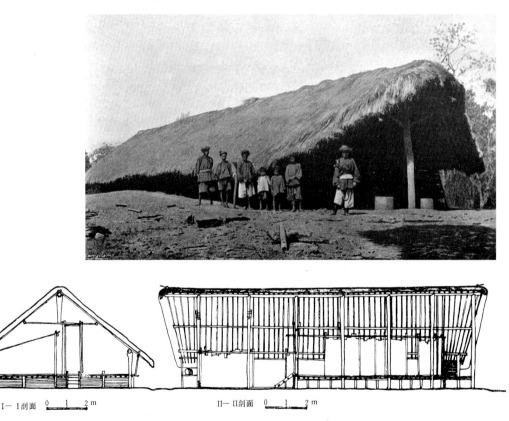

Figure 4.10 a and b A saddle-back-roof Jingpo house in Yunnan province. *Top:* A Jingpo house in 1904. Source: Geil (1904, 280). *Bottom:* Sections of a Jingpo house. Source: Yunnan Sheng Sheji Yuan (1986, 335).

the pile-built structure has any impact on the living situation of this dwelling type. The reason for and myth of a dwelling type, however, needs to be further contextualized. On the one hand, the foregoing discussion of the origin and rationale of the pile-built dwelling is abstract in that it deals with an elevated dwelling type in the broadest and most formal sense. On the other hand, the cultural, geographic, and climatic backgrounds associated with this type are rich and concrete, bringing distinctive qualities and high degrees of specificity. It can readily be argued that the rationale for people living high above the ground may well be some combination of the need for security, protection from wild animals and seasonal floods, good ventilation, a useful space underneath in which to work and to store implements, and other functional reasons—together with a variety of symbolic, social, economic, and other factors. There is little doubt about the historical significance of this particular dwelling type, but merely to trace it back to its origins is not constructive. It is the entanglement of historical myth and present conditions that makes the pile-built dwelling livable and meaningful. But the desire to search for origins could serve the purpose of cultural renewal. The rationale of Corbusier's elevated building type, for example, is substantially different from those advanced for pile-built dwellings in southern China, Southeast Asia, or the Pacific region.

Figure 4.11 A gable-and-hip roof, pile-built Dai house in Ruili, Dehong region, Yunnan province. Source: Photograph by Xing Ruan, 1986.

Type and Formal Structure

The formal structure of Dong pile-built housing exemplifies pile-built dwellings in southern China. The construction and structure of Dong housing are based on an elaborate system in which the overall form is an integrated pillar-and-transverse-tie-beam timber framework. A typical framework is usually described as "three-bay and five-post" *(san jian wu zhu)*, consisting of a structural system four posts wide and five posts deep, with two levels

Figure 4.12 Structural evolution of pile-built dwellings. Source: Yang Changming (1990, 90).

Figure 4.13 A Dong village "boat" profiled by the drum tower as the "mast and sail." Congjiang region, Guizhou province. Source: Photograph by Xing Ruan, 1993.

above the ground (Figure 4.14). Based on this primary structural prototype, and according to specifics of site and need, an additional structure is usually added, as an attachment, to the main structure. The roof covers this "three-bay and five-post" framework, with the additional spaces having their sloped roofs attached to the main structural body. In most cases, a cantilevered overhang is used to enlarge the porch at the first level. A Dong barn, usually constructed as a "one-bay and three-post" framework, can be seen as the basic structural prototype of a Dong house. When a short queen post is used, this structure becomes a "one-bay and two-post" framework. By increasing the number of short queen posts, a Dong house can become rather deep without increasing its load-bearing posts (Figure 4.15). Additions attached to the main structural frameworks are flexible in both plan and section, matching different site conditions and accommodating different sizes of family (Figure 4.16). Based on the main structural framework, for example, a "three-bay and three-post" structural body can be extended into a long house on a linear site.

Along with the integral pillar-and-transverse-tie-beam structural system, the Dong have also developed sophisticated mortise joint construction.

Instead of penetrating the earth, stone column bases support "piles," and these load-bearing posts go upward right through the building. Generally, pile-built dwellings in southern China share similar structural and construction methods, yet each minority group has its own way of building that differs slightly from the others. This slight differentiation is both interesting and critical, giving rise to particular identities and contributing to the diversity of formal features of pile-built housing. Within a Dai house, for example, which shares similar structural principles with the Dong house, the absence of queen posts results in a distinctive roof curve and proportion (Figure 4.17). The specific ways in which the integral pillar-and-transverse-tie-beam structural framework is held together without using nails is a further example: mortising and tenoning, pegging, wedging, binding, and so forth. Among the Dong, the intricate and inhabitable wall surface of their housing is made possible only by their fully developed mortise construction (Figure 4.18).

Apart from the methods of construction, the foundation of the house and the entire resulting structure can be achieved by a variety of means. As with Dong housing, the foundations of most pile-built dwellings in southern China and Southeast Asia use stone column bases to support the piles; foundations piled into the earth are practiced only on waterfronts or in relation to marshy sites. A variation seen in the pile holes at the Hemudu Neolithic site in Zhejiang province proves that they had true pile foundations. Instead of having an entire structural framework with the main feature of load-bearing piles running through the building, a different type of pile-built housing is seen in what might be called a two-phase structure. Here the pile foundation is separated from the upper structure; the piles simply support the upper building rather than running through it. Examples can be found on Southeast Asian islands, but two-phase, pile-built housing is not widely employed in contemporary southern China (although archaeological evidence indicates many instances during early times). According to Huang Caigui (1991b), among the Dong and Miao in the remote mountain areas of Liping, Congjiang, and Rongjiang in Guizhou province, one type of timber house is actually constructed in two phases: first a pile-built framework, ranging from 2 to 3 meters in height, is constructed as a platform; then the structural posts are constructed above it. (Although this type of two-phase structure may look like an integral structural framework, it is not.) Huang also found combinations of an integral framework and two-phase structure in one building.[2]

Archaeological sites of the Yin dynasty (sixteenth century–1028 BC) in Chengdu, Sichuan province, reveal a pile-built house that is believed to have been a two-phase structure; moreover, excavated clay building models of the Han dynasty (220–206 BC) in southern China indicate that a variety of two-phase, pile-built houses were used at that time (Figure 4.19). Cross-log construction, which can be used either as the foundation or as the upper building, is another form of pile-built structure. The high barn of the Gaolite in Heilongjiang province in northeastern China, and others in Alaska, are pile-built platforms that employ a cross-log building on the top (Yang Changming 1990, 63). An excavated tomb painting from Maxiangou in Ji'an, Jilin province, also in northeastern China, reveals that this used to be a housing type in that area (Figure 4.20). Differing from pile foundations, cross-log foundations—which elevate the building but are not pile-built—are commonly seen in Indonesia. An example of this type is the raja's palace in Pematang Purba on the island of Sumatra, which has a cross-log-constructed, richly painted, massive pile foundation (Waterson 1990, 216). Further, a bronze drum engraving from Shizhaishan clearly shows that an elevated building

Figure 4.14 A "three-bay and five-post" Dong house structure. Source: Courtesy of Rong Bing.

Figure 4.15 Dong house elevation showing the use of short queen posts. Source: Fieldwork sketch by Xing Ruan, 1993.

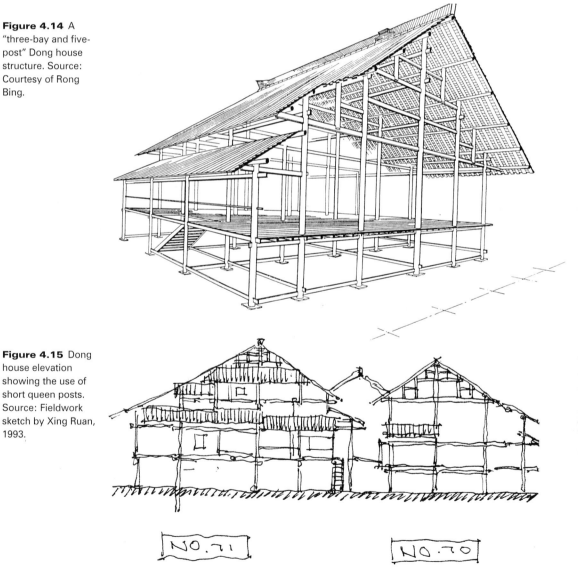

NO. 71   NO. 70

could have been constructed entirely with cross-log construction coexisting with pile-built structures in the area (see Figure 3.17). Even today, cross-log construction is still being employed in the building of Dong drum towers, as well as the foundations of Dong wind-and-rain bridges, all the while coexisting with large numbers of pile-built structures (Ruan 1996a).

These comparisons indicate that pile-built structures can be realized through a variety of technical means. Instead of revealing how the pile-built dwelling's structure and construction were developed, these comparisons

Figure 4.16 Plan fraction of Dong dwellings in Ma'an village, Sanjiang region, Guangxi province, showing the flexible additions attached to the main structural frame. Source: Drawn by Dongmin Zhao and Xing Ruan.

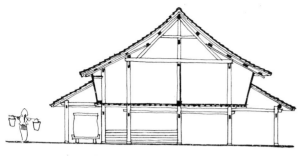

Figure 4.17 Dai house cross-section showing a distinctive roof curve. Source: Yunnan Sheng Sheji Yuan (1986, 239).

are intended to show slight differentiations between different types—differentiations that establish essential qualities relating to both the form and the distinctiveness of each type of pile-built dwelling.

Type and Inhabitation

In contrast to the enclosed courtyard dwelling generally preferred by the Han throughout China, freestanding detached housing forms are commonly built by minorities—and even some Han Chinese—in southern China. For these dwellings, the disposition of living space is described in Chinese as "front hall and back room," or *qian tang hou shi*. The *tang*, or hall, functions as a living room in the Western sense, while *shi* has the connotation of bedroom. The disposition of space in Han Chinese housing is described as "one bright and two dark," meaning that the *tang*, or living room, is a relatively open and bright room between two *shi*, relatively enclosed and dark bedrooms (Figure 4.21). In a

Figure 4.18 The inhabitable wall of a Dong house showing the fully developed mortise construction. Source: Li Changjie et al. (1990, 466).

Figure 4.19 Excavated Han-dynasty clay building models reveal a variety of two-phase, pile-built structures. Source: Drawn by Xing Ruan after Yang Changming (1990, 61).

simple single-courtyard house, this pattern reveals relationships between the courtyard/bright and building/dark, and the *tang*/bright and *shi*/dark, and obviously can be easily expanded into a large multiple-courtyard house. In other words, the "one bright and two dark" pattern plays a key role in housing articulation, but it is difficult to attach "front hall and back room" structures together to form a ramified dwelling.

Han Chinese dwellings, in fact, did not originate with the "one bright and two dark" pattern, and certainly not with a disposition of space around courtyards. In the Yangshao Neolithic settlement ruins found at Banpo, near modern-day Xi'an in Shanxi province in the Huang He (Yellow River) basin, two interesting features can be seen. First, each dwelling is detached; second, the ruined sites of house F3, and particularly house F1 (Figure 4.22), show an explicit "front hall and back room" disposition of interior space, the "hall" being dominated by a fire pit. This is not to suggest a logical relationship between land-based courtyard dwellings and pile-built dwellings, since the spatial disposition of Banpo housing is similar to that of the pile-built dwellings in southern China. But the historical transformation of "front hall and back room" to "one bright and two dark" courtyard has elucidated the instrumental role of the plan, or the disposition of space, in a complex process of social transformation.

Archaeological findings indicate that the half-sunken Banpo housing lasted at least three thousand years, and the radical transformation from the "front hall and back room" detached type to a "one bright and two dark" courtyard type probably occurred between the Western Zhou and the Spring and Autumn periods (1027–476 BC). A Qing-dynasty scholar, Zhang Huiyan, drew a plan of what he believed was the residence of a Spring and Autumn period official (Figure 4.23) (Liu 1978, 36–39). Enclosed within a walled compound, with the front gate on a symmetrical axis, the house itself was also on the axis and detached from the compound wall, thus freestanding. The house was dominated by the central hall, or *tang*, and rooms wrapped around the hall on three sides. Furthermore, a stone tablet at the center of the

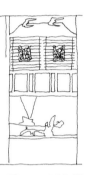

Figure 4.20 Pile-built dwelling from the Maxiangou tomb painting. Source: Sketch drawn by Xing Ruan.

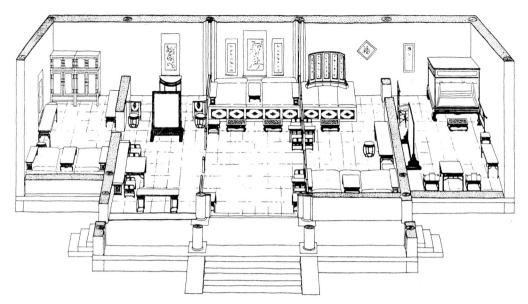

Figure 4.21 The *tang* and *shi* of a Qing-dynasty house. Source: Liu Dunzhen (1978, 349).

overall composition reinforced the symmetrical axis. According to Zhang's literature research, the *tang* was used as the living room, as well as being the family's ritual and ceremonial space. While Zhang's drawing may be viewed as merely schematic in many aspects, the hypothetical disposition of space that he laid out can nevertheless be seen as the prototype of the Han courtyard dwelling.

Security and privacy are the usual reasons given to explain the invention of the walled-courtyard Chinese dwelling. Yet security and privacy are universal concerns, and the minority groups of southern China generally did

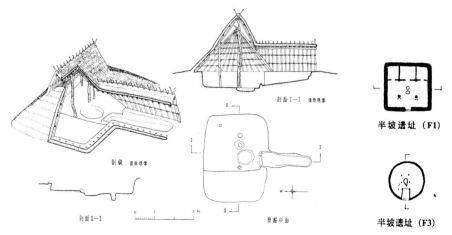

Figure 4.22 Reconstructed Banpo house and the ruin site plans of F1 and F3. The plan clearly indicates the "front hall and back room" spatial disposition. Source: Liu Dunzhen (1978, 24) and Yang Changming (1990, 40).

not come up with these solutions. By the same token, security and privacy do not explain the "one bright and two dark" symmetric composition. Perhaps instead of trying to provide a set of reasons, this issue can be examined from the perspective of the interaction between the spatial disposition within a particular dwelling type and the social relations at the time it was adopted.

The Spring and Autumn period (770–476 BC) was a time during which the social philosophy of Confucianism was emerging. Thus a patriarchal hierarchy, viewed from the emperor at state level down to the master of a family, began to take form in Chinese social relations. It should not be surprising to see that the formal structure of the later walled symmetrical city—with the royal palace on the central axis—also began to emerge. Consistent with this hierarchy is the multiple-courtyard house with the *tang*, or hall/living room, also on the main axis within a large multi-generation family dwelling, serving the ceremonial space for the family's ancestors. By contrast, most of southern China's minority groups never developed a similar type of Confucian patriarchal hierarchy, even though some do venerate their ancestors. For the Dong, for example, the

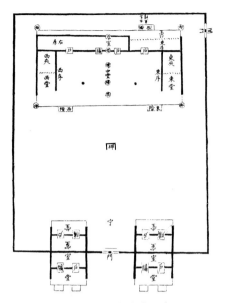

Figure 4.23 Hypothetical plan of a house from the Spring and Autumn period (770–476 BC), drawn by Zhang Huiyan, which may be seen as a prototype of the Han courtyard house. Source: Liu Dunzhen (1978, 37).

ancestor is a mythical figure, either male or female, and the ancestor ceremony is usually held as part of a collective ritual under a particular clan surname by the whole village. The basic unit of that society is the two-generation nuclear family, however, not the large, multigeneration family of Han society.

It seems that "front hall and back room" is a Han Chinese conceptualization that might have been developed from Neolithic Banpo housing. This conceptualization implies at least two things: first, the separation of the *tang* and *shi,* as well as their naming, are not neutral conditions but are related to specific inhabitation; second, the front and back suggest the idea of symmetry and axis. As we shall see, these implications are not applicable to the spatial disposition of pile-built dwellings in southern China. There are, of course, several exceptions in ethnic southern China: the Bai and Naxi ethnic minority groups in Yunnan province, for example, do share common land-based courtyard types with the Han Chinese, a condition that has no doubt arisen through acculturation (Figure 4.24).

Since a two-generation nuclear family is the basic unit of these ethnic minority societies in southern China, their dwellings are usually independent and detached units, as is the case with most Dai houses in Yunnan province. At the settlement level—except for public spaces such as Buddhist temples—the overall disposition of housing in a village is egalitarian, a nonhierarchical

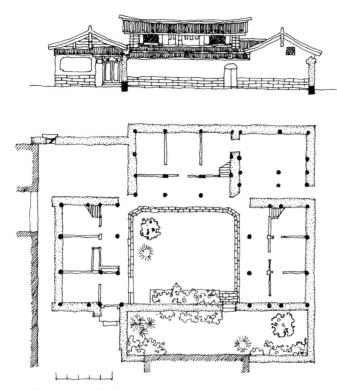

Figure 4.24 Naxi courtyard house. Source: Drawn by Xing Ruan after Zhu Liangwen (1988, 38).

order that probably originated from the house level. In addition to the storage of animals and supplies, as well as workshops for pounding rice and weaving beneath the house, a Dai house is composed of three other parts: balcony and porch; fire pit room; and bedroom. The disposition of these three parts is flexible and completely nonaxial (Figure 4.25). In terms of the relationships between the three parts of a house and the relationship between a house and the settlement, this flexible and nonaxial spatial disposition is more about the possibilities of interchangeable use and the meaning of space than about fixed distinctions between different spaces.

A Dong settlement, as we know, includes a drum tower, a bridge, and a stage for performing opera. Morphologically and visually it may be seen as a hierarchy, but its inhabitation is both nonhierarchical and heterogeneous. Dong architecture is not dominated by vision. Take public space as an example: the making and inhabiting of a drum tower is no more or less significant than that of a Sax altar or a wind-and-rain bridge. Drawing a comparison between housing and public structures, the fire pit in the drum tower is no more important than the fire pit in a Dong house. The dwelling itself is heterogeneous in that each element plays a distinctive and yet significant role in Dong domestic life. At the level of spatial disposition and inhabitation, heterogeneity is not neutral but allows a dynamic, open-ended process of making and inhabiting.

This heterogeneity is about the dissolving of spatial distinctions. One of the most evident features of a Dong house—and pile-built dwellings among the minority groups in southern China in general—is the lack of a sharp duality in its spatial disposition, in which distinctions are vague, ambiguous, and relative. Dual qualities—such as dark and bright, enclosed and open, private and public, female and male, young and old, nuclear family and extended family, individual and society, cold and hot, winter and summer, and so forth—are simultaneously applied and associated with a particular space within a Dong house. A porch can be private and dark in relation to the settlement, for example, but social and bright when compared with the fire pit room in the house (Figure 4.16).

Among the key components of a Dong house—the porch, the fire pit room, the unsurfaced framework within a house, and the ground level space—the bedroom is exceptional in its discrete spatial definition, although the Dong attitude towards the bedroom, and their manner in dealing with it, are not definite. Bedrooms in most cases are "left behind" spaces, usually very small, with room only for a bed, enclosed and

Figure 4.25 Dai house plan showing a flexible disposition of balcony, fire pit room, and bedrooms. Source: Yunnan Sheng Sheji Yuan (1986, 252).

dark, which suggests they are relatively unimportant as inhabitation and serve only as sleeping quarters. Yet bedrooms are also flexible spaces that are easily turned into storage spaces. The Dong in fact do not have a distinction between bedroom and storage. Bedrooms are either behind the fire pit rooms or infill empty areas on the third floor, edge spaces that are neither independent nor definite (Figure 4.26).

In contrast to the Han notion of *shi*, or the bedroom in the Western sense, Dong bedrooms are certainly marginal spaces. The *shi* serves as the counterpart of the *tang*, and, interestingly, the canopy-style bed within it is almost a small room within the larger room. If Banpo is seen as a prototype of Han housing, the separation of the sleeping zone from the fire pit room, or the distinction between *tang* and *shi*, must be a later invention. Even today, a few other minority groups in southern China have not yet developed an enclosed

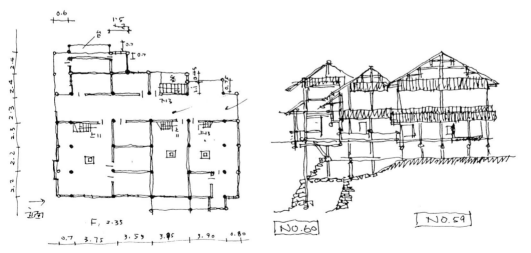

Figure 4.26 Plan and elevation of a Dong house in Ma'an village, Sanjiang county, Guangxi province, showing bedrooms and storage serving as marginal spaces. Source: Fieldwork sketch by Xing Ruan, 1993.

Figure 4.27 Dai house in Xishuangbanna, Yunnan province, showing unfurled mosquito nets used to define sleeping zones. Source: Yunnan Sheng Sheji Yuan (1986, 216).

separate sleeping zone within their dwellings. Yang Changming (1990, 40) found that the sleeping area for the Lahu in Yunnan province is part of the fire pit room; their sleeping zones are defined simply by sleeping mats without any enclosure or apparent need for privacy. The Dai in Xishuangbanna merely use unfurled mosquito nets to define sleeping zones (Figure 4.27)—a definition that is as much a marker of privacy as it is for protection from mosquitoes. In some sense, the enclosure of Dong sleeping zones within the house can be seen as equivalent to the mosquito net of the Dai.

Another feature that gives rise to the ambiguities of spaces, which are not explicitly defined within a Dong house, is asymmetric and nonaxial composition. Spaces for different uses in a Dong house are arranged in a nonsequential way. Sequence and axis are perhaps the two most effective ways in architecture to stage and celebrate a dominant space. Hence in classic Han architecture, the royal palace in the city and the *tang* within a house were placed on the symmetrical axis, while in medieval cities the spatial potency of the dominant church and square, and the link between other public spaces, was realized through a prescribed spatial sequence (Sitte 1965). Spaces in a Dong house are ordered very differently, however, in both vertical and horizontal dispositions relating the ground level, porch, fire pit room, bedroom, storage, and open frameworks on the first and second levels in a variety of sequences (Figure 4.28). Because Dong houses are often built on terraced sites, they can be approached not only from the front porch but also from the back of the house to the fire pit room. Sometimes the porch is bridged to the road or connects with neighboring porches. No space inside a house is essentially more important than another in an absolute way. A Dai house, although built on a level site, is equally asymmetric and nonaxial. Pile-built dwellings in southern China, in other words, are egalitarian in their spatial dispositions—and hence in consequent social relations.

The Dong normally have relatively small two-generation families, and it is only in rare circumstances that three or even four generations live together. Brothers and their families take turns—living separately—to host and feed their elderly parents. As discussed earlier, each family has an open fire pit in the middle of the floor in a room on the second level, and the fire has to be

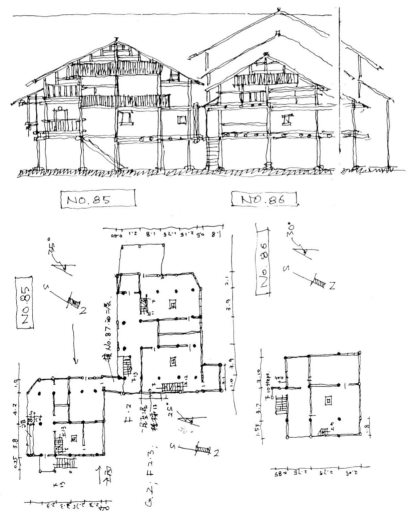

Figure 4.28 Elevation and first-level plans of two Dong houses in Ma'an village, Sanjiang region, Guangxi province, showing rich horizontal and vertical sequences. Source: Fieldwork sketch by Xing Ruan, 1993.

carefully protected at all times—except for the moment of the Sax ritual—to keep the family's genesis alive. The fire pit, in this way, signifies a family. Where brothers and their families share a house, each family has its own fire pit, not only for heating and cooking, but also, more significantly, to establish the hearth of family life. The Dong believe that the fire pit itself is the memorial tablet of the family's ancestor: if the fire were to die out, the family would have no progeny, so nothing is more devastating than destroying a Dong fire pit. The room containing the fire pit is open and spacious for family reunions and daily work. Here women spin and weave, men make fishnets and baskets, young children play, and old people rest and chat. In winter and early spring, when the farmwork is light, this fire pit room becomes the center stage for Dong domestic life. A tea ceremony called "oiled tea" is often carried out for family guests around the fire pit.[3] Young girls spend much time sewing and embroidering the fine trousseaus that will help establish their family's social status when they marry.[4]

The house and how it is lived in are also affected by seasonal changes. In summer, the front part of the house becomes more dominant as activity shifts towards the outside, although the fire is still carefully kept alive in the fire pit room. Wooden porches covered with tiled roofs, another common feature of Dong houses, become the center of family activities during warmer weather

Figure 4.29 A deep Dong house porch in Linxi village, Sanjiang region, Guangxi province. Source: Li Changjie et al. (1990, 387).

(Figure 4.29). These cool, bright, and spacious porches provide superb places for placing spinning wheels and looms for making and displaying Dong textiles. Yards of handwoven black, reddish-purple, or indigo fabric, hung out and shimmering with a metallic sheen after a long dyeing process, billow from the second-story porch of Dong houses, in the process presenting a colorful summer experience that contrasts with the wintertime internal focus around the fire pit.

The significance of a Dong house begins at the announcement of its birth through a building ritual: when the main roof ridgepole is set into place, the entire timber structural framework is completed. Typically the main roof ridgepole is painted red, and its center is wrapped with a piece of black cloth containing valuables (often paper money), a ritual similar to that employed by the Han in southern China. The Dong also hang colorful feather-flowers on this main roof ridge to create a rather distinctive scene (Figure 4.30). Before the house frame is covered with tiles and filled with timber panels, the freshness of the new timber frame set against the weathered dark timber of the older houses, the bright red roof ridge, and the fluttering colorful feather-flowers announce the legitimacy of the new house at the moment when the main roof ridge is ritualistically raised (Figure 4.31). This legitimacy is for both the house and the owner; and so the house becomes, metaphorically, an imitation of the owner.

Type and Heterogeneity

An examination of pile-built dwellings against the background of land-based Han dwellings in China proves that the associations between peoples, cultures, and dwelling types go well beyond a single deterministic link. First, the adoption of pile-built dwellings among minority groups in southern China can hardly be justified by reasons of utility and technicality, be they climate, water site, tree house, or rice cultivation. Second, language, ethnicity, and pile-built dwellings do not constitute consequential relations. Of equal relevance, symbolic connotations—such as cosmology in relation to the three-tiered verticality in a pile-built dwelling as well as the bird, the boat, and the buffalo horns associated with saddle-back roofs—do not afford fixed meanings to this particular type of dwelling. And third, although a type of dwelling is understood as a specific disposition of space, pile-built dwellings are in fact constructed using different methods based on the nature of their siting and the availability of building materials—hence the differences can be caused by their unique technicality. The question then arises: what is the significance of the pile-built dwelling in southern China if its origin is out of our reach, particularly when the twentieth-century reinvention of the pile-built dwelling, Corbusier's *piloti* for example, remains a mystery?

Figure 4.30 The main roof ridgepole of a Dong house in Pingyan village, Sanjiang region, Guangxi province, showing the colorful feather-flowers tied to the ridgepole at the building ritual. Source: Photograph by Xing Ruan, 1993.

Figure 4.31 A new Dong house frame against the background of weathered houses in Pingyan village, Sanjiang region, Guangxi province. Source: Photograph by Xing Ruan, 1993.

Despite the mystery of its origin and the differentiation of its technicalities, the enduring character of the pile-built dwelling exists in its spatial disposition, a verticality that allows the unfolding of asymmetric and non-axial arrangement of spaces. As a result, unlike the land-based Han dwelling in which the hierarchy of center and periphery is explicitly embodied in its courtyard versus room (or *tang* versus *shi*) relationships, the pile-built dwelling is egalitarian and the distinctions between spaces are interchangeable. A type of dwelling, in this sense, is understood as the disposition of space; the pile-built dwelling suggests a way of inhabitation and hence its specific family social relations. The egalitarian and two-generation nuclear family structures in Dai and Dong societies in southern China, and their pile-built dwellings, demonstrate a nice fit between house and society. Likewise, the traditional hierarchical and patriarchal Han society corresponded well with its courtyard dwelling. This, from a different angle, has proved to be the difficulty in preserving courtyard houses when the patriarchal social structure is no longer prevalent in Han society, whereas southern China's pile-built dwellings are still a living heritage, although some of them are now built with bricks and concrete.

Lévi-Strauss, in his late works, increasingly stressed the instrumental power of a house in the construction of social relations, which he terms "house societies" (Carsten and Hugh-Jones 1995). This concept becomes reified when the spatial disposition is analyzed in line with the society it houses. A persuasive example in this regard is Robin Evans' readings of house plans. A matrix of interconnected rooms in a sixteenth-century Italian villa, according to Evans, is not neutral; it is "appropriate to a type of society which feeds on carnality, which recognizes the body as the person, and in which gregariousness is habitual." Nineteenth-century corridors in an English house, where privacy is the paramount concern, tell the opposite story (Evans 1997, 88).

In a similar vein, this chapter has attempted to illuminate the animated interactions between pile-built dwellings and the social relations they accommodate in southern China. But between the universal, enduring character of pile-built dwellings and their contextualizations into specific localities, this chapter has also shown another series of dynamic interactions between type and heterogeneity. A type of dwelling, after all, is only materialized in its making and becomes legible in its inhabiting. As such, the heterogeneity of a dwelling type is forever subject to renewal. Corbusier's obsession with the myth of Swiss lake dwellings and their romanticized capacity in hygiene and clearness—the inhabitation is elevated above the water—has been symbolically transformed into *piloti* and a modernist aesthetic of whitewashed walls. A pile-built dwelling, for Corbusier, is an allegory that does not have to accommodate any "authentic" way of life but does yield to imagination. Like the notion of "ruin"—Walter Benjamin's material analogy of allegory—it is "an always-disappearing structure that invites imaginative reconstruction" (quoted by Clifford 1986b, 119). Beyond the subject of pile-built dwellings in ethnic southern China, a deeper concern in this chapter is methodology, which involves the study of architecture in general. In other words: in order to understand the significance of an architectural type and its allegorical heterogeneity, it is necessary to combine spatial and material analyses of a type with its social interactions.

5

OUT OF TIME
Ahistorical Architecture and Cultural Renewal

In 1985, an exhibition of "Dong Architecture and Customs in Guizhou" was staged in Beijing by the Guizhou provincial government. In the planning stages, the curators wanted to borrow the drum from the drum tower in Zengchong village as a significant item among the exhibits, for the Zengchong drum tower is considered the oldest in the entire Dong region. As the oldest, of course, it was assumed to carry a sense of tradition and authenticity.

Drum beating is either trivial or nonexistent nowadays in Dong society, so the drum, as we already know, does not form an essential part of the drum tower inhabitation. But the idea of staging an exhibition had never occurred to the Dong, and loaning their drum to someone was perhaps equally unprecedented. The proposal was first rejected by the *nyens laox* in Zengchong. After apparently difficult negotiations, the curators finally received permission from the Dong in Zengchong under one condition: the drum had to be adorned with red silk when it was taken to Beijing. This, ironically, can be regarded as a Han custom with nothing quintessentially Dong about it.[1]

An ad hoc ritual was performed on the day the villagers parted with their drum. The ritual was the usual one with *lusheng* playing and cannon firing at the drum tower square. After this routine Dong ritual, all the villagers formed a long procession to escort the drum to the road (Zengchong village is about 1.5 kilometers from the main road) where the government vehicles were waiting. The crowd remained silent at the reluctant moment of saying goodbye, as if they were parting from a family member (Chen Moxi 1989). The event, newly invented and staged like a masquerade, spontaneously unfolded as a time-honored ritual, which must have been endorsed in the name of tradition before the eyes of the villagers in Zengchong.

There may have been an undertone of romanticization in the book when I emphasized the ritualistic inhabiting and making of architecture among the minority groups in southern China. I may also have created an impression that their architecture is "traditional" and their life and society have not yet been largely infiltrated by modernization. Any intelligible view, of course, would regard this as what James Clifford has called "ethnographic pastoral" (1986b, 118). Considering the newly invented ritual for the farewell of the drum and the many thousands of years contact with the Han, the Dong could not possibly have maintained an "unbroken and stable" tradition that we now see as Dong ethnicity. But ethnicity for a minority group in the majority Han context is, historically as well as contemporarily, a necessity for both the warmth of their own home and a legitimate position in the Han world. Yet the desire for ethnicity comes from outsiders as well, for the majority population seems always to expect minority groups to be exotic. Romanticism does, however, help minority groups imagine an "authenticity" in the name of tradition, although the whole thing could be an invention.

In his studies of the invention of Maori tradition, Allan Hanson argues "that 'culture' and 'tradition' are anything but stable realities handed down from generation to generation. Tradition is now understood quite literally to be an invention designed to serve contemporary purposes" (1989, 890). But what is architecture's role in the invention of tradition? Or is architecture instrumental, not only within minority groups in southern China, as I have argued, but also in the cultural renewal during growth and progress—a modernization influence imposed by the "outside world"? The answer must be yes. For the architecture of minority groups has a continuing validity that is largely due, quite literally, to its different role from that of the text.

An Accidental Drive for Ethnicity

Minority groups in southern China, largely nonliterate peoples, evidently have admired the Han and their literary culture. Throughout the course of history, the Dong, for example, have made numerous attempts to fabricate an ethnicity through textualization—a writing of their history and culture. Some critical historical moments can be singled out when Dong ethnicity was an issue and textualization was attempted to achieve such a goal.

Since the first emperor of the Qin dynasty, Qinshihuangdi, imperial Han "nationality policy" has often been envisaged to unite nationalities through assimilation. Textualization from imperial authorities as well as later Western missionaries was first and foremost intended to make minority populations literate, which has been perceived as one of the most powerful means of assimilation. But for most of the minority groups in southern China, this proved to be a very difficult task—for they simply did not have a written language to be retextualized. Efforts were made in a variety of ways. Western missionaries created the Latin alphabetic text for the Jingpo in Yunnan province, for example, and the Chinese central government attempted to romanize the Dong language in the early 1950s. Neither of these efforts made a minority group literate or to any degree culturally "elevated." Both the Guomindang government and the Communist government made further attempts to change the "primitive" customs of the minority groups; but certain ethnic customs are resilient.[2]

As mentioned in Chapter 1, from the late Republican period until the early 1950s, scholars conducted a number of ethnographic and anthropological investigations of the Dong. This surely was one moment when the Dong themselves became aware of their distinctive cultural customs and artifacts. These studies and investigations, unfortunately, withered when the political climate became highly restricted from the 1950s until the early 1980s. The beginning of the 1980s was perhaps the least politically and ideologically controlled period since the Communist government took over the country from the Guomindang government in 1949. Motivated once again by a self-consciousness of ethnic identity, as well as a liberal economic environment and a matching expectation from the Han and the central government, a variety of activities—including ethnographic and anthropological studies and performances and exhibitions of customs, art, and architecture—were conducted and organized by an elite group of Dong people.[3] They were elite in the sense that they were the few indigenous Dong who were selected, educated, and politically trained as local officials and scholars by the Communist ruling power. They were, as such, textualized by the Han in Chinese. Their education, by any measure, could hardly have been a liberal one. Yet ironically it is this group of Dong people who initially and self-consciously tried to express their ethnic identity through textual materials: writing the first Dong history, recording oral literature, publishing ethnographic and anthropological studies. All were written, of course, in Chinese.

The topics of these Dong studies are summarized by Xiang Ling, one of the first Chinese-educated Dong scholars who started the Dong investigations in the 1950s and continued this mission in the 1980s, as follows:

- The ethnic origin of the Dong and their evolution
- Dong culture—mainly Dong oral literature, art, and customs
- Dong religious belief and national psyche
- Dong oral language and its written form, which is the Latin alphabetic system created in 1958

- Dong society and politics
- Socialist modernization in the Dong region

The Dong, by and large, are still illiterate in Chinese and hence are not able to understand, or enhance, a self-conscious identity and ethnicity through the works of this group of Dong scholars. Historically, the Dong as a relatively small minority group in southern China never drew much attention from the Han and others. In the Qing dynasty, as mentioned in Chapter 1, the Dong were simply regarded as a branch of the Miao. This is perhaps the reason why very few studies were produced prior to the 1950s. The interference of Western missionaries, limited to the Rongjiang area, disappeared soon after 1949.[4] The intense investigations of the early 1980s, and the written works of these Dong scholars, did not initially change this situation.

The activities generated by the Dong scholars, quite unexpectedly, had a rather accidental effect on the renewal of Dong architecture and their built world in general. Since the primary tool for fabricating a Dong ethnicity was, for the literate Dong scholars, writing, they did not anticipate that their work, in the form of a series of events rather than publications, would have triggered a collective enthusiasm for remaking the Dong habitat. It was almost an exuberant ambience—not unlike that of a medieval European society when building a cathedral. The result of this cultural renewal is a Dong ethnicity marked by an architectural identity.

Although research into architecture was by no means emphasized in the tasks of Dong studies by local scholars, in 1982 they recorded a few old drum towers that had survived from the Cultural Revolution and successfully lobbied to have them placed on a list of "Ancient and Historical Monumental Architecture" that should be preserved as cultural relicts in Guizhou province, including the Zengchong drum tower and Xindi drum tower of Congjiang and the Jitang drum tower of Liping.[5] The local scholars' presence in the field, their attention to the Dong artifacts, the fact that some drum towers were recorded and included on the list of provincial cultural relics—all this encouraged the Dong to express themselves through material culture. Singing, dancing, opera, rituals, artifacts, and indeed an inventive reconstruction of their architecture, the stage for these cultural practices, flourished in the 1980s.

Just a few years after the three drum towers were first recorded on the list of cultural relics in Guizhou province, a group of investigators returned to the Dong region in Guizhou and tried to determine the exact number of drum towers in this area. To their surprise, they found the drum towers had substantially mushroomed in number, from a few up to approximately three hundred, since their first visit. They soon realized that it was impossible to get an accurate total, for almost every village at the time was engaged in building a drum tower. This second visit resulted in a photographic exhibition of

Dong architecture in Guiyang, capital city of Guizhou province. The Beijing exhibition of Dong architecture and customs in 1985, as mentioned earlier, was initiated due to the success of the Guiyang exhibition. The 1985 Beijing exhibition made the Dong one of the few minority groups adored by the Han, which had not been the case prior to the 1980s. There always have been mutual collaborations between the Han and these few privileged minority groups. On the one hand, the Han showcase the "cultures" of national minorities, especially singing and dancing, in order to paint a "happy together" family album of the Han living in harmony with the minority nationalities. On the other hand, individual minority groups appear to take pride in participating in such activities since it helps elevate their sociopolitical status vis-à-vis other minority nationalities. The discovery of distinctive Dong architecture now added an architectural element to the "singing and dancing" cultural repertoire.

The reciprocal reaction from the Dong caused by these exhibitions exceeded anything that writing could possibly have achieved. Take the building of drum towers as an example. In fact, there are very few drum towers that survived various political campaigns and the Cultural Revolution (Wu and Chen 1985). Thus the entire period of the 1980s was an enlightenment era during which the Dong almost completely rebuilt their habitat, displaying much playful invention in their drum towers and wind-and-rain bridges. The Dong scholars who organized the two exhibitions had only modest goals at the outset, one of which was to draw the attention of local provincial governors in order to raise money for a book. Guizhou has long been considered one of the poorest and least developed provinces in China. Local officials first came across Dong architecture at the Guiyang exhibition and quickly saw it as a potential resource for bringing tourists from other provinces and, better still, additional funds from the central government. The 1985 Beijing exhibition, with its models and pictures of Dong architecture and the performance of Dong customs, was designed to serve this purpose.

Although viewers may have gained a sense of age and tradition from the architectural images included in these exhibitions, Dong architecture, as well as its making and inhabiting, are essentially contemporary. Accidental fire had been the main threat to the Dong habitat, especially because of the fire pits in drum towers, bridges, and houses, as well as the fact that entire settlements, from public structures to housing, were built with timber. Over time, fires had damaged and more often destroyed not only drum towers but also entire settlements. Moreover, timber structures and components, due to accidental damage and natural rotting, need to be periodically replaced. Thus repairing and rebuilding had been both routine and essential activities for the Dong. Unlike the Han, the Dong rarely paint their buildings, leaving timber largely untreated and in a natural state. As a result, raw timber frames weather quickly,

Figure 5.1 Smoke from the fire pit in the Zengchong drum tower accelerates the ageing of the timber frame. Congjiang region, Guizhou province. Source: Photograph by Xing Ruan, 1993.

especially since the smoke from widespread fire pits in buildings in fact accelerates the ageing process. It is not surprising, then, that Dong buildings appear weathered and old soon after they are erected (Figure 5.1).

Perhaps the aged appearance of Dong architecture does not give the impression that it is in fact part of the drive for Dong cultural renewal and the fabrication of a Dong ethnicity. But consider this: due to the nonliterate nature of Dong culture, they simply do not have historically recorded textual protocols to follow when building and rebuilding their habitat. Oral traditions, handed down via storytelling, singing, and dancing, are inevitably playful and inventive. A building type, such as a drum tower or a wind-and-rain bridge, remains loosely a spatial disposition and its imagined (and often romanticized) use. By contrast, the Han had already produced a building manual, *Yingzao Fashi,* in the eleventh century, which for several centuries had given instructions to builders on standardization ranging from building types to dimensions. The inventive nature of Dong architecture is thus accidentally camouflaged by time-honored masks; paradoxically, it becomes a significant drive for cultural renewal in the name of tradition.

Foreign Forms, Old Shells, New Uses

New building types and forms are occasionally seen in Dong settlements, but they have not yet had any sweeping effect in changing settlement patterns. In the Dong region of Guizhou province, the primary school is usually the only brick and concrete building within a Dong settlement (Figure 5.2). Its power-ful presence, against the background of an idyllic Dong village silhouette, is a heavily invested symbol, by both the Han and the Dong, of moderniza-tion and progress. A school is the only hope for literacy. Although the 1950s romanization of the Dong language is to some degree taught, the real measure of literacy is gaining command of the Chinese language. The growing num-ber of Chinese-educated youth among the Dong is the evidence of success in this endeavor. But the position of school architecture seems to pose an uneasy situation: this modern building stands apart from, rather than merg-ing into, the village's built fabric. It is a relationship between foreground and background. The distinctive roles that textualization and architecture play in Dong cultural renewal are once again made tangible.

Old Han buildings are also seen in Dong settlements (Figure 5.3). The enclosed masonry courtyard house—a type with narrow light-well courts typically found in eastern China in Anhui, Jiangsu, Zhejiang, and Jiangxi provinces—is adopted in some Dong areas. Although very few in number, these masonry Han houses, mixed with timber housing, can be found in the Sanjiang region of Guangxi and the Congjiang region of Guizhou province. Unlike the school buildings, the Han-look, land-based, masonry houses sim-ply juxtapose with Dong pile-built, timber houses with intimate proximity and yet uncompromised contrast.

Han masonry courtyard houses, arguably, can be related to the story of Dong migration from Jianfu in Jiangxi province; they also can be easily related

Figure 5.2 The primary school is usually a brick and concrete modern building that stands out in a Dong settlement. The primary school in Gaozeng village, Congjiang region, Guizhou province. Source: Photograph by Xing Ruan, 1992.

to the Republican-period theory, which saw the Dong as living examples of ancient Han Chinese. But opposite interpretations can be applied to this phenomenon. For example, Han houses can be seen as evidence of the historical remains proving Dong migration and their ethnic origin. In reverse, Han houses can be viewed as the outcome, or material reconstruction, of the migration theories. But it is more likely that some well-off Dong built Han houses because they admired Han culture or pretended they had a Han origin.[6] An almost foreign type, either adopted or imposed, could coexist within its old context. Nevertheless, it is reassuring to witness that architecture is instrumentally empowering in cultural renewal.

Other events in the late 1980s promoted tourism to Dong areas, including the architectural and ethnographic investigations carried out by Japanese scholars. Motivated by the migration theories and a fascination with tracing their cultural traits back to their origins, Japanese ethnographers and architects searched for Japanese roots in southern and southwestern China, particularly among the Tai linguistic groups such as the Dai in Yunnan province. Three collaborative Sino-Japanese architectural investigations were conducted between 1989 and 1990 in the Guizhou Dong region, and many Japanese ethnographers also went to the Sanjiang area of Guangxi province (Huang 1991a). Their presence in the field, compounded with the exhibitions on Dong customs and architecture, have drawn a wide range of scholarly

Figure 5.3 Masonry land-based Han houses can be seen within Dong settlements in some areas. Two houses in Heli village, Sanjiang region, Guizhou province. Source: Photograph by Xing Ruan, 1992.

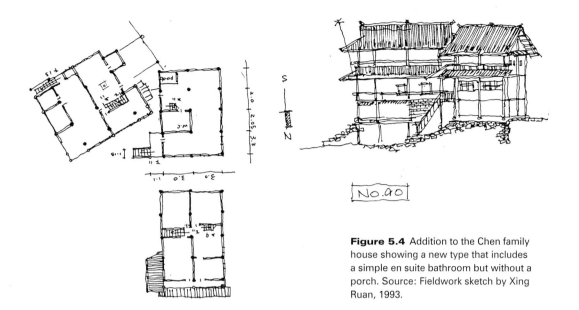

Figure 5.4 Addition to the Chen family house showing a new type that includes a simple en suite bathroom but without a porch. Source: Fieldwork sketch by Xing Ruan, 1993.

interest as well as general tourists to the Dong region, particularly in the more accessible areas such as the Sanjiang region. Hosting and entertaining tourists thus increasingly became routine for the Dong to the degree that both the specialists' interest and general tourism further stimulated building activities.

This cultural reconstruction does not stop primarily at a physical level in building. Rather, it is a reconstruction of "cultural authenticity" through the making and inhabiting of architecture—that is, a transformation from a society structured on honor to one based on capital. As visitors and tourists bring money because of Dong architecture and related material culture, the Dong realize that their architecture has capital value in addition to making their ethnicity visible. In my 1989 fieldwork, our informant, a local tourist guide, usually took visitors to the Chen family in Ma'an village to have a Dong meal. The Chen family was privileged to have the opportunity to entertain tourists, simply because both the Chengyang wind-and-rain bridge and the Ma'an drum tower could be viewed from their house. As a result of this "special locality" of their house, the social and economic status of the Chen family changed over the next couple of years. In 1993 when I returned to Ma'an, the Chen family had become one of the better off and most prestigious families in the village. With the help of the Sanjiang tourist bureau, the family built an extension to their family house. This new addition is not quite a Dong house any more. It is a Dong house with modest modern facilities—a simple en suite bathroom—but the internal fire pit is missing (Figure 5.4).[7] This addition is used as a small hostel for tourists; the income from it is shared by the Chen family and the local tourist bureau. When it was

Figure 5.5 A
duoye performed to
entertain tourists in
Ma'an village, San-
jiang region, Guangxi
province. Source:
Photograph by Xing
Ruan, 1993.

realized that my wife and I are architects, Chen's neighbor approached us and requested remodeling drawings for his house, which he hoped to convert into tourist accommodations as well since the Chengyang bridge could be seen from his house too. We persuaded him not to transform his house into a hostel, however, because most tourists do not stay overnight at Ma'an but prefer to stay in the town of Sanjiang, an hour and a half away, which has plenty of tourist hotels.

In Ma'an, these value transformations are often made evident in architecture. At the front of the settlement, the Chengyang bridge is well preserved for tourists. The family head, Mr. Chen, had been offered a job from the tourist bureau to look after the bridge. From his well-located house, every time he saw visitors approaching the Chengyang bridge from the road Chen would rush down and stop them from crossing the bridge until they agreed to buy tickets for visiting the architecture in Ma'an. Temples and shrines in the Chengyang bridge are not functioning any more but are kept as tourist curiosities. Women and children sit in the bridge to sell colorful feather-flowers as souvenirs. Feather-flowers, traditionally, are supposed to be hung from the roof ridge beam in building rituals (Figure 4.30). Other ritual dancing and singing now also serve tourists. *Duoye* and *lusheng* can be performed anytime at the drum tower to entertain visitors (Figure 5.5). In this scenario, the drum tower does not play a role in Sax ceremony or serve as a traditional village council; yet it still plays a significant and dominant role, like a village heart, in disposing the Dong's new cultural practices. The drum tower, and the bridges as well, have thus acquired a new "authenticity," which is the power of economic capital. Architecture as "old shells" remains, but the new use for it has once again enacted legible and meaningful relationships between the

Dong and their built world. The change in social status of the Chen family in Ma'an, both symbolically and instrumentally, has been achieved through their specific and yet meaningful interaction with the Ma'an drum tower and the Chengyang bridge.[8]

In sharp contrast to the areas of Ma'an that are adjacent to the drum tower and the Chengyang bridge, the architecture and settlements at the upper reach of the Linxi River remain much less affected by tourists and their capital. There the earth god shrines and temples in bridges are still in use and contact with visitors is more spontaneous. People in Ma'an, on the contrary, must contend with the curiosity of outsiders whose questions are based on preconceptions—what might be called the linguistic pairing of "form/meaning" questions. Strategically, but not necessarily calculatingly, the Dong are known to make up meanings to "explain" their architecture as well as other cultural activities. On the one hand, these fabrications appear to satisfy and please visitors; on the other hand, new meanings are necessarily evoked in the name of tradition and authenticity. One example is the master builder of Ma'an, who coordinated the villagers to rebuild the drum tower in 1985 and made up "mythical" building codes for us when we agreed to pay for an interview with him. These "mythical" building codes may well be applied to future building and rebuilding in Ma'an, themselves resulting in inventions and creations concerning their cultural practices.[9]

Cultural fabrication can indeed be detected in various aspects of Dong society today, and the issue of authenticity is in fact debated among the Dong themselves. One controversial event was the creation of a Dong epic in which a Dong scholar, Yang Baoyuan, originally from the Chengyang area, wrote *Ga Man Man Dao Shi Jia*. When the epic was first published in Chinese, he claimed that it was his translation from the only surviving Dong-language epic that is phonetically recorded in Chinese characters, a work that was kept in his family. Although this Dong epic received wide criticism by local Dong scholars as a fake, the general public accepted it soon after its publication. Indeed the epic was used as a textbook of Dong traditional literature in the Central Institute of Nationalities in Beijing. The real irony, however, is that it began to be accepted by the local Dong as their "authentic tradition." Even the master builder of Ma'an believed that the epic had been created by the ancestors of the Dong.

The new drum tower in Sanjiang town, the capital of the Sanjiang Dong Nationality Autonomous County, is a nondisguised architectural invention in that it was built as a tourist attraction in order to promote Dong culture and ethnicity. Designed by a Dong local builder and some government officials from Sanjiang county,[10] the drum tower is a hybrid of a Dong drum tower, a wind-and-rain bridge, and an opera stage. Another playful feature is that the drum is architecturally addressed by a central column on the ground floor:

Figure 5.6 The new drum tower in Sanjiang town showing a drum supported by a central column underneath the opera stage. Source: Photograph by Xing Ruan, 1993.

the drum is supported by this central column on the ground level underneath the opera stage (Figure 5.6). No such feature is found among existing Dong architecture. The inhabitation of this drum tower surely is not meant to be a traditional one but is in fact a stage setting, a Dong cultural showcase, an identifying device for the urbanized Dong living in Sanjiang. Although the making and inhabiting of this drum tower has been displayed in the light of "traditional authenticity," poetically the symbolic power of its architecture is remotivated and revoked—which makes this drum tower as instrumental in the rural context as it is in contemporary Dong society.

EPILOGUE

Appraisals of the splendor of architecture deal only with spatial and dispositional conditions to the degree that what is behind the "exterior" image is neglected altogether. To discern the life of the "interior," circumstantial social conditions need to be considered in relation to physical laws of form and space. After a selective tour of not only the exterior but also periodically the interior of what goes on in the architecture of minority groups in southern China, I shall now turn the attention of my readers to the symbolic center of China—Tiananmen Square, or the Square of the Gate of Heavenly Peace—to sum up how the symbolization of architecture, often against the intent of its designer, actually works.

Tiananmen is the southern gate of the Forbidden City, which was the imperial palace in Beijing and now is the "museum of the old palace." The massive square in front of Tiananmen was built after 1949 by the Communist government for large-scale celebrations and rallies. Bound by the grand scale of the Great Hall of the People and the equally monumental Museum of Chinese History, the square was envisaged as the "political and cultural center" of the country ever since it was created in the early 1950s. After the death of Chairman Mao in 1976, his monolithic mausoleum was erected along the central axis on the southern portion of the square.

As it says clearly with Chairman Mao's script, "Serve the People," on the wall of Xinhuamen (Gate of New China, west of Tiananmen along Chang'an Avenue), the intention of expanding the space before Tiananmen was to create a place for people to rally. Neither the Communist government nor

Chairman Mao in their wildest dreams wanted to recreate another imperial palace. But at the beginning of the Cultural Revolution, millions of Red Guards, waving Mao's "little red book" in their hands, rallied in Tiananmen Square to worship Chairman Mao. Mao, standing on the gate facing a sea of red books and flags, clearly enjoyed the status of an emperor. This "imperial power" of architecture never ceased to radiate after the decline of the emperor in the early twentieth century, not even after the death of Chairman Mao in 1976. In April 1989, three student representatives attempted to present a petition in Tiananmen Square; they did so on their knees, and on the steps in front of the Great Hall of the People, a gesture that mimicked the usual ritual of prostration that ordinary people performed before emperors in the past (Zhang Longxi 1992, 125). Even the literal meaning of Tiananmen—Gate of Heavenly Peace—bears little of the truth of its quiet witness to the twentieth century: "While the name of the gate, with its rich historical echoes and its evocations of a timeless sphere beyond politics, has seemed across the last century to bring a promise of solace to the Chinese people dreaming of escape from current realities, the gate itself in the same period came to stand implacably for the power of the state" (Spence 1981, 18).

The implacable power of architecture that recurrently works on inhabitants is the theme of this book, but the way it works depends on an understanding, bodily as well as conceptually, even at the level of subconsciousness, of the built work by the inhabitants. This understanding is the evidence of the extraordinary capacity of human beings to engage symbolically with the built world. I have thus far, I hope, persuaded my readers to believe that, first of all, architecture is symbolic in the sense that it is empowering in the disposition of actions, and to a certain degree the thinking, of its inhabitants. Michel Foucault's reading of Jeremy Bentham's panopticon is perhaps the most pervasive example on this point (1975, 195–228). The panopticon is a round prison where the periphery is divided as individual backlit cells and the center is a surveillance tower that has a direct view of each cell. Foucault calls it an apparatus or a machine; but the power is only exercised when the inmate is conscious that he is under constant surveillance. This visibility is also compounded by invisibility—he is not aware of his fellow inmates in the cells next to him. Bentham's panopticon is designed to cause anxiety in the inmate; it affects his psyche, hence his behavior. A surveillance camera, unlike a spatial apparatus, does not necessarily create the same effect, for one is often unaware of its existence.

The panopticon cannot be used as a universal analogy for architecture, for its very goal is control, which can be reliably applied only at the conscious level of animals. Foucault in fact suspects that Bentham's panopticon is inspired by Le Vaux's menagerie at Versailles: "One finds in the programme of the Panopticon a similar concern with individualizing observation, with characterization and classification, with the analytical arrangement of space" (Foucault 1975, 203). But the animals cannot be simply replaced by human beings. The Dong interact with their architecture with anxiety and awareness, as we already know, although this interaction often occurs at the level of subconsciousness. If architecture is not reduced to the level of control used in sheep farming, a recurrent theme of this book is that making and inhabiting are essential processes within which a reification of architectural meaning becomes possible. And indeed the engagement between the inhabitants and the making of their habitat is the key.

Bentham's panopticon has never been tested in its entire built reality. The reason is that a building does not work as an animal trap. The precise workings of the panopticon can only be given, through text, as instructions to an apparatus. The Dong, by contrast, being a nonliterate people, gain a bodily as well as mental understanding of their architecture through making and inhabiting. A conceptual frame throughout the book is that architecture is not as didactic as text; its meaning, rather, is tacit like that of an allegory.

An allegory, literally, is a story that carries a moral message. It works—the message gets across—through the story itself rather than any direct didactic teaching. It is all too easy to say, as an English dictionary often tells us, that the meaning embedded in an allegory is symbolically represented. This, however, does not tell the "technical" process of symbolization in which the meaning, though tacit, is made knowable. This technical process, as James Clifford sees it, is that "allegory prompts us to say of any cultural description not 'this represents, or symbolizes, that,' but rather, 'this is a (morally charged) story about that'" (1986b, 100). If "any cultural description," in the form of text, works allegorically, architecture, which possesses little linguistic capacity, must work in a nondidactic manner. The spatial disposition of architecture, unlike language, demands imaginative engagement from the inhabitants. Benjamin's "ruin," as mentioned earlier, is thus a fitting analogy for an architectural allegory. For the nature of making and inhabiting is driven by our urge and imagination to renew, and to reconstruct, which is indeed what a "ruin" yields to.

What I have attempted to demonstrate, through my biased excursions into the process of making and inhabiting architecture among the minority groups in southern China, is that those inhabitants, who are still the creators of their built world, habitually maintain, as well as renew, a lively relationship with their architecture. Within such processes, they gain meaningful reassurance of their creation, and they hence are encouraged to become aware of the sense of their own place and even to imagine the places of others—the space beyond their own place. This, indeed, is an allegorical process. For the narratives of Dong architecture are on the one hand made meaningful through collective rituals. On the other hand, such narratives are not fixed on their "shells"—the architecture. The renewal of their architecture is achieved, not through a complete reinvention of new forms, but by injecting new narratives into the old "shells." If an allegory is a story that has the potential to generate another story, allegorical architecture is enduring: the life of a building can be renewed by engaging with new meanings. The key for the creator and the inhabitant, however, is the imagining of the "figure" and his/her animated relationship with the built world. But like the scientist in the Salk Institute contemplated by Kahn, or the emperor of Tiananmen Square imagined by the student representatives in the 1989 protest, this imagined figure is not always understood or even subconsciously felt by the inhabitants.

This book, from the viewpoint of allegorical architecture, is a reimagining of the minority groups in southern China as a collective figure and its living relationship with the built world, which was created with an allegory in the first place. Far from being nostalgic, the writing of this book should be seen as one attempt at architectural renewal. My ultimate purpose is to offer hope to the built world of our time, where form and fabric are conceived and materialized without much involvement from citizens. It is a reminder of our primordial and yet romantic urge to imagine a paradisial way of life—our fantasy—when we build. This romanticism often becomes hopelessly vain (just consider Kahn's Salk Institute) if it fails to receive a legibly loving care and maintenance from its inhabitants. It is for this reason that making and inhabiting among the minority groups in southern China provide a valuable lesson not only to planners and architects but also to citizens in our time.

To receive corporeal as well as mental discernment from its inhabitants, architecture in our time needs luck. The Sydney Opera House is one of the very few lucky ones, for both its image and idea, or form and meaning, have been accepted and understood by the citizens of the world. The "shell" will remain universally admired, just like the pure beauty of the Kantian *flower*. The flower, for Immanuel Kant, is universally admired as "free beauty." But what Kant fails to discern is that a flower is almost always instrumental under, to paraphrase Louis Kahn, "circumstantial conditions." A flower, therefore, can rarely be free from interest or concept; the beauty of a flower is not free from metaphorical connotations. The meaning of the Sydney Opera House, like a red rose on Valentine's Day, is thus circumstantially engaged due to a willingness from its inhabitants. To prove this, one only needs to consider the instrumental role of the Opera House during New Year celebrations these days, which often turn Sydney's harbor into an exuberant public arena on New Year's Eve. This surely would not occur if the architecture were not conceived as an allegory in the first place.

Notes

PROLOGUE

1. According to Joseph Rykwert's recollection, the panel had twenty-one jurors including architectural historians, Rykwert himself, Françoise Choay, architects Vittorio Gregotti, Renzo Piano, and Arata Isozaki, composer Luigi Nona, abstract painter Gottfried Honnegger, and scientist Henri Laborit (Joseph Rykwert, pers. comm.).

2. Generally speaking, these six Tai linguistic groups include Zhuang, Buyi, Dai, Dong, Shui, and Li. According to contemporary linguistic usage, there are four language affiliations in southern China:

- The Tibeto-Burman group of the Sino-Tibetan family includes Hani, Li, Lahu, Tibetan, Bai, Naxi, Lisu, Primi, Jinpo, Achang, and Qiang.
- The Zhuang-Dai group of the Sino-Tibetan family includes Zhuang, Dai, Dong, Shui, Buyi, and Maonan.
- The Miao-Yao group of the Sino-Tibetan family includes Miao and Dong.
- The Austro-Asiatic family includes Blang, Wa, Benglong (also called Deang), and Kemu.

Most of these groups share common architectural features, such as pile-built structures, and have ties with Austronesian culture. Linguistically, however, these groups do not belong to the Austronesian family.

CHAPTER 1. ARCHITECTONIC FABRICATIONS OF MINORITIES

1. The *lusheng* is a mouth organ made of bamboo pipes. It is one the most popular musical instruments among many minority groups in southern China. Probably in reference to the Han, Eberhard (1986, 197) has this to say about its symbolism: "The word *sheng* is phonetically identical with the word *sheng* meaning 'to rise in rank,' so the

mouth organ symbolizes preferment. Another way of expressing this is to show a child holding a lotus seed capsule *(lian)*. This symbolizes the wish that one may 'rise further and further *(lian)*.'"

2. For a different hypothesis of Dong ethnic origins, see *Dongzu jianshi bianxie zu* and various articles by Zhang Min.

3. During my 1993 fieldwork in the Congjiang region of Guizhou province, I discovered that a few villages with Dong language and Dong architecture, such as drum towers, have been classified as Miao. For unknown reasons, these villages either did not choose to be identified as Dong when the reclassification of "minority nationalities" was conducted by the central government in the 1950s or they were arbitrarily or purposefully designated as such by the government.

4. Legend has it that Zhou Enlai, the premier at that time, made the decision. Similar situations happened with other minority nationalities, such as the Dai, a Tai linguistic group in southern China that was given a character "傣," with the *ren* as the radical.

5. See "2000 National Population Census," *China Statistical Yearbook* (2004, 46).

6. See "1982 National Population Census," *China Statistical Yearbook* (1986, 97f).

7. If a case is not covered by the customary law, the "gods' arbitration" is applied. The most popular form is "chicken killing." The procedure is this: a line is drawn to separate two parties; a chicken is slaughtered right on the line by the executive; the party on whose side the chicken finally dies loses; the arbitration becomes reconciled if the chicken dies exactly on the line.

8. As a real person, his name was Guanyu. He was one of those who helped Liu Bei to become emperor of western China and to found a short-lived dynasty there in the third century AD. Guanyu was subsequently given the honorific name Guan-gong. He fell from power after the death of Liu Bei but was gradually elevated to divine status in the centuries that followed. Today temples to Guandi (his name as a god) are to be found in almost all of China's towns and counties. In the Han Chinese theater, he was a protagonist in the many plays based on the "Romance of the Three Kingdoms," where he is portrayed in the uniform of a general on horseback. He is instantly recognizable by his red face.

9. In spare moments a few more inches are added to embroidered edgings and squares used to decorate bags (worn at the waist), baby carriers, apron yokes, and jacket sleeves. As with their architecture, the Dong as an ethnic group are identified through the type, making, and wearing of such textiles. The styles of these textiles vary from place to place, however. Each group, sometimes each village, produces its own distinctive style of dress and architecture. Rituals, festivals, and market days reveal this richness of dress. Much can be gleaned from a glance at a woman's costume: not only does it illustrate how diligent she is as a worker and how creative she is as craftswoman, but also more importantly where she comes from.

CHAPTER 2. MYTH AND RITUALISTIC POSTURES

1. For the Han, the emperor was regarded as "the son of heaven" *(tianzi)*; what was below heaven *(tianxia)*, a long-established term, simultaneously meant the Chinese empire and the civilized world.

2. Many scholars believe that the notion of "water-based" culture, from Buckminster Fuller and thence from Sumet Jumsai, is highly speculative and unsupported by either archaeological or linguistic evidence. The pile-built structures shared by southern ethnic groups in China and Austronesian cultures in Southeast Asia may have nothing to do with water, for example, and could well be a cosmological model. As Waterson

(1990, 93) among others (Wessing 1984; Dall 1982) has pointed out, the concept of a three-tiered cosmos—consisting of a middle world, inhabited by humans, sandwiched between an upper and lower world—is common among Asian cultures. These issues are further discussed in Chapter 4. There are obviously many assumptions regarding the migrations too. Regardless of the migration routes (from the Asian coast to the interior of the mainland, for example, or in the opposite way), Dong culture is in many aspects closely related to water.

3. Most of the Dong myths of origin and migration cited in this chapter are taken from a collection of Dong folk songs by Yang Guoren and Wu Dingguo (1981).

4. The following Dong myth of human origin, extermination, rebirth, and settlement is based on Yang Guoren and Wu Dingguo (1981): The first boy, Songen, and first girl, Songsang, were born from eggs hatched by tortoise mothers. Songen and Songsang then married and produced a big family of twelve children. The youngest, Wangsu, was a smart boy but also very naughty. One day, he played with fire and the king snake, causing a huge forest fire. The king snake went into the earth, the king dragon dived into the river, the king tiger hid in the cave, but the thunder shrew (because thunder is unpredictable, the Dong believe that thunder is a bad-tempered woman called the thunder shrew) had nowhere to hide. She flew back to the sky where the fire was flying, her clothes damaged and one foot burnt. To demonstrate her anger to Wangsu, the thunder shrew destroyed nine new houses he had built. Wangsu then built an iron house with timber and moss as camouflage. The thunder shrew was finally trapped in this iron house by Wangsu when she tried to destroy it.

Trying to starve her to death, Wangsu did not give the thunder shrew any food and water. On a day when Wangsu wanted to go out, he exhorted two of his brothers and sisters, Zhang Liang and Zhang Mei, to guard the thunder shrew. Zhang Liang and Zhang Mei were very kindhearted and gave the thunder shrew some water when she begged for it. Zhang Liang and Zhang Mei did not realize that water was the only source of her energy. The thunder shrew became shiny and extremely powerful after drinking some water and easily broke through the iron house and escaped. She left a melon seed for Zhang Liang and Zhang Mei, however, and told them this seed could save their lives in the future.

After she escaped, the thunder shrew caused a continuous nine-month rain. The whole world was flooded and all living beings were almost exterminated. The seed from the thunder shrew grew into a huge melon floating on the water. Zhang Liang and Zhang Mei survived by living in this floating melon. They also saved seven hundred snakes and seven thousand bees by getting them into the melon. These snakes and bees were very grateful to Zhang Liang and Zhang Mei and attacked the thunder shrew. To save her life, the thunder shrew promised to end the flood. She then created suns to dry the flood. The bees removed ten of the suns when the land was dry; the two remaining became the sun for the day and the moon for the night.

A pair of surviving hawks told Zhang Liang and Zhang Mei that they were the only surviving human beings. The two hawks sincerely advised Zhang Liang and Zhang Mei to marry each other so that they could procreate and produce human beings. Zhang Liang and Zhang Mei had no choice. After nine months, a strange baby with many eyes, noses, and mouths was born. Zhang Liang and Zhang Mei felt ashamed. They thought it was the incarnation of ghosts. Therefore they chopped it into pieces and threw them into the mountains.

A strange thing happened. After a few days, Zhang Liang and Zhang Mei saw innumerable children all over the mountains. These children spoke different languages, such as Han, Miao, Dong, Yao, and so on. But they all called the brother and sister father and mother.

5. The stories of Dong origins vary from place to place. The two folk songs about the origin in Yang Guoren and Wu Dingguo (1981) are also slightly different from each other. But one thing is common: the Dong were transformed from flesh, and mountain river valleys are the most appropriate sites for them to settle.

6. From my own fieldwork observations, I find that the Dong's sense of cultural superiority to the Miao is pervasive. They usually see the Miao as a brave, even warlike, but straightforward and uncultivated people. This kind of attitude to the Miao also exists among the southern Chinese. A crude and rash person is usually described as *miaozi,* literally a Miao person.

7. The boat metaphor and its influence on houses and settlements can be seen in Southeast Asia and the Pacific region. See a detailed study of "the building in the form of the boat" and "the village in the form of the boat" in Ronald Lewcock and Gerard Brans' "The Boat as an Architectural Symbol" in Oliver (1975). See also Chapter 3 on this point.

8. During my fieldwork in the Dong region, I had no problem in finding my way in and out of a new village because of the identifying devices, such as the gate, the drum tower, and the wind-and-rain bridges. But it was not always possible to determine the location of a Sax altar without the guidance of informants.

9. See "The Study of Dong Village Form" in *Jianzhu Shi* (The Architect) 41: 74–87. I did not, however, find any trees as Sax altars in my fieldwork.

10. Exceptions are found in some villages where the old drum tower was destroyed, usually by accidental fire. In these cases, the village often could not afford to build another one and instead built a simple, low shelter to serve as the drum tower.

11. Multistory structures are widely used as stages by the Han and others. In the Qing dynasty, for example, Cixi had one such opera structure in the Summer Palace.

12. During my fieldwork in the village of Heli in the Sanjiang region, when a Dong realized that we had come from far away, he took my wife and me to a Tudi shrine and burnt incense for our safe journey.

13. Maybe because of the linguistic affiliation, the Thai are believed to be culturally and historically related to the Tai linguistic groups in southern China, particularly the Dai in Xishuangbanna.

14. The information on Sax rituals comes mainly from three sources:

- My own fieldwork, including participation in annual Sax worship in the village of Longtu in the Congjiang region, Guizhou province, on 23 January 1993, the Chinese New Year
- "Introduction of 'Sax' Activities in the Jiudong Region" by Shi Tinzhang (1989), who was originally from the Jiudong area of the Congjiang region
- Wu Quanxin (1992): "Field Report on the Establishment of the Sax Altar in Zhanli Village"

15. One of the Dong migration legends tells the story of the Dong's grandmother, Sax, leading the migration from the coast to the interior. She always held a huge umbrella to protect her people, and she finally died during the migration journey (Gong Jie 1989).

16. Unlike the umbrella and boxwood tree, the significance of white stone pieces and their numbers has never become clear to me. These stone pieces do not seem to play any meaningful role in the ritual performance.

17. According to my observation in the village of Longtu, the Dong dance and sing hand in hand in a procession of *duoye*, repeating a series of clockwise and counter-clockwise movements in a way which, it seems, replicates the coiled movement that is part of their Sax ritual. Wu Quanxin recorded Zhanli village's *duoye* as a south-to-north and west-to-east route in the Sax ritual, which I think forms a coil diagram. Whether the coil diagram in the *duoye* is nautically related is once again possible but highly speculative.

18. In Chinese medicine, many diseases are described as *feng*: catching a cold is *shangfeng*, which literally means "hurt by wind"; apoplexy is *zhongfeng*, which means "shot by the wind."

CHAPTER 3. CHORAL SYMBOLIZATION

1. Regarding the analogies of village heart and the rituals of founding villages, particularly among minority groups in southern China, see Yang Changming (1990, 114–120). Yang's writing on this topic includes contributions from my own fieldwork material in the Dai area of Yunnan province.

2. An example is found in the village of Boa Wae, Nage district, West Flores (Waterson 1990, 20). It seems that the forked offering stake *(peo)* in the village gives rise to the form of the village heart. Buffaloes offered to male clan ancestors are tied to the post before being slaughtered.

3. I could not manage to visit this village. However, my informant Wu Quanxin, from the Congjiang region, described his observations and fieldwork findings in Shudong village to me when I was in Congjiang (December 1992).

4. This practice is perhaps similar to the sacrifice offered to male clan ancestors that Waterson described in Southeast Asia. See note 2.

5. This is believed to be a similar ritual to She, which was practiced by the ancient Chinese as a ceremony to the earth god. In ancient Chinese mythology the snake was seen as a spirit and was thought to have an intimate connection with the earth (Huang 1983, 218).

6. I shall return to this later when I discuss what Sumet (1988) sees as a Naga-related coil motif, which he proposes is common to water-related customs.

7. In ancient China, the drum was one of the eight musical instruments. Moreover, a drum was usually beaten to solicit attention. Drums gave the signal for attack in battle (their noise was compared to rolling thunder); drums were beaten at many festive occasions, before the city gates were closed at night, and before a market shut down; outside the courthouse hung the "complaint drum," which was there for anyone to beat who wanted to bring a lawsuit.

8. When I conducted my fieldwork in Ma'an village of the Sanjiang region, I found that gong beating is a daily routine in winter to remind the villagers to be careful with fires.

9. The bronze drums unearthed in the southern minority area, including the Dong region, are well known. The image of frogs sitting round the outer rim, figures of men who are sailing in ships or taking part in processions, call for more interpretations. These bronze drums have been in use for more than two thousand years and are among the most valuable possessions of these people. But it is unclear whether the bronze drums are related to the Dong drum tower.

10. The people of Baxie village in the Sanjiang region of Guangxi province are believed to be migrants from Guizhou province. As already shown, *dougong* support is used in their drum tower and even in the village gate. (See Figures 3.30 and 2.24.)

11. Chi is a Chinese measurement; 1 chi is equal to 0.33 meter.

12. See note 3.

13. Waterson (1990, 20) notes the skepticism regarding boat associations in Southeast Asia from people like Forth. Rather than imposed images, I found the boat analogies throughout Dong architecture and other artifacts.

14. A tower is conventionally believed to have upper floors.

15. Interview with Shi Tinzhang in Congjiang in December 1992.

16. Ibid.

17. In the past, each zhai had its own price controls, while the exchange of commodities with other zhai was based on market prices.

18. See Chapter 1 on Lu You's description of the *duoye*.

19. Interview with Wu Quanxin in Congjiang in December 1992.

20. Interview with Wu Chengfang in February 1993.

CHAPTER 4. TYPE, MYTH, AND HETEROGENEITY

An early version of this chapter appeared in a different form in *Asia's Old Dwellings* (Knapp 2003).

1. One of the meanings of *ganlan* in Chinese is "a nest dwelling in a tree."

2. In my own fieldwork of the Dong and other Tai linguistic groups in southern China, I did not find any two-phase, pile-built housing examples.

3. Into a pot hanging above the fire basin, the woman of the house pours a little tea oil, dried puffed glutinous rice, soya beans, and peanuts. After stirring a while, this mixture is placed into each tea bowl. The leaves, known as "mist tea," are then placed in the pot and hot water is added. When boiled, this is poured into each bowl. Every guest, by custom, should drink three bowls of such tea.

4. Generally the Dong are very free in choosing their love partners. In the evenings of late winter and early spring, young girls get together to weave, spin, and embroider in a fire pit room. Young boys come with the *pipa*, a four-stringed lute, to sing antiphonally with girls until late evening or even early next morning. In Leli, Rongjiang, however, girls and boys do not have direct contact. Girls sit at windows in the room, while boys use ladders to climb up outside the windows to sing with the girls. Courtship occurs through the antiphonal ritual. The Dong usually marry at the age of seventeen or eighteen. Traditionally the best marriage was considered to be the girl marrying her maternal uncle's son. If the girl wanted to marry someone else, she had to get permission from her uncle. The girl did not live with her husband permanently after the wedding. Following a period of alternating residence, once the girl is pregnant she then goes to live with her husband. Divorce is relatively easy among the Dong. If the chief fails to settle the marital dispute, a divorce is done with a simple ritual.

CHAPTER 5. OUT OF TIME

1. Another interesting example: the two new concepts of "legal ownership" and "cultural ownership" were created by the Maori before the "Te Maori" exhibition. "Legal ownership" was vested in the museums that held them; "cultural ownership" remained with the tribes. As Allan Hanson points out: "The concept of cultural ownership of art objects, which had not been enunciated prior to 'Te Maori,' has enriched the significance of tribal membership for Maori people and represents an important step towards Maori Tanga's goal of bringing the Maori heritage under Maori control" (Hanson 1989, 896).

2. Personal communication with Yang Tongshan in Sanjiang, January 1993.

3. Most Dong literature in Chinese included in the bibliography is from this period.

4. Personal communication with Long Yuxiao in the Research Institute of Guizhou Nationalities, Guiyang, December 1992.

5. Although included in this list, the Xindi drum tower was later accidentally destroyed by fire. I found that a shelter was built on the site to replace the drum tower when I was doing my fieldwork there.

6. Through my personal contact with local officials and during my fieldwork in the minority regions in southern China, I found that it is not unusual for them to feel that, even now, they are still more or less discriminated against by the Han.

7. My wife and I stayed in this room during our fieldwork. Without a fire pit, we had to use a small stove at night to withstand the winter chill. The thin timber paneling of a Dong house simply does not provide any insulation.

8. Tim Oakes has made similar observations of tourism in rural Guizhou. He argues that commercial and cultural tourism, rather than rendering the ethnic identity "flat" and inauthentic, in fact becomes an important factor in the ongoing construction of place identity (1997; 1999).

9. During our fieldwork in Baxie, a Danish anthropology student was living there to conduct his fieldwork. He used his notebook computer to show villagers the globe map; he interviewed people every day; his question was how the Dong community is symbolically constructed. He wanted to know why. Locals knew how to make up answers to please him.

10. The master builder of the Sanjiang drum tower is from Baxie village, another tourist attraction in the Sanjiang region. Baxie people have had frequent contact with outsiders. This builder is in his forties, an age considered to be very young in Dong society. Energetic and highly regarded in the area, he is often commissioned to build "minority culture villages," replicas of Dong villages in large cities. This particular builder is able to produce architectural drawings, such as plans and elevations, and builds according to his drawings. This modern way of creating architecture makes it a lot easier for him to invent and be playful. Because of his master builder reputation, he has gained a high social status in Baxie. Apart from the Communist administrative system, this builder plays the role of a real leader of Baxie.

Bibliography

Aasen, Clarence
    1990. "Dai Lue Settlements and Architecture in Xishuanbanna, China: The Composite Order of Cultural Identity." Unpublished conference paper.

Abidin, Wan Burhanuddin Bin Wan
    1981. *The Malay House: Rationale and Change.* Cambridge, MA: MIT Press.

Alkire, William H.
    1972. "Concepts of Order in South-East Asia and Micronesia." *Comparative Studies of Society and History* 14 (4): 484–493.

Altman, Irwin, and Amos Rapoport
    1980. *Environment and Culture.* New York: Plenum.

An Zhimin [Chih-min] 安志敏
    1963. "'*Gan Lan' shi jianzu de kaogu yanjiu*" '干栏'式建筑的考古研究 [The Ganlan (Pile Dwellings) in Ancient China]. *K'ao Ku Hsueh Pao* 考古学报 [Journal of Archaeology] 2: 65–85.

Anderson, Benedict Richard O'Gorman
    1972. "The Idea of Power in Javanese Culture." In Claire Holt, ed., *Culture and Politics in Indonesia.* Ithaca: Cornell University Press.

Bachelard, Gaston
    1969. *The Poetics of Space.* Translated by Maria Jolas. Boston: Beacon.

Barth, Fredrik
    1969. *Ethnic Groups and Boundaries.* London: Allen & Unwin.

Barthes, Roland
    1970. *S / Z.* Paris: Senil.

Beauclair, Inez de
    1956. "Ethnic Groups." In Hellmut Wilhelm, ed., *A General Handbook of China.* HRAF Subcontractor's Monograph No. 55, New Haven (mimeographed).

1960. "A Miao Tribe of Southeast Kweichow (Guizhou) and Its Cultural Configuration." *Bulletin of the Institute of Ethnology* 10: 127–199.

Benedict, Paul K.

1975. *Austro-Thai Language and Culture: With a Glossary of Roots.* New Haven: HRAF Press.

Benedikt, Michael

1991. *Deconstructing the Kimbell: An Essay on Meaning and Architecture.* New York: Cambridge University Press.

Blier, Suzanne Preston

1987. *The Anatomy of Architecture: Ontology and Metaphor in Batammaliba Architectural Expression.* New York: Cambridge University Press.

Bloomer, Jennifer

1993. *Architecture and the Text: The Scrypts of Joyce and Piranesi.* New Haven: Yale University Press.

Blust, Robert

1976. "Austronesian Culture History: Some Linguistic Inferences and Their Relations to the Archaeological Record." *World Archaeology* 8: 19–43.

Bognar, Botond

1989. "The Place of Nothingness: The Japanese House and the Oriental World Views of the Japanese." In Jean-Paul Bourdier and Nezar AlSayyad, eds., *Dwellings, Settlements, and Traditions: Cross-Cultural Perspectives.* Lanham, MD: University Press of America.

Bourdier, Jean-Paul, and Nezar AlSayyad, eds.

1989. *Dwellings, Settlements, and Traditions: Cross-Cultural Perspectives.* Lanham, MD: University Press of America.

Bourdieu, Pierre

1971. "The Berber House or the World Reversed." In *Échanges et communications: Mélanges offerts à Claude Lévi-Strauss à l'occasion de son 60 anniversaire.* The Hague: Mouton.

1973. "The Berber House." In M. Douglas, ed., *Rules and Meanings.* Harmondsworth: Penguin.

1977. *Outline of a Theory of Practice.* Cambridge: Cambridge University Press.

1984. *Distinction: A Social Critique of the Judgment of Taste.* Cambridge, MA: Harvard University Press.

1990. *In Other Words: Essays Towards a Reflexive Sociology.* Cambridge: Polity Press.

1993. *The Field of Cultural Production: Essays on Art and Literature.* Cambridge: Polity Press.

Boyd, Andrew

1962. *Chinese Architecture and Town Planning: 1500 BC–1911 AD.* London: Alec Tiranti.

Broadbent, Geoffrey, et al., eds.

1980a. *Meaning and Behaviour in the Built Environment.* Chichester: Wiley.

1980b. *Signs, Symbols, and Architecture.* Chichester: Wiley.

Bruk, Solomon Il'ich

1960. *Peoples of China, Mongolian People's Republic, and Korea.* Moscow Academy of Sciences USSR, Institute of Ethnography imeni N. N. Miklukho-Maklay. Translated by US Joint Publications Research Service, No. 3710, Washington, DC.

Burns, Carol
   1991. "On Site." In Andrea Kahn, ed., *Drawing Building Text*. New York: Princeton Architectural Press.
Buttimer, Anne, and David Seamon, eds.
   1980. *The Human Experience of Space and Place*. London: Croom Helm.
Caraveli, Anna
   1985. "The Symbolic Village: Community Born in Performance." *Journal of American Folklore* 98 (389): 259–286.
Carsten, Janet, and Stephen Hugh-Jones
   1995. *About the House: Lévi-Strauss and Beyond*. Cambridge: Cambridge University Press.
Castells, Manuel
   1978. *City, Class, and Power*. New York: St. Martin's Press.
Chang, Amos Ih Tiao
   1981. *The Tao of Architecture*. Princeton: Princeton University Press.
Charernsupkul, Anuvit, and Vivat Temiyabandha
   1979. *Northern Thai Domestic Architecture and Rituals in House Building*. Bangkok: Fine Arts Commission of the Association of Siamese Architects.
Chen Guoqian 陈国强 et al.
   1988. *Bai Yue minzu shi* 百越民族史 [History of Bai Yue Nationalities]. Beijing: Zhongguo Shehui Kexue Chubanshe 中国社会科学出版社.
Chen Moxi 陈默溪
   1983. "Dongzu de zhixiu yishu" 侗族的织绣艺术 [The Art of Dong Weaving and Embroidering]. *Guizhou minzu yanjiu* 贵州民族研究 [Ethnic Studies in Guizhou] 13: 127–131.
   1989. "Guanyu Dongzu 'Sa chongbai' de diaocha he tantao" 关于侗族'萨崇拜'的调查和探讨 [Investigation and Discussion of Dong "Sax Worship"]. Unpublished paper, Sax Conference, Rongjiang, Guizhou province.
   1990. "Guanyu Dongzu 'Sa chongbai' de diaocha he tantao" 关于侗族'萨崇拜'的调查和探讨 [Investigation and Discussion of Dong "Sax Worship"]. *Miao Dong Wentan* 苗侗文坛 [Miao and Dong Forum] 6: 13–28.
Chen Ruochen 陈若尖 and Qi Jiaju 戚家驹
   1991. "Lusheng yu sangzang xisu he dui zishen de fazhan" 芦笙与丧葬习俗和对自身的发展 [*Lusheng* and Funeral Customs]. *Miao Dong Wentan* 苗侗文坛 [Miao and Dong Forum] 9: 61–66.
Chen Weigang 陈维刚
   1981. "Dongzu mingcheng kao" 侗族名称考 [Studies of the Name of Dong (Gamel)]. *Minzu Yanjiu* 民族研究 [Ethnic Studies] 5.
Clément, Pierre, and Sophie Charpentier-Clément
   1974. "Notes sur l'Habitation sur Pilotis en Asie du Sud-Est" (Notes on the Pile Dwelling in Southeast Asia). *Asie du Sud-Est et Monde Insulindien* 5 (2): 13–24.
   1975. "Pour une Approche Ethno-architecturale de l'Habitation" [Towards an Ethno-architectural Approach to the Dwelling]. In *Histoire et Theories de l'Architecture*. Paris: Institut de l'Environnement.
Clifford, James
   1986a. "Introduction: Partial Truths." In James Clifford and George E. Marcus, eds., *Writing Culture: The Poetics and Politics of Ethnography*. Berkeley: University of California Press.

1986b. "On Ethnographic Allegory." In James Clifford and George E. Marcus, eds., *Writing Culture: The Poetics and Politics of Ethnography*. Berkeley: University of California Press.

1988. *The Predicament of Culture: Twentieth-Century Ethnography, Literature, and Art*. Cambridge, MA: Harvard University Press.

Colquhoun, Alan

1981. *Essays in Architectural Criticism: Modern Architecture and Historical Change*. Cambridge, MA: MIT Press.

Conklin, Harold C.

1998. *Ethnographic Atlas of Ifugao: A Study of Environment, Culture, and Society in Northern Luzon*. New Haven: Yale University Press.

Cooper, Clare Marcus

1974. "The House as Symbol of Self." In Jon Lang et al., eds., *Designing for Human Behavior*. Strousberg, PA: Dowden, Hutchinson, and Ross.

Dai Yixuan 戴裔煊

1948. *Gan Lan—xinan Zhongguo yuanshi zhuzhai de yanjiu* 干栏一西南中国原始住宅的研究 [Gan Lan—Research on Primitive Houses in Southwest China]. Guangzhou: Lingnan Daxue Xinan Shehui Jingji Yanjiusuo 岭南大学西南社会经济研究所.

Dall, Greg

1982. "The Traditional Acehnese House." In John Maxwell, ed., *The Malay-Islamic World of Sumatra*. Melbourne: Monash University Center of South-East Asian Studies.

Danto, Arthur

1999. *Philosophizing Art: Selected Essays*. Berkeley: University of California Press.

Davis, Richard Bernard

1984. *Muang Metaphysics: A Study of Northern Thai Myth and Ritual*. Bangkok: Pandora.

Deng Minwen 邓敏文

1990. "'Sax' sheng shixi" '萨'神试析 [Analyzing the Sax Goddess]. *Guizhou minzu yanjiu* 贵州民族研究 [Ethnic Studies in Guizhou] 42: 18–24.

Deng Minwen 邓敏文 and Wu Hao 吴浩

1989. "Lun Dongzu 'yue fa kuan'" 论侗族《约法款》[Studies on Dong "Kuanx of Laws and Regulations"]. *Zhongnan Minzu Xueyuan Xuebao* 中南民族学院学报 [Journal of South-Center Nationalities Institute] 2.

Deng Yan 邓焱

1981. "Miao Dong shanzhai kaocha" 苗侗山寨考查 [Investigation of Miao and Dong Mountain Villages]. *Jianzu Shi* 建筑师 [The Architect], vol. 9. Beijing: Zhongguo Jianzu Gongye Chubanshe 中国建筑工业出版社.

Derrida, Jacques

1978. *Writing and Difference*. London: Routledge & Kegan Paul.

Dodd, William Clifton

1923. *The Tai Race*. Cedar Rapids: Torch Press.

Domenig, Gaudenz

1980. *Tektonik im Primitiven Dachbau*. Zurich: Institut Gaudenz/Eidgenossische Technische Hochschule.

Dongzu Jianshi Bianxie Zu 侗族简史编写组 [Brief History of the Dong Compilers' Group]

1985. *Dongzu jianshi* 侗族简史 [Brief History of the Dong]. Guiyang: Guizhou Minzu Chubanshe 贵州民族出版社.

Dongzu Wenxue Shi Bianxie Zu 侗族文学史编写组 [History of Dong Literature Compilers' Group]

1988. *Dongzu wenxue shi* 侗族文学史 [History of Dong Literature]. Guiyang: Guizhou Minzu Chubanshe 贵州民族出版社.

Dongzu wenzi fangan caoan

1959. *Dongzu wenzi fangan caoan* 侗族文字方案草案 [Draft of Dong Alphabetic Writing]. Guiyang: Guizhou Minzu Chubanshe 贵州民族出版社.

Donley, Linda Wiley

1982. "House Power: Swahili Space and Symbolic Markers." In Ian Hodder, ed., *Symbolic and Structural Archaeology*. Cambridge: Cambridge University Press.

Douglas, Mary

1972. "Symbolic Orders in the Use of Domestic Space." In Peter John Ucko et al., eds., *Man, Settlement, and Urbanism*. Cambridge, MA: Schenkman.

Duan Xiaoming 段晓明译, trans.

1985. *Wo zu zhiyuan—Yunnan* 倭族之源—云南 [Search for the Origin of the Japanese—the Route from Southern Yunnan]. Kunming: Yunnan Renmin Chubanshe 云南人民出版社. Originally published as Torigoe Kenzaburo et al., *Unnan kara no michi: Nihonjin no rutsu o saguru* (Tokyo: Kodansha, 1983).

Dumarçay, Jacques

1985. *The House in South-East Asia*. Singapore: Oxford University Press.

Duncan, James S.

1973. "Landscape Taste as a Symbol of Group Identity: A Westchester County Village." *Geography Review* 63: 334–355.

1976. "Landscape and the Communication of Social Identity." In Alec Rapoport, ed., *The Mutual Interaction of People and Their Built Environment: A Cross-Cultural Perspective*. The Hague: Mouton.

1981. "From Container of Women to Status Symbol: The Impact of Social Structure on the Meaning of the House." In James S. Duncan, ed., *Housing and Identity: Cross-Cultural Perspectives*. London: Croom Helm.

1985. "Individual Action and Political Power: A Structuration Perspective." In Ronald John Johnston, ed., *The Future of Geography*. London: Methuen.

Duncan, James S., and Nancy G. Duncan

1976. "Social World, Status Passage, and Environmental Perspectives." In Gary T. Moore and Reginald G. Golledge, eds., *Environmental knowing: Theories, Research, and Methods*. Stroudsburg: Dowden, Hutchinson & Ross.

Durkheim, Emile

1965. *The Elementary Forms of the Religious Life*. Chicago: University of Chicago Press. Originally published in 1915.

Durkheim, Emile, and Marcel Mauss

1963. *Primitive Classification*. Chicago: University of Chicago Press. Originally published in 1903.

Eberhard, Wolfram

1986. *A Dictionary of Chinese Symbols: Hidden Symbols in Chinese Life and Thought*. London: Routledge.

Eco, Umberto

 1972. "The Componental Analysis of the Architectural Sign/Column." *Semiotica* 5 (2): 97–117.

 1976. *A Theory of Semiotics*. Bloomington: Indiana University Press.

 1980. "Function and Sign: The Semiotics of Architecture." In Geoffrey Broadbent et al., eds., *Signs, Symbols, and Architecture*. Chichester: Wiley.

Edelman, Murray

 1978. "Space and the Social Order." *Journal of Architectural Education* 32: 2–7.

Eisenman, Peter

 1971. "From Object to Relationship II: Casa Giuliani Frigerio in Perspecta." *Yale Architectural Journal* 13/14: 36–65.

Eliade, Mircea

 1957. *The Sacred and the Profane: The Nature of Religion*. New York: Harcourt, Brace, and World.

Evans, Robin

 1997. *Robin Evans: Translations from Drawing to Building and Other Essays*. London: Architectural Association.

Fathy, Hassan

 1973. *Architecture for the Poor*. Chicago: University of Chicago Press.

Feng Yuzhao 冯玉照 and Wu Zhenguang 吴正光

 1985. *Guizhou Dongzhai gulou fengyuqiao* 贵州侗寨鼓楼风雨桥 [Drum Towers and Wind-and-rain Bridges in Guizhou's Dong Villages]. Guiyang: Guizhou Renmin Chubanshe 贵州人民出版社.

Fernandez, James William

 1977. *Fang Architectonics*. Philadelphia: Institute for the Study of Human Issues.

 1984. "Emergence and Convergence in Some African Sacred Places." *Geoscience and Man* 24: 31–42.

 1986. *Persuasions and Performances: The Play of Tropes in Culture*. Bloomington: Indiana University Press.

Foucault, Michel

 1970. *The Order of Things: An Archaeology of the Human Sciences*. New York: Random House.

 1975. *Discipline and Punish: The Birth of the Prison*. New York: Vintage Books.

 1984. "Des Espace Autres." *Architectura, Mouvement, Continuité*, October: 46–49.

Frampton, Kenneth

 1985. *Modern Architecture: A Critical Architecture*. London: Thames & Hudson.

Fraser, Douglas

 1968. *Village Planning in the Primitive World*. London: Studio Vista.

Fu Zuosen 傅作森

 1981. "Da you cha" 打油茶 [Oil Tea]. *Zhongyang Minzu Xueyuan Xuebao* 中央民族学院学报 [Journal of Central Nationalities Institute], 1.

Geertz, Clifford

 1959. "Form and Variation in Balinese Village Structure." *American Anthropologist* 61: 991–1012.

 1966. *Person, Time, and Conduct in Bali: An Essay in Cultural Analysis*. New Haven: Southeast Asia Studies, Yale University.

 1973. *The Interpretation of Cultures: Selected Essays*. New York: Basic Books.

 1974. *Myth, Symbol, and Culture*. New York: Norton.

Geil, William Edgar

    1904. *A Yankee on the Yangtze: Being a Narrative of a Journey from Shanghai Through the Central Kingdom to Burma.* New York: Armstrong & Son.

Gell, Alfred

    1996. "Vogel's Net: Traps as Artworks and Artworks as Traps." *Journal of Material Culture*, vol. 1. London: Sage.

    1998. *Art and Agency: An Anthropological Theory.* Oxford: Clarendon.

    1999. *The Art of Anthropology: Essays and Diagrams.* Edited by Eric Hirsch. London: Athlone Press.

Gibbs, Phillip

    1987. *Building a Malay House.* Singapore: Oxford University Press.

Giddens, Anthony

    1976. *New Rules of Sociological Method: A Positive Critique of Interpretive Sociologies.* New York: Basic Books.

    1979. *Central Problems in Social Theory: Action, Structure, and Contradiction in Social Analysis.* Berkeley: University of California Press.

    1984. *The Constitution of Society: Outline of the Theory of Structuration.* Berkeley: University of California Press.

Gong Jie 公节

    1989. "'Wa,' 'Sax' wenhua chuyi" '娲' '萨' 文化刍议 [Discussions on "Wa" and "Sax" Culture]. Unpublished paper, Sax Conference, Rongjiang, Guizhou province.

Guangxi Sanjiang Dongzu Zizhixian Zhi Bianzuan Weiyuanhui 广西三江侗族自治县志编纂委员会编纂 [Guangxi Sanjing Dong Nationality Autonomous County Organization], ed.

    1992. *Sanjiang Dongzu Zizhixian Zhi* 三江侗族自治县志 [Annals of Sanjing Dong Nationality Autonomous County]. Beijing: Zhongyang Minzu Xueyuan Chubanshe 中央民族学院出版社.

Guidoni, Enrico

    1978. *Primitive Architecture.* London: Faber.

Guizhou Minorities Social and History Investigation Group, Ethnic Research Institute of China Science Academy 贵州少数民族社会历史调查组，中国社会科学院民族研究所合编, eds.

    1963. *Dong zu jianshi jianzhi hebian (chugao)* 侗族简史简志合编（初稿）[Brief History and Annals of the Dong Nationality (Draft)]. Beijing: Zhongguo Kexueyuan Minzu Yanjiusuo 中国社会科学院民族研究所.

Guizhou Sheng Wenguanhui Bangongshi, Guizhou Sheng Wenhua Chubanting Wenwuchu 贵州省文管会办公室，贵州省文化出版厅文物处 [Guizhou Provincial Office for Cultural Administration, Cultural Relics Division of Guizhou Provincial Cultural Publishing Office], eds.

    1985. *Guizhou Dongzhai gulou fengyuqiao* 贵州侗寨鼓楼风雨桥 [The Drum Tower and Wind-and-Rain Bridges in Dong Villages of Guizhou Province]. Guiyang: Guizhou Renmin Chubanshe 贵州人民出版社.

Guizhou Sheng Wenwu Guangli Weiyuan Hui and Guizhou Wenhua Chubanting 贵州省文物管理委员会及贵州文化出版厅编 [Guizhou Cultural Relics Bureau and Guizhou Provincial Cultural and Publishing Bureau], eds.

    1987. *Guizhou gu jianzhu* 贵州古建筑 [Guizhou Ancient Architecture]. Guiyang: Guizhou Meishu Chubanshe 贵州美术出版社.

Guo Hushen 郭湖生

    1962. "Xishuangbanna Daizu de fosi jianzhu" 西双版纳傣族的佛寺建筑 [The Buddhist Temple of Dai in Xishuangbanna]. *Wenwu* 文物 [Cultural Relics] 2.

Gusevich, Miriam

    1991. "The Architecture of Criticism." In Andrea Kahn, ed., *Drawing Building Text.* New York: Princeton Architectural Press.

Han Shen Zazhi She 汉声杂志社 [Echo Magazine Publisher]

    1991. *Han Shen* 汉声 [Echo Magazine (Taipei)] 32.

Hanson, F. Allan

    1975. *Meaning in Culture.* London: Routledge & Kegan Paul.

    1989. "The Making of the Maori: Culture Invention and Its Logic." *American Anthropologist* 91: 890–902.

Hanson, F. Allan, and Louise Hanson, eds.

    1990. *Art and Identity in Oceania.* Honolulu: University of Hawaiʻi Press.

He Guangyue 何光岳

    1988. "Manren de laiyuan he qianxi" 蛮人的来源和迁徙 [The Source and Migration of *Man* (Barbarian)]. *Zhongnan Minzu Xueyuan Xuebao* 中南民族学院学报 [Journal of South-Center Nationalities Institute] 5.

He Xiaoxin 何晓昕

    1990. *Feng shui tanyuan* 风水探源 [The Source of *Fengshui*]. Nanjing: Dongnan Daxue Chubanshe.

Heidegger, Martin

    1971. *Poetry, Language, Thought.* New York: Harper & Row.

Herdeg, Klaus

    1990a. *Formal Structure in Indian Architecture.* New York: Rizzoli.

    1990b. *Formal Structure in Islamic Architecture of Iran and Turkistan.* New York: Rizzoli.

Hobart, Mark

    1978. "The Path of the Soul: The Legitimacy of Nature in Balinese Conceptions of Space." In George Milner, ed., *Natural Symbols in South-East Asia.* London: School of Oriental and African Studies.

Howe, Leo

    1983. "An Introduction to the Cultural Study of Traditional Balinese Architecture." *Archipel* 25: 137–158.

Huang Caigui 黄才贵

    1982. "Dongzu de xiguanfa" 侗族的习惯法 [Customary Law of the Dong]. *Guizhou Wenshi Congkan* 贵州文史丛刊 [Corpus of Guizhou Literature and History] 3.

    1983. "Dongzu mingcheng chutan" 侗族名称初探 [Initial Investigation of the Dong's Name]. *Guizhou minzu yanjiu* 贵州民族研究 [Ethnic Studies in Guizhou] 13: 94–102.

    1986. "Liping xian Zhaodong Dongzu shehui diaocha" 黎平县肇洞侗族社会调查 [The Investigation of Dong Society in Zhaodong Village, Liping County]. *Guizhou minzu diaocha* 贵州民族调查 [Ethnic Investigations in Guizhou] 4.

    1987. "Qiantan Dongzu youcha he riben chadao de tongyuan guanxi" 浅谈侗族油茶和日本茶道的同源关系 [Dong Oil Tea and Japanese Tea Ceremony Share the Same Origin]. *Guizhou minzu yanjiu* 贵州民族研究 [Ethnic Studies in Guizhou] 31: 165–171.

1990. "Dongzu tang Sax de zongjiao xingzhi" 侗族堂萨的宗教性质 [Religious Quality of the Dong Sax Altar]. *Guizhou minzu yanjiu* 贵州民族研究 [Ethnic Studies in Guizhou] 42: 25–32.

1991a. "Riben xuezhe dui Guizhou Dongzu Gan Lan minju de diaocha yu yanjiu" 日本学者对贵州侗族干栏民居的调查与研究 [Investigations and Studies of Guizhou Dong Pile-Built Houses by Japanese Scholars]. *Guizhou minzu yanjiu* 贵州民族研究 [Ethnic Studies in Guizhou] 46: 23–30.

1991b. "Zhong ren Gan Lan shi jianzhu de tongyuan guanzi chutan" 中日干栏式建筑的同源关系初探 [Genetic Relations of Pile-Built House in China and in Japan]. *Guizhou minzu yanjiu* 贵州民族研究 [Ethnic Studies in Guizhou] 48: 108–118.

1992. "Dongzu fu xi dajiazu yicun yu Gan Lan changwu—laizi Rongjiang xian Baoli dazhai de baogao" 侗族父系大家族遗存与干栏长屋—来自榕江县保里大寨的报告 [Historical Remains of the Dong Patriarchy Big Family and Pile-Built Long House: Fieldwork Report from Baoli Dazhai in Rongjiang County]. *Guizhou minzu diaocha* 贵州民族调查 [Ethnic Investigations in Guizhou] 9.

Huang Ze 黄泽

1992. "Xinan shaoshu minzu mugu wenhua chutan" 西南少数民族木鼓文化初探 [Initial Investigation of Timber Drum Tower Cultures of Southwest Minorities]. *Guizhou minzu yanjiu* 贵州民族研究 [Ethnic Studies in Guizhou] 52: 58–64.

Inn, Henry

1950. *Chinese Houses and Gardens*. New York: Bonanza Books.

Jiang Daqian 姜大谦

1990. "Shi lun Dongzu fangzhi wenhua" 试论侗族纺织文化 [Dong Textile Culture]. *Miao Dong Wentan* 苗侗文坛 [Miao and Dong Forum] 7: 105–115.

Jiang Yiliang 江应梁

1990. *Zhongguo minzu shi (shang, zhong)* 中国民族史 (上，中) [China Nationalities History, vols. 1 and 2]. Beijing: Beijing Minzu Chubanshe 北京民族出版社.

Jilin Sheng Bowuguan Ji-an Kaogu Tui 吉林省博物馆辑安考古队 [Ji-an Archaeology Team and Jilin Provincial Museum]

1964. "Jilin Ji-an Maxiangou yi hao bihua mu" 吉林辑安麻线沟一号壁画墓 [Fresco Tomb No. 1 in Maxiangou, Ji-an, Jilin]. *Kao Gu* 考古 [Archaeology] 10.

Jin Yu 金珏

1992. "Luelun Dongzu minju de zhuangshi xianxiang" 略论侗族民居的装饰现象 [The Decoration Phenomenon of Dong Housing]. *Guizhou minzu yanjiu* 贵州民族研究 [Ethnic Studies in Guizhou] 51: 67–72.

Jung, Carl Gustav

1968. *The Archetypes and the Collective Unconscious*. Princeton: Princeton University Press.

Kahn, Andrea, ed.

1991. *Drawing Building Text*. New York: Princeton Architectural Press.

Kant, Immanuel

1952. *The Critique of Judgement; Translated with Analytical Indexes by James Creed Meredith*. Oxford: Clarendon Press.

Kent, Susan

    1984. *Analyzing Activity Areas: An Ethnoarchaeological Study of the Use of Space.* Albuquerque: University of New Mexico Press.

King, Anthony D.

    1980. "A Time for Space and a Space for Time: The Social Production of the Vacation House." In Anthony D. King, ed., *Buildings and Society: Essays on the Social Development of the Built Environment.* London: Routledge & Kegan Paul.

    1984. "The Social Production of Building Form: Theory and Research." *Environment and Planning D: Society and Space* 2: 429–446.

    1987. "Cultural Production and Reproduction: The Political Economy of Societies and Their Built Environment." In David Canter et al., eds., *Ethnoscapes: Transcultural Studies in Action and Place.* Gower: Hampshire.

    1989. "Review of Architecture of the British Empire: The History and Design of the Australian House, The Railway Station." *Environment and Planning B: Planning and Design* 15: 226–229.

King, Victor Turner

    1980. "Symbols of Social Differentiation: A Comparative Investigation of Signs, the Signified, and Symbolic Meanings in Borneo." *Anthropos* 80: 125–152.

Knapp, Ronald G.

    1986. *China's Traditional Rural Architecture: A Cultural Geography of the Common House.* Honolulu: University of Hawai'i Press.

    1989. *China's Vernacular Architecture: House Form and Culture.* Honolulu: University of Hawai'i Press.

    1999. *China's Living Houses: Folk Beliefs, Symbols, and Household Ornamentation.* Honolulu: University of Hawai'i Press.

    2000. *China's Old Dwellings.* Honolulu: University of Hawai'i Press.

Knapp, Ronald G., ed.

    2003. *Asia's Old Dwellings: Tradition, Resilience, and Change.* New York: Oxford University Press.

Kostof, Spiro

    1985. *A History of Architecture: Settings and Rituals.* New York: Oxford University Press.

Kuang Lu 邝露

    1985. *Chi Ya* 赤雅. Beijing: Zhonghua Shuju 中华书局.

Kundera, Milan

    1984. *The Unbearable Lightness of Being.* London: Faber & Faber.

Kuper, Hilda

    1972. "The Language of Sites in the Politics of Space." *American Anthropologist* 4: 411–425.

Langer, Susanne

    1953. *An Introduction to Symbolic Logic.* New York: Dover.

Lawrence, Denise, and Low Setha

    1990. "The Built Environment and Spatial Form." *Annual Review of Anthropology* 19: 453–505.

Lawrence, Roderick J.

    1981. "The Social Classification of Domestic Space: A Cross-Cultural Study." *Anthropos* 76 (5/6): 649–664.

1982. "Domestic Space and Society: A Cross-Cultural Study." *Comparative Studies in Society and History* 24 (1): 104–130.

1989. "Structuralist Theories in Environment-Behavior-Design Research: Applications for Analyses of People and the Built Environment." In Ervin H. Zube and Gary T. Moore, eds., *Advances in Environment, Behavior, and Design*, vol. 2. New York: Plenum.

Le Corbusier

1987. *Journey to the East.* Cambridge, MA: MIT Press. Originally published in 1966 as *Le Voyage d'Orient.*

Leach, Edmund Ronald

1978. "Does Space Syntax Really 'Constitute the Social'?" In David Green et al., eds., *Social Organization and Settlement: Contributions from Anthropology, Archaeology, and Geography*, pt. 2. BAR International Series (supplementary) 47 (11). Oxford: British Archaeological Reports.

LeBar, Frank M., ed.

1972. *Ethnic Groups of Insular South-East Asia*, vol. 1: *Indonesia, Andaman Islands, and Madagascar.* New Haven: HRAF Press.

LeBar, Frank M., et al.

1964. *Ethnic Groups of Mainland Southeast Asia.* New Haven: HRAF Press.

Lee, Sang Hae

1989. "Siting and General Organization of Traditional Korean Settlements." In Jean-Paul Bourdier and Nezar AlSayyad, eds., *Dwellings, Settlements, and Traditions: Cross-Cultural Perspectives.* Lanham, MD: University Press of America.

Lethaby, William

1974. *Architecture, Mysticism, and Myth.* London: Architectural Press. Originally published in 1881.

Lévi-Strauss, Claude

1963. *Structural Anthropology.* Translated by Claire Jacobson and Brooke Grundfest Schoepf. Garden City, NY: Doubleday Anchor.

1983. *The Way of the Masks.* London: Cape.

1991. *Conversations with Claude Lévi-Strauss.* Chicago: University of Chicago Press.

Li Changjie 李长杰 et al.

1990. *Gui bei minju* 桂北民居 [Vernacular Architecture of Northern Guangxi Province]. Beijing: Zhongguo Jianzhu Gongye Chubanshe 中国建筑工业出版社.

Li Fangkuei 李方桂

1943. *Notes on the Mak Languages.* Monograph Series A, no. 20. Shanghai: Academia Sinica, Institute of History and Philology.

1965. "The Tai and the Kam [Dong, Gamel]–Shui Language." *Lingua* 14: 148–179.

1987. "Tai yu he Dong, Shui yu" 台语和侗，水语 [The Tai and the Kam (Dong, Gamel)-Shui Language. Translated by Shi Lin 石林. *Guizhou minzu yanjiu* 贵州民族研究 [Ethnic Studies in Guizhou] 29: 47–67.

Li Qiangmin 李强民

1988. "Yeche ren de jianzhai lisu" 叶车人的建寨礼俗 [The Village Founding Ritual of the Yeche]. *Yunnan Shehui Kexue* 云南社会科学 [Yunnan Social Science] 3.

Li Ruiqi 李瑞岐

    1989. *Guizhou Dong xi* 贵州侗戏 [Guizhou Dong Opera]. Guiyang: Guizhou Minzu Chubanshe 贵州民族出版社.

Li Shixue 李时学

    1992. "Dongzu gulou ji gulou wenhua guanjian" 侗族鼓楼及鼓楼文化管见 [Dong Drum Towers and Drum Tower Culture]. *Guizhou minzu yanjiu* 贵州民族研究 [Ethnic Studies in Guizhou] 52: 65–70.

Li Xiankui 李先逵

    1989. "Lun Gan Lan shi jianzhu de qiyuan yu fazhan" 论干栏式建筑的起源与发展 [Origin and Development of *Ganlan* (Pile-Built Dwellings)]. *Sichuan Jianzhu* 四川建筑 [Sichuan Architecture] 2: 8–11.

Li Yih-Yuan

    1957. "On the Platform-House Found Among Some Pingpu Tribes in Formosa." *Bulletin of the Institute of Ethnology* (Academia Sinica) 3: 139–144.

Liang, Ssu-cheng [Liang Shicheng]

    1984. *A Pictorial History of Chinese Architecture*. Cambridge, MA: MIT Press.

Liang Zhaotao 梁钊韬 et al.

    1985. *Zhongguo minzu xue gailun* 中国民族学概论 [Introduction to Chinese Ethnology]. Kunming: Yunnan Renmin Chubanshe 云南人民出版社.

Lim, Jee Yuan

    1987. *The Malay House: Rediscovering Malaysia's Indigenous Shelter System*. Pulau Penang, Malaysia: Institut Masyarakat.

Lin Huicheng 林会承

    1984. *Xianqin shiqi Zhongguo juzhu jianzhu* 先秦时期中国居住建筑 [Chinese Dwellings in Early Qin]. Taipei: Taiwan Liuhe Chubanshe 台湾六合出版社.

Linzey, Mott

    1988. "Speaking To and Talking About: Maori and European-Educated Comportments Towards Architecture." Paper presented at the International Symposium on Traditional Dwellings and Settlements in a Comparative Perspective, Berkeley, April.

Liscák, Vladimír

    1993. "Some Approaches to the Classification of Small Ethnic Groups in South China." *Thai-Yunnan Project Newsletter* (Australian National University) 20: 12–16.

Littlejohn, James

    1967. "The Temne House." In John Middleton, ed., *Myth and Cosmos: Readings in Mythology and Symbolism*. Garden City, NY: Natural History Press. Originally published in 1960.

Liu Dunzhen 刘敦桢

    1957. *Zhongguo zhuzhai gaishuo* 中国住宅概说 [Introduction to Chinese Dwellings]. Beijing: Jianzhu Gongchen Chubanshe 建筑工程出版社.

    1978. *Zhongguo gudai jianzhu shi* 中国古代建筑史 [History of Ancient Chinese Architecture]. Beijing: Zhongguo Jianzhu Gongye Chubanshe 中国建筑工业出版社.

Liu, Laurence G.

    1989. *Chinese Architecture*. New York: Rizzoli.

Liu Yangwu 刘扬武 and Deng Qiyao 邓启耀

    1985. "Achang zu yuanshi zongjiao canyu" 阿昌族原始宗教残余 [Traces of the

Achang Primitive Religion]. In *Zhongguo shaoshu minzu zongjiao chubian* ‘中国少数民族宗教’初编 [China’s Minority Religions, 1st ed.]. Kunming: Yunnan Renmin Chubanshe 云南人民出版社.

Long Senlin 龙森林
  1991. “Shi lun Dongzu zhi san chongbai” 试论侗族纸伞崇拜 [Preliminary Studies on Dong Worship of Paper Umbrellas]. *Miao Dong Wentan* 苗侗文坛 [Miao and Dong Forum] 9: 44–51.

Luchinger, Arnulf
  1981. *Structuralism in Architecture and Urban Planning*. Stuttgart: Karl Kramer Verlag.

Maki, Fumihiko
  1979. “Japanese City Spaces and the Concept of Oku.” *Japanese Architect* 265: 51–62.

Mauss, Marcel, and Henri Beuchat
  1979. *Seasonal Variations of the Eskimo: A Study in Social Morphology*. London: Routledge & Kegan Paul. Originally published in 1906.

Mo Junqing 莫俊卿
  1986. “Yue wu jibu yuanliu kao” 越巫鸡卜源流考 [Origin of Yue’s (Yueh) Chicken Divination]. *Zhongnan Minzu Xueyuan Xuebao* 中南民族学院学报 [Journal of South-Center Nationalities Institute], 1986 supplement.

Moore, Henrietta L.
  1986. *Space, Text, and Gender: An Anthropological Study of the Marakwert of Kenya*. Cambridge: Cambridge University Press.

Morgan, Lewis Henry
  1965. *Houses and House-Life of the American Aborigines*. Chicago: University of Chicago Press. Originally published in 1881.

Mubin Sheppard and Tan Sri Haji
  1969. “Traditional Malay House Forms in Trengganu and Kelantan.” *Journal of the Malayan Branch of the Royal Asiatic Society* 42 (2): 1–28.

Needham, Joseph
  1965. *Science and Civilization in China*. Vol. 1. Cambridge: Cambridge University Press.

Ni Dabai 倪大白
  1990. *Dong-Tai yu gailun* 侗台语概论 [Outline of the Kam (Dong)-Tai Language]. Beijing: Zhongyang Minzu Xueyuan Chubanshe 中央民族学院出版社.

Oakes, Tim
  1997. “Ethnic Tourism in Rural Guizhou: Sense of Place and Commerce of Authenticity.” In Michel Picard and Robert E. Wood, eds., *Tourism, Ethnicity, and the State in Asian and Pacific Societies*. Honolulu: University of Hawai‘i Press.
  1999. “Selling Guizhou: Cultural Development in an Era of Meketization.” In Hans Hendrischke and Chongyi Feng, eds., *The Political Economy of China’s Provinces*. London: Routledge.

Oliver, Paul, ed.
  1969. *Shelter and Society*. London: Barrie & Jenkins.
  1971. *Shelter in Africa*. London: Barrie & Jenkins.
  1975. *Shelter, Sign, and Symbol*. London: Barrie & Jenkins.
  1987. *Dwellings: The House Across the World*. Oxford: Phaidon.

1997. *Encyclopedia of Vernacular Architecture of the World*. Cambridge: Cambridge University Press.

Pan Nianying 潘年英

1985. "Dongzu rennin de kongjian yuyan—lun gulou de shehui gongneng he meixue yiyi" 侗族人民的空间语言—论鼓楼的社会功能和美学意义 [The Spatial Language of Dong People: Social Function and Aesthetic Meaning of the Drum Tower]. *Guizhou Shehui Kexue (Wen Shi Zhe)* 贵州社会科学（文史哲）[Guizhou Social Science] 5.

1988. "Dongzu de yu tuteng kao" 侗族的鱼图腾考 [Investigation of the Dong Fish Totem]. *Minjian Wenxue Luntan* 民间文学论坛 [Folk Literature Forum] 5 (6).

Pérez-Gómez, Alberto

1983. *Architecture and the Crisis of Modern Science*. Cambridge, MA: MIT Press.

Pirazzoli-T'Serstevens, Michele

1972. *Living Architecture: Chinese*. London: Macdonald.

Pred, Allan

1985. "The Social Becomes the Spatial, the Spatial Becomes the Social: Enclosures, Social Change, and the Becoming of Places in Skane." In Derek Gregory and John Urry, eds., *Spatial Relations and Spatial Structures*. New York: St. Martin's Press.

1986. *Place, Practice, and Structure: Social and Spatial Transformation in Southern Sweden, 1780–1850*. Totowa, NJ: Barnes & Noble.

Prussin, Labelle

1969. *Architecture in Northern Ghana: A Study of Forms and Functions*. Berkeley: University of California Press.

Pu Hong 普虹

1992. "Dongxi ying zou ziji fazhan zhi lu" 侗戏应走自己发展之路 [Dong Opera Should Develop Its Own Direction]. *Guizhou minzu yanjiu* 贵州民族研究 [Ethnic Studies in Guizhou] 52: 71–76.

Qia Mingzi 潜明兹

1989. "Shilun Dongzu 'Ga mang mang dao shi jia'" 试论侗族《嘎茫莽道时嘉》 [Comments on Dong "Ga Mang Man Dao Shi Jia" (Dong Ancient Epic)]. *Zhongnan Minzu Xueyuan Xuebao* 中南民族学院学报 [Journal of South-Center Nationalities Institute] 2.

Rabinow, Paul, ed.

1984. *The Foucault Reader*. New York: Pantheon Books.

Rapoport, Amos

1969a. "The Pueblo and the Hogan: A Cross-Cultural Comparison of Two Responses to an Environment." In Paul Oliver, ed., *Shelter and Society*. London: Barrie & Jenkins.

1969b. *House Form and Culture*. Englewood Cliffs, NJ: Prentice-Hall.

1976. "Socio-cultural Aspects of Man-Environment Studies." In Amos Rapoport, ed., *The Mutual Interaction of People and Their Built Environment: A Cross-Cultural Perspective*. The Hague: Mouton.

1977. *Human Aspects of Urban Form*. Oxford: Pergamon.

1982. *The Meaning of the Built Environment: A Nonverbal Communication Approach*. Beverly Hills: Sage.

1985. "Thinking About Home Environments: A Conceptual Framework." In

Irwin Altman and Carol M. Werner, eds., *Home Environments*. New York: Plenum.

 1986. "Culture and Built Form—a Reconsideration." In David G. Saile, ed., *Architecture in Cultural Change: Essays in Built Form and Culture Research*. Lawrence: Built Form and Culture Studies, School of Architecture and Urban Design, University of Kansas.

 1989. "On the Attributes of Tradition." In Jean-Paul Bourdier and Nezar AlSayyad, eds., *Dwellings, Settlements, and Traditions: Cross-Cultural Perspectives*. Lanham, MD: University Press of America.

 1990. "Systems of Activities and Systems of Settings." In Susan Kent, ed., *Domestic Architecture and the Use of Space—an Interdisciplinary, Cross-Cultural Study*. Cambridge: Cambridge University Press.

Rawson, Jessica

 1983. *The Chinese Bronzes of Yunnan*. London: Sidgwick & Jackson; Beijing: Cultural Relics Publishing House.

Reid, Anthony

 1980. "The Structure of Cities in South-East Asia, 15th to 17th Centuries." *Journal of South-East Asian Studies* 11 (2): 235–250.

Ruan, Xing

 1996a. "Empowerment in the Practice of Making and Inhabiting: Dong Architecture in Cultural Reconstruction." *Journal of Material Culture* 1 (2): 211–238.

 1996b. "Making and Inhabiting a Cultural Milieu: An Architectural Study of Meaning and Dong Architecture in Southern China." Ph.D. dissertation, Victoria University of Wellington.

 1997. "Choral Symbolic Power: An Architectural Study of Meaning on Dong Drum Towers." *Exedra* 7 (1): 14–23.

Rudofsky, Bernard

 1964. *Architecture Without Architects: A Short Introduction to Non-pedigreed Architecture*. London: Secker & Warburg.

 1977. *The Prodigious Builders*. London: Secker & Warburg.

Rykwert, Joseph

 1981. *On Adam's House in Paradise: The Idea of the Primitive Hut in Architectural History*. Cambridge, MA: MIT Press.

 1988. *The Idea of a Town: The Anthropology of Urban Form in Rome, Italy, and the Ancient World*. Cambridge, MA: MIT Press.

 1996. *The Dancing Column: On Order of Architecture*. Cambridge, MA: MIT Press.

 2000. *The Seduction of Place: The City in the Twenty-First Century*. London: Weidenfeld & Nicolson.

Sahlins, Marshall

 1976. *Culture and Practical Reason*. Chicago: University of Chicago Press.

Said, Edward William

 1975. *Beginnings: Intention and Method*. New York: Basic Books.

 1978. *Orientalism*. New York: Pantheon Books.

 1993. *Culture and Imperialism*. London: Chatto & Windus.

Schwimmer, Eric

 1990. "The Anthropology of the Ritual Arts." In Allan Hanson and Louise

Hanson, eds., *Art and Identity in Oceania*. Honolulu: University of Hawai'i Press.

Shen Xu 申旭 and Liu Zhi 刘稚

1988. *Zhongguo xinan yu dongnan ya de kuajing minzu* 中国西南与东南亚的跨境民族 [Border Minorities of Southwest China and Southeast Asia]. Kunming: Yunnan Renmin Chubanshe 云南人民出版社.

Shi Bozhou 石波舟

1991. "Jiudong Dongzu de rensheng yili" 九洞侗族的人生仪礼 [Life Rites of the Dong in the "Jiudong" Area]. *Miao Dong Wentan* 苗侗文坛 [Miao and Dong Forum] 11: 100–106.

Shi Ruoping 石若屏

1981. "Dongzu kuan zuzhi de yidian yanjiu" 侗族款组织的一点研究 [Preliminary Study of Dong *Kuanx*]. *Guangxi minzu yanjiu cankao ziliao* 广西民族研究参考资料 [Reference of Guangxi Ethnic Studies]. Nanning: Guangxi Minzu Yanjiu Suo.

1984. "Dongzu zuyuan yu qianxi" 侗族族源与迁徙 [Dong's Ethnic Origin and Migration]. *Guizhou minzu yanjiu* 贵州民族研究 [Ethnic Studies in Guizhou] 20: 75–88.

Shi Tingzhang 石庭章

1985. "Tan Dongzhai gulou jiqi shehui yiyi" 谈侗寨鼓楼及其社会意义 [The Drum Tower and Its Social Meanings in a Dong Village]. *Guizhou minzu yanjiu* 贵州民族研究 [Ethnic Studies in Guizhou] 24: 115–119.

1989. "Jiudong diqu 'Sax' huodong de jieshao" 九洞地区'萨'活动的介绍 [Introduction of "Sax" Activities in the Jiudong Region]. Paper presented at the Sax Conference, Rongjiang, Guizhou Province.

Sitte, Camillo

1965. *City Planning According to Artistic Principles*. New York: Random House. Originally published in 1889.

Soebadio, Haryati

1975. "The Documentary Study of Traditional Balinese Architecture: Some Preliminary Notes." *Indonesian Quarterly* 3: 86–95.

Spence, Jonathan

1981. *The Gate of Heavenly Peace: The Chinese and Their Revolution, 1895–1980*. New York: Viking Press.

Sperber, Dan

1975. *Rethinking Symbolism*. Cambridge: Cambridge University Press.

1985. *On Anthropological Knowledge: Three Essays*. Cambridge: Cambridge University Press.

Steinhardt, Nancy Shatzman

1990. *Chinese Imperial City Planning*. Honolulu: University of Hawai'i Press.

Stierlin, Henri

1977. *Encyclopedia of World Architecture*. London: Macmillan.

Sumet, Jumsai

1988. *Naga: Cultural Origins in Siam and the West Pacific*. Singapore: Oxford University Press.

Tambiah, Stanley Jeyaraja

1985. *Culture, Thought, and Social Action: An Anthropological Perspective*. Cambridge, MA: Harvard University Press.

Tan Shaoshan 覃绍山

1992. "Zhongguo nanfan minzu qiao su qiantan" 中国南方民族桥俗浅谈 [Initial Investigation of Customs of China's Southern Nationalities]. *Zhongnan Minzu Xueyuan Xuebao* 中南民族学院学报 [Journal of South-Center Nationalities Institute] 5.

Thomas, Nicholas

1991. "Against Ethography." *Cultural Anthropology* 3: 306–322.

Thongchai, Winichakul

1994. *Siam Mapped: A History of the Geo-Body of a Nation.* Honolulu: University of Hawai'i Press.

Tong Enzheng 童恩正

1983. "Shilun zhaoqi Tonggu" 试论早期铜鼓 [On the Early Bronze Drum]. *Kaogu Xuebao* 考古学报 [Journal of Archaeology] 3.

Torigoe Kenzaburo

1983. *Unnan kara no michi: Nihonjin no rutsu o saguru.* Tokyo: Kodansha.

Tschumi, Bernard

1986. *La Case Vide: La Villette 1985.* London: Architectural Association.

1987. *Cinegram Folie: Le Parc de la Villette.* Princeton: Princeton Architectural Press.

Tuan, Yi-Fu

1972. "Structuralism, Existentialism, and Environmental Perception." *Environment and Behavior* 4 (3): 319–331.

1974. *Topophilia: A Study of Environment Perception, Attitudes, and Values.* Englewood Cliffs, NJ: Prentice-Hall.

1996. *Cosmos and Hearth: A Cosmopolite's Viewpoint.* Minneapolis: University of Minnesota Press.

Turner, Victor

1967. *The Forest of Symbols: Aspects of Ndembu Ritual.* Ithaca: Cornell University Press.

1969. *The Ritual Process: Structure and Anti-Structure.* Ithaca: Cornell University Press.

1974. *Dramas, Fields, and Metaphors: Symbolic Action in Human Society.* Ithaca: Cornell University Press.

Turton, Andrew

1978. "Architectural and Political Space in Thailand." In George Bertram Milner, ed., *National Symbols in South-East Asia.* London: School of Oriental and African Studies.

Van Eyck, Aldo

1969. "Basket-House-Village-Universe." In Charles Jencks and George Baird, eds., *Meaning in Architecture.* London: Barrie & Jenkins.

Vesely, Dalibor

1985. *Architecture and the Conflict of Representation.* AA Files 8. London: Architectural Association.

Vogt, Adolf Max

1998. *Le Corbusier, the Noble Savage.* Cambridge, MA: MIT Press.

Wang Ningsheng 汪宁生

1983. "Zhongguo kaogu faxian zhong de 'da fan zhi'" 中国考古发现中的'大房子' [The "Big House" in China Archaeology Findings]. *Kaogu Xuebao* 考古学报 [Journal of Archaeology] 3.

Wang Shengxian 王胜先

1984. "Dongzu zuyuan kaolue" 侗族族源考略 [Studies of Dong Ethnic Origin]. *Guizhou minzu yanjiu* 贵州民族研究 [Ethnic Studies in Guizhou] 18: 95–103.

1990a. *Yueyi yisu xintan: Dongzu lishi wenhua luncong* 越裔遗俗新探：侗族历史文化论丛 [New Investigations of Yue Descendant Customs: Dong Historical and Cultural Treatises]. Guiyang: Guizhou Renmin Chubanshe 贵州人民出版社.

1990b. "Dongzu dou niu jie" 侗族斗牛节 [Dong Buffalo Fighting Festival]. *Minjian Wenhua* 民间文化 [Folk Literature] 8.

Wang Shengxian 王胜先 and Luo Tinghua 罗廷华

1989. *Dongzu lishi wenhua xisu* 侗族历史文化习俗 [History, Culture, and Customs of the Dong People]. Guiyang: Guizhou Renmin Chubanshe 贵州人民出版社.

Waterson, Roxana

1990. *The Living House: An Anthropology of Architecture in South-East Asia.* Singapore: Oxford University Press.

Watson, William

1961. *China Before the Han Dynasty.* London: Thames & Hudson.

1971. *Cultural Frontiers in Ancient East Asia.* Edinburgh: Edinburgh University Press.

Wessing, Robert

1984. "Acehnese." In Richard V. Weekes, ed., *Muslim Peoples: A World Ethnographic Survey.* Westport: Greenwood Press.

Whorf, Benjamin Lee

1956. "Linguistic Factors in the Terminology of Hopi Architecture." In *Language, Thought, and Reality: Selected Writings of Benjamin Lee Whorf.* Cambridge, MA: MIT Press.

Willetts, William

1965. *Foundations of Chinese Art from Neolithic Pottery to Modern Architecture.* London: Thames & Hudson.

Woolard, D. S.

1988. "Traditional Dwellings of the South Pacific." Paper presented at the International Symposium on Traditional Dwellings and Settlements in a Comparative Perspective, University of California, Berkeley.

Wu Chenglin 吴泽霖 and Ch'en Kou-Chiin 陈国钧

1942. *Guizhou Miao-Yi shehui Yanjiu* 贵州苗夷社会研究 [Studies of Miao-I Societies in Kweichow (Guizhou)]. Kweiyang (Guiyang): Wentong Shuju 文通书局.

Wu Dingguo 吴定国

1989. "Guanyu 'Sax' de xingxiang" 关于'萨'的形象 [The Image of Sax]. Paper presented at the Sax Conference, Rongjiang, Guizhou Province.

Wu Hao 吴浩

1989. "Dongzu Sasui chongbai tanyuan" 侗族萨岁崇拜探源 [Tracing the Origins of Dong Sax Worship]. *Miao Dong Wentan* 苗侗文坛 [Miao and Dong Forum] 5: 54–65.

1990. "Dongzu geyao yu Dongzu minsu" 侗族歌谣与侗族民俗 [Dong Folk Songs and Dong Social Customs]. *Minzu Yishu* 民族艺术 [Ethnic Arts] 4.

Wu, Nelson Ikon

1963. *Chinese and Indian Architecture: The City of Man, the Mountain of God, and the Realm of the Immortals.* New York: Braziller.

Wu Nengfu 吴能夫

1989. "Lue tan Dongzu de 'ge yang xin' shuo" 略谈侗族的'歌养心'说 [The Dong Concept of "Song Nourishing the Heart"]. *Guizhou minzu yanjiu* 贵州民族研究 [Ethnic Studies in Guizhou] 39: 89–91.

Wu Quanxin 吴佺新

1992. "Zhanli jian Sax tan de diaocha baogao" 占里建萨坛的调查报告 [Field Report on the Establishment of the Sax Altar in Zhanli Village]. *Miao Dong Wentan* 苗侗文坛 [Miao and Dong Forum] 13: 105–114.

Wu Quanxin 吴佺新 and Chen Chunyuan 陈春园

1985. "Youxiu de chuantong jianzhu yishu—Conjiang gulou qun" 优秀的传统建筑艺术—从江豉楼群 [Fine Traditional Architectural Arts: Drum Tower Cluster in Congjiang]. *Guizhou minzu yanjiu* 贵州民族研究 [Ethnic Studies in Guizhou] 24: 120–123.

Wu Shancheng 吴善诚

1989. "Dongzu chuantong jianzhu yishu tese chutan" 侗族传统建筑艺术特色初探 [Initial Investigation of Artistic Characteristics of Traditional Dong Architecture]. *Zhongnan Minzu Xueyuan Xuebao* 中南民族学院学报 [Journal of South-Center Nationalities Institute] 2.

Wu Shihua 吴世华

1988. "Dongzu yuanshi zhixi chutan" 侗族原始支系初探 [Preliminary Studies of Dong Original Ethnic Branches]. *Guizhou minzu yanjiu* 贵州民族研究 [Ethnic Studies in Guizhou] 34: 125–127.

1989. "Chengyang qiao de jianzhu yishu he Dongzu de chuantong daode" 程阳桥的建筑艺术和侗族的传统道德 [Architectural Art of Chengyang Bridge and Traditional Morals of the Dong]. *Zhongnan Minzu Xueyuan Xuebao* 中南民族学院学报 [Journal of South-Center Nationalities Institute] 2.

1990. "Dong 'Sax' shidai chutan—Sanjiang Linxi Sax shen yiji diaocha" 侗'萨'时代初探—三江林溪萨神遗迹调查 [Dong Sax Times: Investigation of Historical Remains of the Sax Goddess in the Linxi Area of the Sanjiang Region]. *Guizhou minzu yanjiu* 贵州民族研究 [Ethnic Studies in Guizhou] 42: 41–43.

1991. "'Ga mang man dao shi jia' bushi Dongzu minjian shishi" '嘎茫莽道时嘉'不是侗族民间史诗 ["Ga Mang Man Dao Shi Jia" Is Not a Dong Folk Epic]. *Miao Dong Wentan* 苗侗文坛 [Miao and Dong Forum] 12: 39–54.

Wu Zhengguang 吴正光

1992. "Guizhou minzu jianzu de leixing he neihan" 贵州民族建筑的类型和内涵 [Types and Content of Guizhou Ethnic Architecture]. *Guizhou Minzu Xueyuan Xuebao* 贵州民族学院学报 [Journal of Guizhou Nationalities Institute] 1.

Wu Zhide 吴治德

1989. "'Gan Lan' kao" '干栏'考 [The Study of *Ganlan* (Pile-Built House)]. *Guizhou minzu yanjiu* 贵州民族研究 [Ethnic Studies in Guizhou] 37: 128–129.

1992. "Tongdao Dong xiang sangsu" 通道侗乡丧俗 [Funeral Customs of the Dong in Tongdao County]. *Miao Dong Wentan* 苗侗文坛 [Miao and Dong Forum] 13: 115–120.

Wu Zhizhu 吴支柱 and Wang Chengzu 王承祖

　　1989. "Dongzu yinyue de chengwei yu fenlei" 侗族音乐的称谓与分类 [Names and Classification of Dong Music]. *Guizhou minzu yanjiu* 贵州民族研究 [Ethnic Studies in Guizhou] 37: 130–134.

Wurm, Stephen Adolphe, and Basil Wilson

　　1975. *English Finderlist of Reconstructions in Austronesian Languages (Post Brandstetter)*. Canberra: ANU Press.

Xi Dingke 席定克

　　1990. "Shi lun Guizhou shaoshu minzu minjian zhuzhai jianzhu" 试论贵州少数民族民间住宅建筑 [Vernacular Housing of Guizhou Minorities]. *Guizhou minzu yanjiu* 贵州民族研究 [Ethnic Studies in Guizhou] 41: 61–68.

Xiang Lin 向零

　　1985. "Congjiang xian jiudong Dongzu shehui zuzhi yu xiguanfa" 从江县九洞侗族社会组织与习惯法 [Dong Social Organization and Customary Law in Jiudong of Congjiang County]. *Guizhou Minzu Diaocha* 贵州民族调查 [Ethnic Investigations in Guizhou] 3.

　　1989. "Dong Kuan xianggui jiqi yanbian—dui Dongzu shehui zuzhi xingshi gongneng jiqi yanbian de tantao" 侗款乡规及其演变—对侗族社会组织形式功能及其演变的探讨 [Village Regulations of Dong *Kuanx* and Their Evolution: Exploring the Form, Function, and Evolution of Dong Social Organization]. *Guizhou minzu yanjiu* 贵州民族研究 [Ethnic Studies in Guizhou] 39: 6–13.

　　1991. "Liudong Dongzu shehui zuzhi diaocha—yi ge gudai junshi lianmeng zuzhi de yiji" 六洞侗族社会组织调查——一个古代军事联盟组织的遗迹 [Investigation of Liudong Dong Social Organization: Historical Remains of Ancient Military Alliance]. *Guizhou Minzu Diaocha* 贵州民族调查 [Ethnic Investigations in Guizhou] 8.

Xin Gongwan 邢公畹

　　1985. *Sanjiang Dong yu* 三江侗语 [Sanjiang Dong Language]. Tianjin: Nankai Daxue Chubanshe 南开大学出版社.

Xu Jiesun 徐杰舜 and Wei Rike 韦日科, eds.

　　1992. *Zhongguo minzu zhengce shijian* 中国民族政策史鉴 [History of China's Minority Ethnic Policy]. Nanning: Guangxi Renmin Chubanshe 广西人民出版社.

Xu Jiesun 徐杰舜 et al., eds.

　　1992. *Chengyang qiao fengsu* 程阳桥风俗 [Social Customs of the Chengyang Bridge Region]. Nanning: Guangxi Minzu Chubanshe 广西民族出版社.

Xu Songshi 徐松石

　　1959. "Dongnanya minzu zhong de Zhongguo xueyuan" 东南亚民族中的中国血缘 [The Chinese Clan in the Southeast Asia Nationalities]. *Yuandong Minzushi Yanjiu* 远东民族史研究 [Far East Ethnography History Research] 3.

Yang Baoyuan 杨保愿

　　1982. "Tan Dongzhai jianzhu yishu" 谈侗寨建筑艺术 [Architectural Arts of Dong Villages]. *Guangxi Minzu Xueyuan Xuebao* 广西民族学院学报 [Journal of Guangxi Nationalities Institute] (Social Science Addition 2).

　　1988. *Ga mang man dao shi jia: Dongzu yuanzu ge* 嘎茫莽道时嘉：侗族远祖歌 [*Ga Mang Man Dao Shi Jia*: Dong Ancient Epic]. Beijing: Zhongyang Minjian Wenxue Chubanshe 中央民间文学出版社.

1990a. "Dongzu 'Sa wenhua' Kaoshi" 侗族'萨'文化考释 [Investigation and Interpretation of Dong "Sax Culture"]. *Miao Dong Wentan* 苗侗文坛 [Miao and Dong Forum] 7: 10–29.

1990b. "Dongzu jisi wudao ji minsu gaishu" 侗族祭祀舞蹈及民俗概述 [General Introduction to Dong Customs and Dances for Offering Sacrifices to Gods and Ancestors]. *Miao Dong Wentan* 苗侗文坛 [Miao and Dong Forum] 6: 72–88.

Yang Changming 杨昌鸣

1990. "Dongnan ya zaoqi jianzhu wenhua chutan" 东南亚早期建筑文化初探 [Preliminary Study of Early Southeast Asian Architectural Culture]. Ph.D. dissertation, Dongnan Daxue, Nanjing.

1992. "Zhaizhuang • jihuisuo • gulou—Dongzu gulou fasheng fazhan guocheng shi wo jian" 寨桩，集会所，鼓楼—侗族鼓楼发生发展过程之我见 [Village Pillar, Meetinghouse, Drum Tower: Emergence and Evolution of the Dong Drum Tower]. *Guizhou minzu yanjiu* 贵州民族研究 [Ethnic Studies in Guizhou] 51: 73–78.

Yang Chuan 扬川

1985. "Zaoqi Dongxi de duandai jiqi tedian chutai" 早期侗戏的断代及其特点初探 [Dynastic History of Early Dong Opera and Its Characteristics]. *Guizhou minzu yanjiu* 贵州民族研究 [Ethnic Studies in Guizhou] 21.

Yang Guoren 杨国仁

1986. *Dongzu xushi ge* 侗族叙事歌 [Dong Narrative Songs]. Guiyang: Guizhou Renmin Chubanshe 贵州人民出版社.

Yang Guoren 杨国仁 and Wu Dingguo 吴定国

1981. *Dongzu zuxian nali lai (Dongzu gu ge)* 侗族祖先哪里来（侗族古歌）[Where Dong Ancestors Came From (Dong Ancient Songs)]. Art and Literature Research Institute of Southeast Guizhou Miao and Dong Autonomous Prefecture, Guizhou Provincial Folk Art and Literature Research Institute. Guiyang: Guizhou Renmin Chubanshe 贵州人民出版社.

1985. *Dongzu lisu ge* 侗族礼俗歌 [Dong Folk Songs of Rites and Customs]. Guiyang: Guizhou Renmin Chubanshe 贵州人民出版社.

Yang Hao 杨豪 and Yang Yaolin 杨耀林

1983. "Guangdong Gaoyao xian Maogang shui shang mugou jianzhu yizhi" 广东省高要县茅岗水上木构建筑遗址 [The Ruin of Water Timber Architecture in the Maogang Area of Gaoyao County, Guangdong]. *Wenwu* 文物 [Cultural Relics] 12.

Yang Quan 杨权

1992. *Dongzu minjian wenxue shi* 侗族民间文学史 [History of Dong Folk Literature]. Beijing: Zhongyang Minzu Xueyuan Chubanshe 中央民族学院出版社.

Yang Shunqing 杨顺青

1990. "Guanyu Dongzu gulou wenhua de jidian sikao" 关于侗族鼓楼文化的几点思考 [Some Comments on Dong Drum Tower Culture]. *Zhongnan Minzu Xueyuan Xuebao* 中南民族学院学报 [Journal of South-Center Nationalities Institute] 6.

Yang Tongshan 杨通山

1990. "Sanxiang Sax shen chongbai diaocha" 三乡萨神崇拜调查 [Investigation of Sax Worship in Three Villages]. *Guizhou minzu yanjiu* 贵州民族研究 [Ethnic Studies in Guizhou] 42: 38–40.

1991. "'Sa Tian Ba' shuyu dangdai ren bianzao de gudai shen" '萨天巴'属于当代人编造的古代神 ["Sax Tian Ba" Is an Imaginary Ancient God of Modern People]. *Minzu Yishu* 民族艺术 [Ethnic Arts] 2.

Yang Tongshan 杨通山 et al.

1980. *Dongzu minge xuan* 侗族民歌选 [Selected Dong Folk Songs]. Shanghai: Shanghai Wenyi Chubanshe 上海文艺出版社.

1982. *Dongzu minjian gushi xuan* 侗族民间故事选 [Selected Dong Folk Stories]. Shanghai: Shanghai Wenyi Chubanshe 上海文艺出版社.

Yang Tongshan 杨通山 et al., eds.

1983. *Dong xiang fengqing lu* 侗乡风情录 [Record of Dong Customs]. Chengdu: Sichuan Minzu Chubanshe 四川民族出版社.

Yang Xiguang 杨锡光 et al., eds.

1988. *Dong kuan—Zhongguo shaoshu minzu guji Dongzu guji zhiyi* 侗款—中国少数民族古籍侗族古籍之一 [Dong *Kuanx*—Vol. 1 of Dong Books in the Classic Series of China's Minority Nationalities]. Changsha: Yuelu Shushe 岳麓书社.

Yates, Timothy

1989. "Habitus and Social Space: Some Suggestions About Meaning in the Saami (Lapp) Tent ca. 1700–1900." In Ian Hodder, ed., *The Meaning of Things: Material Culture and Symbolic Expression*. London: Unwin Hyman.

You Zhong 尤中

1991. "Zhuang-Dong yu zhu minzu de lishi fazhan yanbian" 壮侗语诸民族的历史发展演变 [The Course of History of Zhuang-Dong (Kam) Linguistic Nationalities]. *Sixiang Zhanxian* 思想战线 [Ideology Battle Line] 4.

Yu Xiao 宇晓

1990. "Guanyu Dongzu zucheng de yinwen yimin wenti" 关于侗族族称的英文译名问题 [The Issue of the Dong's Name in English]. *Guizhou minzu yanjiu* 贵州民族研究 [Ethnic Studies in Guizhou] 44: 94–96.

1991. "Dongzu qin cong siming zhi yanjiu" 侗族亲从嗣名制研究 [Ethnicity in Nomenclature: An Anthropological Study of Teknonymy of the Dong]. *Guizhou minzu yanjiu* 贵州民族研究 [Ethnic Studies in Guizhou] 48: 36–43.

Yuan Youzhen 袁有真

1987. "Dongzu yin er-huan" 侗族银耳环 [Silver Earrings of the Dong]. *Guizhou Sheng Bowuguan Guankan* 贵州省博物馆馆刊 [Guizhou Provincial Museum Periodical] 4.

Yunnan Sheng Lishi Yanjiu Suo Diaoca Zu 云南省历史研究所调查组 [Yunnan History Research Institute]

1966. "Yunnan Cangyuan yanhua" 云南沧源岩画 [The Cave Painting in Cangyuan, Yunnan]. *Wenwu* 文物 [Cultural Relics] 2: 7–27.

Yunnan Sheng Sheji Yuan 云南省设计院 [Yunnan Provincial Design Institute]

1986. *Yunnan minju* 云南民居 [Vernacular Dwellings of Yunnan]. Beijing: Zhongguo Jianzhu Gongye Chubanshe 中国建筑工业出版社.

Zerner, Charles

1983. "Animate Architecture of the Toraja." *Arts of Asia* Sept.–Oct.: 96–106.

Zhang, Longxi

1992. "Western Theory and Chinese Reality." *Critical Inquiry* 19: 105–130.

Zhang Min 张民

1980. "Chong 'jizu ge' tantao Dongzu de qianxi" 从'祭祖歌'探讨侗族的迁徙

[Probing Dong Migration Through "Ancestor Worship Songs"]. *Guizhou minzu yanjiu* 贵州民族研究 [Ethnic Studies in Guizhou] 3: 71–82.

1983. "Qiantan Dongzu yu Ge Lin he Lin" 浅谈侗族与仡伶和伶 [Dong, Ge Lin, and Lin]. *Guizhou minzu yanjiu* 贵州民族研究 [Ethnic Studies in Guizhou] 13: 86–93.

1985. "'Dong yi lao lei' zhiyi–jianzheng Dongzu zuyuan yu qianxi" '侗亦僚类' 质疑—兼证侗族族源与迁徙 [Question "the Dong Is Also the Liao"—On Dong Ethnic Origin and Migration]. *Guizhou minzu yanjiu* 贵州民族研究 [Ethnic Studies in Guizhou] 24: 1–14.

1986. "Guanyu Dongzu gulou de diaocha" 关于侗族鼓楼的调查 [Investigation of the Dong Drum Tower]. *Zhongyang Minzu Xueyuan Xuebao* 中央民族学院学报 [Journal of Central Nationalities Institute] 2.

1987a. "Dongzu sangzang—Rongjiang xian Chejiang xiang Chezhai zirancun" 侗族丧葬—榕江县车江乡车寨自然村 [Dong Funerals: Investigation in the Chezhai Village of Chejiang Xiang in Rongjiang County]. *Guizhou minzu diaocha* 贵州民族调查 [Ethnic Investigations in Guizhou] 5.

1987b. "Dongzu shi yanjiu pingshu" 侗族史研究评述 [Review of Dong History Studies]. *Guizhou minzu yanjiu* 贵州民族研究 [Ethnic Studies in Guizhou] 31: 103–111.

1989. "Sasui yanjiu jiankuang" 萨岁研究简况 [Brief Introduction to "Sax Sis" Studies]. Paper presented at the Sax Conference, Rongjiang, Guizhou Province.

1990a. "Guanyu Rongjiang xian Chejiang de 'Sasui' diaocha" 关于榕江县车江的'萨岁'调查 [Investigation of Chejiang's "Sax Sis" in Rongjiang County]. *Guizhou minzu diaocha* 贵州民族调查 [Ethnic Investigations in Guizhou] 7.

1990b. "'Sa Tian Ba' zhiyi—jianshuo Dongzu de zhigao wushang nüshen Saxsi" '萨天巴'质疑—兼说侗族的至高无上女神萨岁 [Question "Sa Tian Ba": The Most Lofty Dong Goddess Saxsi]. *Guizhou minzu yanjiu* 贵州民族研究 [Ethnic Studies in Guizhou] 42: 10–17.

1991a. "Guanyu Dongzu yuanshi zongjiao de diaocha" 关于侗族原始宗教的调查 [Investigations of Dong Primitive Religions]. *Guizhou minzu diaocha* 贵州民族调查 [Ethnic Investigations in Guizhou] 8.

1991b. "Shi jiao Dong su yu gu Yue su de yuanyuan guanxi" 试较侗俗与古越俗的渊源关系 [Comparisons Between Dong Customs and Ancient Yue (Yueh) Customs and Their Origins]. *Guizhou minzu yanjiu* 贵州民族研究 [Ethnic Studies in Guizhou] 45: 30–37.

1991c. "Shitan 'Sasui' shentan yuanliu" 试探'萨岁'神坛源流 [Origin and Evolution of "Sax Sis" Altars]. *Guizhou minzu yanjiu* 贵州民族研究 [Ethnic Studies in Guizhou] 48: 27–35.

1992. "Guanyu Dongzu 'Sa' shen de diaocha baogao" 关于侗族'萨'神的调查报告 [Fieldwork Report on the Dong "Sax" Goddess]. *Guizhou minzu diaocha* 贵州民族调查 [Ethnic Investigations in Guizhou] 9.

Zhang Min 张民 et al.

1985. *Dong zhai gulou yanjiu* 侗寨鼓楼研究 [Dong Drum Tower Study]. Guiyang: Guizhou Renmin Chubanshe 贵州人民出版社.

Zhang Renwei 张人位

1988. "Jicheng fayang Miao Dong wenhua de juchu gongzuo—shuang yuwen jiaoxue de qishi" 继承发扬苗侗文化的基础工作—双语文教学的启示 [The

Fundamental Work of Furthering and Developing Dong Culture: Bilingual Teaching]. *Miao Dong Wentan* 苗侗文坛 [Miao and Dong Forum] 2: 86–90.

Zhang Shishan 张世珊 and Yang Chang si 杨昌嗣

    1992. *Dongzu wenhua gailun* 侗族文化概论 [General Outline of Dong Culture]. Guiyang: Guizhou Renmin Chubanshe 贵州人民出版社.

Zhao Fuxing 赵复兴

    1984. "È-lun-chun ren de Ao-lun shi chaoju de yicun" 鄂论春人的奥论是巢居的遗址 [Historical Remains of the Nest Dwellings of the Oroqen]. *Minzuxue Yanjiu* 民族学研究 [Ethnology Research] 7.

Zhejiang Sheng Wenguan Hui Deng 浙江省文管会等 [Bureau of Cultural Relics of Zhejiang]

    1980. "Zhejiang Hemudu di-er qi fajue de zuyao shouhuo" 浙江省河姆渡第二期发掘的主要收获 [Second Report on the Historical Findings at Hemudu]. *Wenwu* 文物 [Cultural Relics] 5: 1–15.

Zhejiang Sheng Wenwu Guanli Weiyuanhui 浙江省文化管理委员会 [Bureau of Cultural Relics of Zhejiang]

    1978. "Hemudu yizhi diyiqi fajue baogao" 河姆渡遗址第一期发掘报告 [First Report on the Historical Findings at Hemudu]. *Kaogu Xuebao* 考古学报 [Journal of Archaeology] 1: 39–107.

Zheng Guoqiao 郑国乔

    1983. "Dongzu de yuyin" 侗族的语音 [Tones of the Dong Language]. *Guizhou minzu yanjiu* 贵州民族研究 [Ethnic Studies in Guizhou] 15.

Zhong Nian 钟年

    1988. "Lusheng wenhua chutan" 芦笙文化初探 [Initial Investigation of *Lusheng* Culture]. *Guizhou minzu yanjiu* 贵州民族初探 [Ethnic Studies in Guizhou] 33: 97–101.

Zhou Hongcan 邹洪灿

    1983. "Dongzu cunzhai xingtai yanjiu" 侗族村寨形态研究 [Studies on Dong Village Forms]. *Jianzu Shi* 建筑师 [The Architect], vol. 14. Beijing: Zhongguo Jianzu Gongye Chubanshe 中国建筑工业出版社.

Zhu Changsheng 祝长生 and Sun Jianxiong 孙建雄

    1991. "Cong guihua jiaodu tantao Longsheng minju" 从规划角度探讨龙胜民居 [Probing Longsheng Vernacular Houses from the Planning Point of View]. *Jianzu Shi* 建筑师 [The Architect], vol. 43. Beijing: Zhongguo Jianzu Gongye Chubanshe 中国建筑工业出版社.

Zhu Hueizhen 朱慧珍

    1988a. *Dongzu minjian wenyi meilun* 侗族民间文艺美论 [Aesthetic Criticism of Dong Arts and Literature]. Nanning: Guangxi Renmin Chubanshe 广西人民出版社.

    1988b. "Dongzu minjian gushi de langman zhuyi tese jiqi sixiangxing" 侗族民间故事的浪漫主义特色及其思想性 [Romanticism and Its Political Tendency in Dong Folk Stories]. *Guizhou minzu yanjiu* 贵州民族研究 [Ethnic Studies in Guizhou] 33: 108–112.

Zhu Junming 朱俊明 et al., eds.

    1987. *Bai Yue shi yanjiu* 百越史研究 [Studies of Bai Yue (Pai Yueh) History]. Guiyang: Guizhou Renmin Chubanshe 贵州人民出版社.

Zhu Liangwen 朱良文

    1988. *Lijiang Naxi zu minju* 丽江纳西族民居 [The Vernacular Architecture of the Naxi in Lijiang]. Kunming: Yunnan Keji Chubanshe 云南科技出版社.

Index

coil, 43, 75–76, 87, 97, 109, 111, 128.
See also dragon
collective figure, 182
Congjiang, 17, 19, 21–22, 46–47, 49, 55,
63, 71, 117, 123, 127–129, 151, 170,
173
constitution of a human person, 12
cosmos and cosmological beliefs, 3–4,
7–9, 11, 89–90, 107, 126, 132, 135,
146, 163
courtship, 35, 130
cowrie-shell container, 96, 147
cultural affinities, 23, 142
cultural authenticity, 175
cultural fabrication, 108, 177
cultural reconstruction, 175
cultural relics, 170
cultural renewal, 11–12, 108, 132, 135,
144, 149, 167–168, 170, 172–174
cultural repertoire, 171
Cultural Revolution, 5, 131, 136,
170–171, 180
customary law, 25–26, 123, 125–127

Dai, 18, 61, 67–68, 91, 141–142, 144,
146–147, 151, 157–158, 160–161,
165, 174
Dian Lake, 97
diaojiaolou, 141–142
didacticism, 2, 9, 130, 181
Dong epic, 177
Dong ethnicity, 168, 170, 172
Dong patriarchy, 25, 93
Dong scholars, 20, 102, 169–171, 177
dougong (eave bracket set), 54, 104–105,
113, 117
dragon, 55, 57, 78–79, 81, 97, 109
drum tower, 10, 12, 16, 24–28, 30, 33,
35, 37, 40, 43, 46–47, 49, 51–52,
54–55, 60–61, 63, 72–76, 83, 87,
89–97, 101–105, 107–109, 111,
113–117, 119–120, 122–123,
125–137, 147–148, 153, 158, 167,
170–172, 175–178
drum tower funeral, 129
drum tower square, 47, 49, 51–52, 60, 75,
113, 115, 126, 128, 131–132, 134, 167
duoye, 75, 87–88, 128, 134, 176
Durand, Jacques-Nicolas-Louis, 3

economy and efficiency, 3, 40
efficiency and efficacy, 5
egalitarian, 157, 161, 165
Eisenman, Peter, 4
empowerment, 12, 23, 25, 40–41, 49, 74,
95, 126, 136–137, 180
entertaining tourists, 88, 175–176
ethnicity, 10–12, 14, 16–17, 22, 37,
39–40, 55, 61, 104, 126, 142–144,
147, 157, 163, 166, 168–170, 172,
174–175, 177
ethnocentrism, 13–14
ethnographer, 6, 174
ethnographic findings and research, 2, 8,
15, 20, 108, 169, 174
ethnographic pastoral, 168
ethnography, 8, 11
Evans, Robin, 165
exoticism, 13–14

fabrications, 6, 11–14, 16, 23, 39, 90, 93,
108, 133–134, 168, 170, 172, 177
feather flowers, 163, 176
fengshui (Daoist *fengshui*), 23, 30, 39–40,
57, 60, 78–81, 83, 88
Fernandez, James, 7–8
figurative meanings, 10, 12, 38, 76, 78,
81, 88, 139
fire pit, 26, 33, 68, 74–75, 81, 91, 93–94,
97, 107, 113, 115, 119–120, 122, 130–
131, 134–137, 145, 155, 158–163,
171–172, 175
folk songs, 15, 20–21, 26, 35, 65, 67, 107,
130
form: as formal analysis, 9, 11; as formal
language, 4; as formal problem, 3–4,
6; as formal structure, 38, 45, 49, 55,
70–71, 75–76, 80, 114, 135, 149, 157
Foucault, Michel, 113, 180
front hall and back room, 154–155, 157

ganlan, 30, 139, 141–142
Gell, Alfred, 122
grandeur and splendor, 2–3
graveyard, 22–23, 40, 62, 65, 72, 78
guan. *See* watchtower
Guangxi, 10, 17, 21, 26, 40–42, 62–63, 81,
103, 107, 116, 119, 127, 135, 141–142,
173–174

single-column drum tower, 92–93, 107

skyline, 43, 89, 116, 122

snake, 97, 109

social anthropologist, 2, 4, 7–9

social status, 62, 162, 177

social template, 2, 38

Song dynasty, 13, 15, 19, 128

spatial disposition, 1, 9–11, 23, 37, 49, 63, 66, 111, 113, 139, 155, 157–158, 161, 165, 172, 181

spatial syntax, 4

Spring and Autumn period, 155, 157

stone tablets, 25–26, 125, 132, 136, 155

storytelling, 130, 172

structuralism and structuralist, 3–4, 7

subconsciousness, 5, 180–182

Sumet, Jumsai, 40, 108, 111, 144–145

Sydney Opera House, 182

symbolic capital, 129, 135

symbolization, 89, 95, 122, 128, 131, 179, 181

tacit meaning, 2, 75, 96, 101, 107–108, 135, 181

Tai linguistic groups, 10, 18, 23, 40, 61, 67–68, 91, 105, 141, 174

Tang (hall or living room), 154–157, 159–160, 165

Tang dynasty, 19, 21, 105

tanmo (flicking ink), 134

Terragni, Giuseppe, 38

textual protocols, 172

textualized culture, 102, 149, 169

thick description, 10

three-bay and five-post, 149–150

Tiananmen Square, 179–180, 182

topographic focal point, 49, 55, 83, 137

tourism and tourist, 1, 12, 88–89, 131–132, 136–137, 171, 174–177

transliteration, 21, 104, 107

Tschumi, Bernard, 2

Turner, Victor, 108

tutanshi, 141–142

umbrella, 27, 45–47, 71, 74, 93, 96–97

unfurled mosquito nets, 160

universal human conditions, 11

Van Eyck, Aldo, 6

vernacular architecture, 2, 5–6, 8–9, 11

verticality, 89–90, 97, 128, 163, 165

Villa Savoye, 138

village heart, 90–92, 96, 101, 107, 123, 128, 176

village pillar, 91–92, 94–96, 101, 123

visual appreciation, 5

Vogt, Adolf, 139

watchtower (*wang lou*), 103–104

water-associated analogies, 42–43, 76, 111

Waterson, Roxana, 9, 105, 143–144, 148

Wazoku, 145

weathering, 163, 172

Western Zhou dynasty, 155

willingness, 182

wind-and-rain bridge, 10, 12, 24, 30, 33, 40, 55, 57, 60–61, 63, 79–80, 105, 109, 132, 136, 153, 158, 171–172, 175, 177

workings of architecture, 2, 9–11, 23, 37–38, 70, 90, 111, 122–123, 181

Xi'an, 155

Xiang Ling, 169

Xishuangbanna, 61, 67, 91, 142, 160

Yangshao, 155

Yanzhou, 103

Yeche, 91

Yuan dynasty, 15, 22

Yunnan, 10, 18, 91, 96–97, 105, 141–142, 145–148, 157, 160, 169, 174

Zengchong, 47, 117, 125, 167–168, 170

zhai, 24–28, 30, 81, 87, 93, 123, 125–128, 130–131

Zhang Huiyan, 155–156

Zhaoxin, 43, 49, 64, 93, 108–109, 123, 129

Zhuang, 16–18, 131, 141–142

zoomorphism, 38, 40–41, 57, 81

Zurich, Lake of, 139

About the Author

XING RUAN is professor of architecture at the University of New South Wales in Sydney. He is the author of *New China Architecture* (2006) and coeditor (with Paul Hogben) of *Topophilia and Topophobia: Reflections on Human Habitat in the Twentieth Century* (forthcoming). Xing Ruan has published on architecture and anthropology, architectural education, China's modern and contemporary architecture, as well as Australian contemporary architecture in both scholarly and professional journals. He is coeditor, with Ronald Knapp, of the book series Spatial Habitus: Making and Meaning in Asia's Architecture, which is published by the University of Hawai'i Press. Born in China, he received his architecture education at the Southeast University in Nanjing.

PRODUCTION NOTES
Ruan, *Allegorical Architecture*

Design and composition by Diane Gleba Hall
Text set in Minion with display type in Univers
Printing and binding by Thomson-Shore, Inc.
Printed on 70 lb. Fortune Matte, 556 ppi